Garfield
NUTTY AS A FRUITCAKE

BY JIM DAVIS

Ballantine Books • New York

A Ballantine Books Trade Paperback Original

Published in the United States by Ballantine Books, an imprint of Random House,
a division of Penguin Random House LLC, New York.

BALLANTINE and the HOUSE colophon are registered trademarks of Penguin Random House LLC.

ISBN 978-0-425-28576-3
Ebook ISBN 978-0-425-28577-0

Printed in China on acid-free paper

randomhousebooks.com

9 8 7 6 5 4 3 2 1

Fat Cat Fan Art

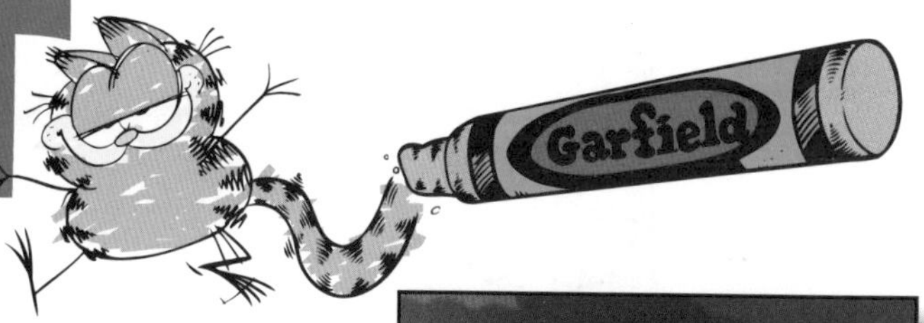
Garfield

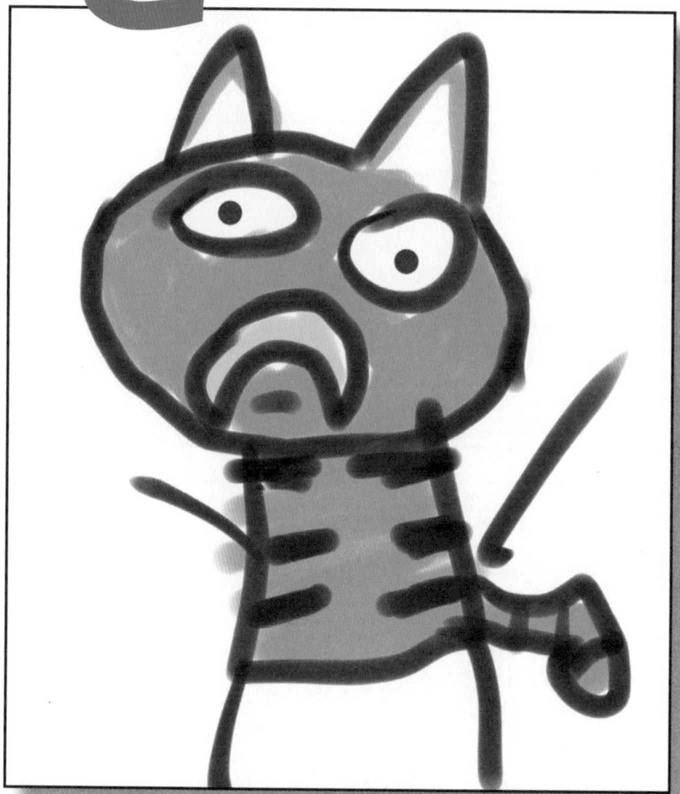

Jonathan G.
Age 17
Michigan

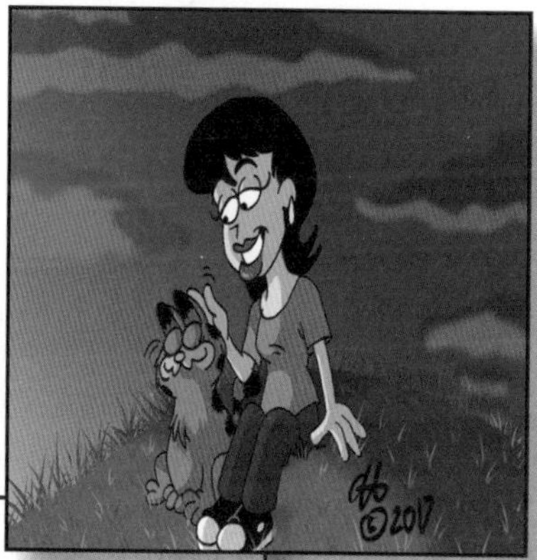

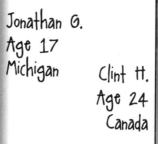

Clint H.
Age 24
Canada

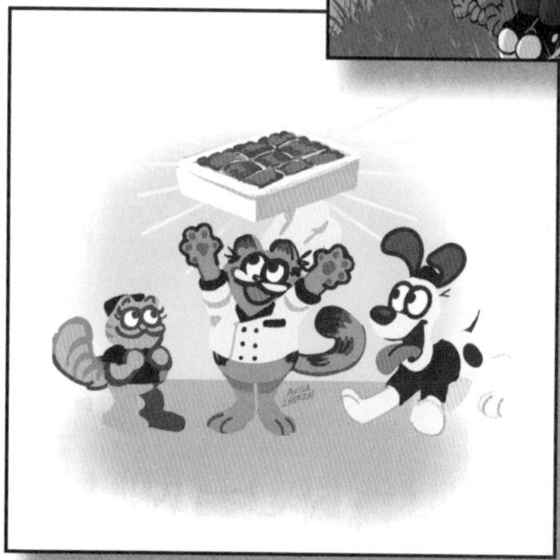

Anisa S.
Age 20
Massachusetts

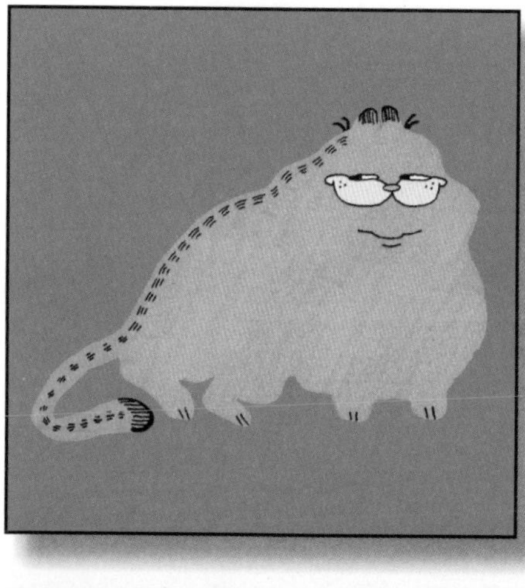

Zoe M.
Age 19
Texas

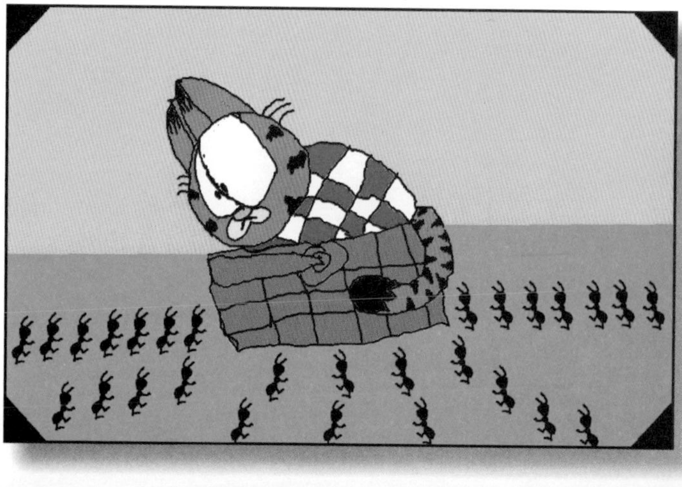

Elijah B.
Age 16
Ohio

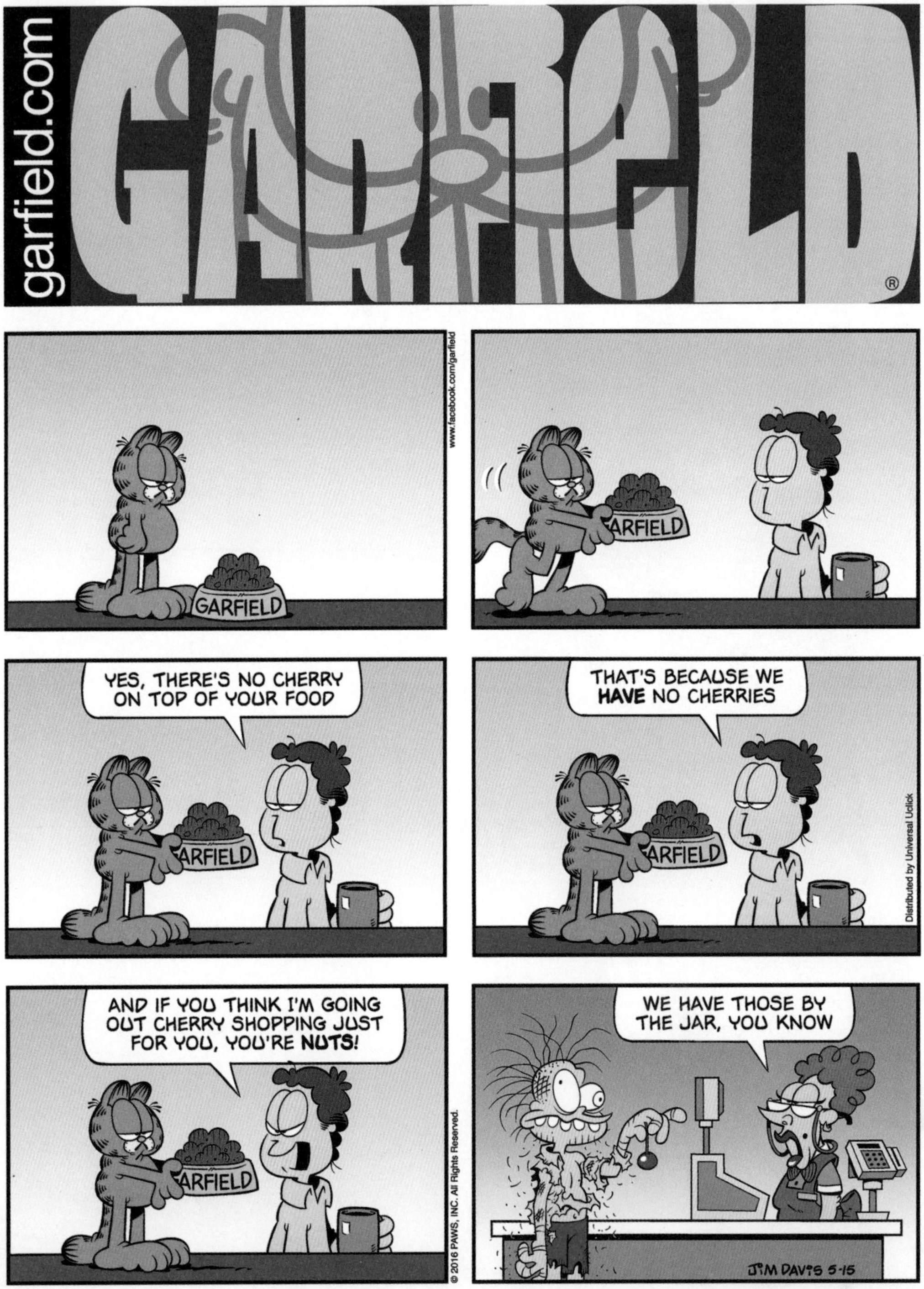
garfield.com
GARFIELD
www.facebook.com/garfield
GARFIELD
GARFIELD
YES, THERE'S NO CHERRY ON TOP OF YOUR FOOD
GARFIELD
THAT'S BECAUSE WE **HAVE** NO CHERRIES
GARFIELD
Distributed by Universal Uclick
AND IF YOU THINK I'M GOING OUT CHERRY SHOPPING JUST FOR YOU, YOU'RE **NUTS**!
GARFIELD
© 2016 PAWS, INC. All Rights Reserved.
WE HAVE THOSE BY THE JAR, YOU KNOW
JIM DAVIS 5-15

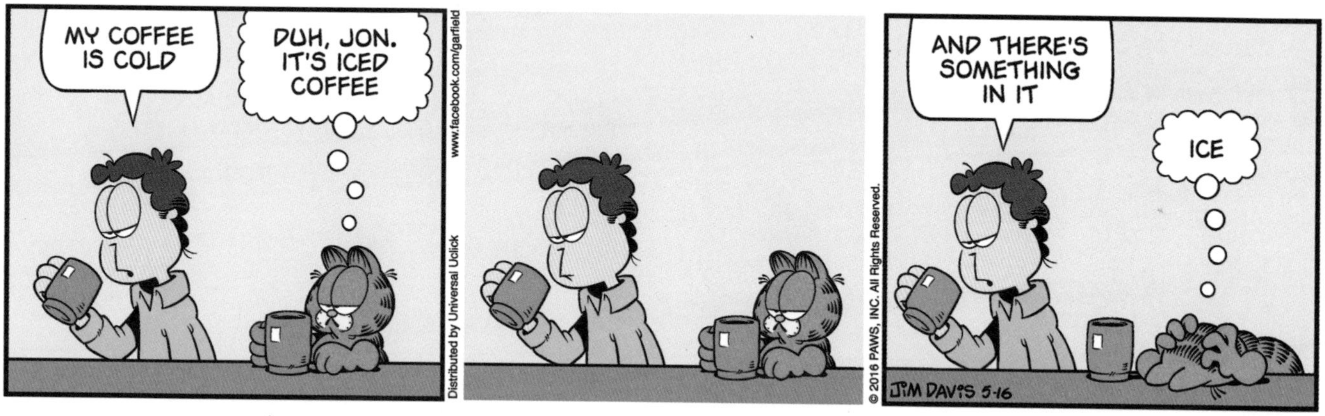
MY COFFEE IS COLD
DUH, JON. IT'S ICED COFFEE
Distributed by Universal Uclick www.facebook.com/garfield
© 2016 PAWS, INC. All Rights Reserved.
AND THERE'S SOMETHING IN IT
ICE
JIM DAVIS 5-16

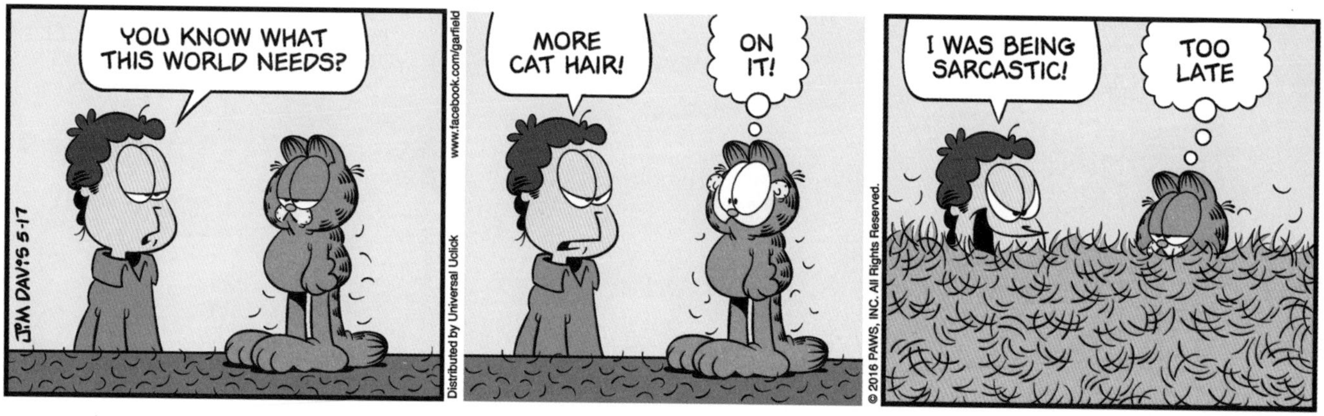
JIM DAVIS 5-17
YOU KNOW WHAT THIS WORLD NEEDS?
Distributed by Universal Uclick www.facebook.com/garfield
MORE CAT HAIR!
ON IT!
© 2016 PAWS, INC. All Rights Reserved.
I WAS BEING SARCASTIC!
TOO LATE

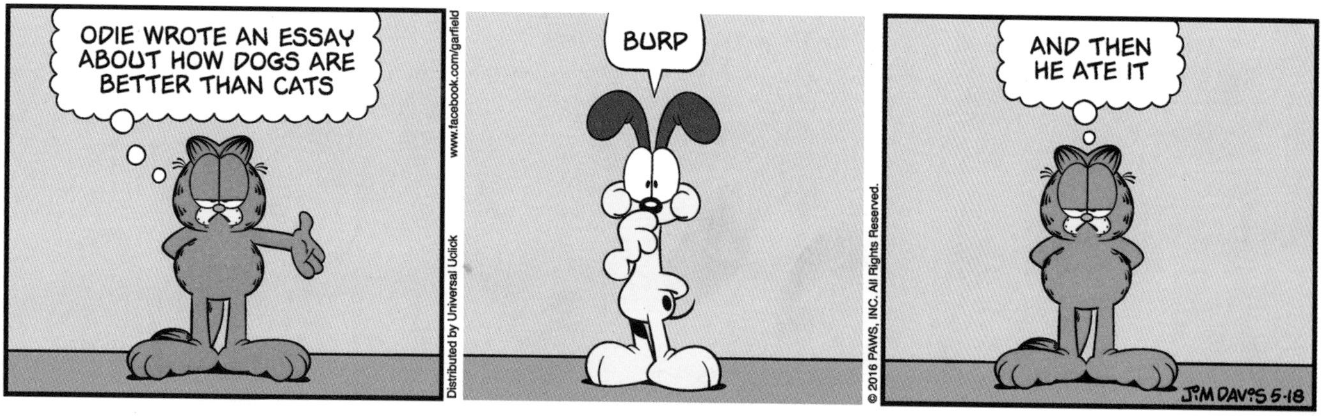
ODIE WROTE AN ESSAY ABOUT HOW DOGS ARE BETTER THAN CATS
Distributed by Universal Uclick www.facebook.com/garfield
BURP
© 2016 PAWS, INC. All Rights Reserved.
AND THEN HE ATE IT
JIM DAVIS 5-18

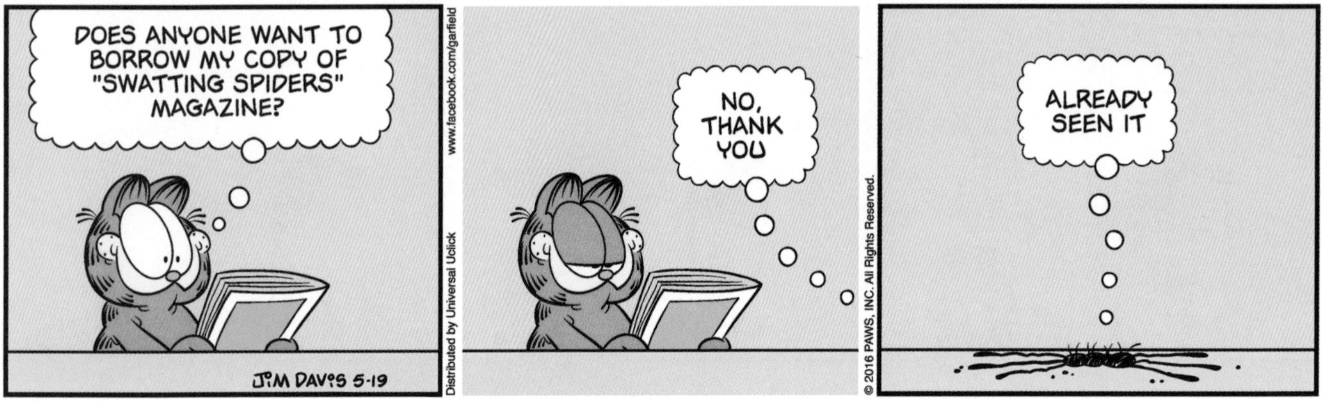
DOES ANYONE WANT TO BORROW MY COPY OF "SWATTING SPIDERS" MAGAZINE?
JIM DAVIS 5-19
www.facebook.com/garfield
Distributed by Universal Uclick
NO, THANK YOU
ALREADY SEEN IT
© 2016 PAWS, INC. All Rights Reserved.

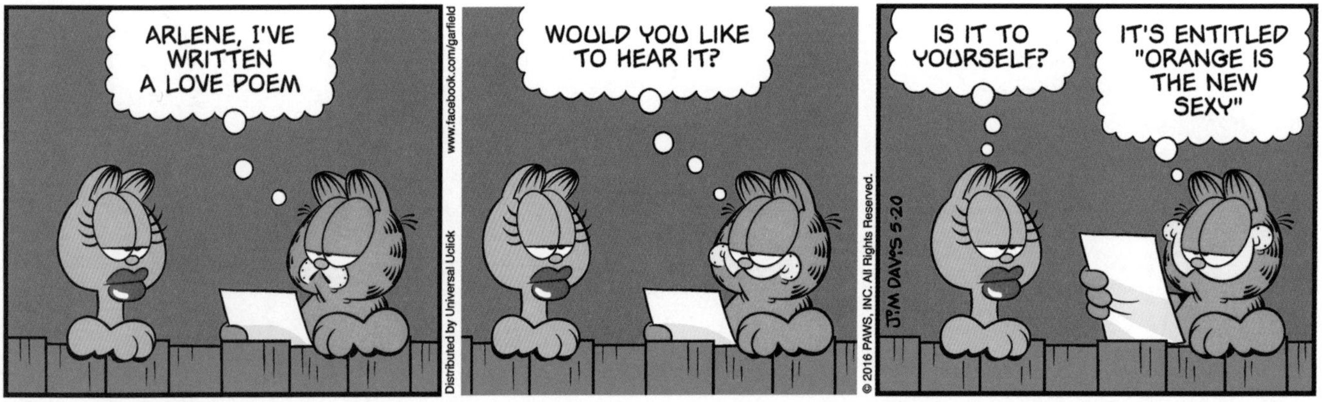
ARLENE, I'VE WRITTEN A LOVE POEM
www.facebook.com/garfield
Distributed by Universal Uclick
WOULD YOU LIKE TO HEAR IT?
IS IT TO YOURSELF?
IT'S ENTITLED "ORANGE IS THE NEW SEXY"
JIM DAVIS 5-20
© 2016 PAWS, INC. All Rights Reserved.

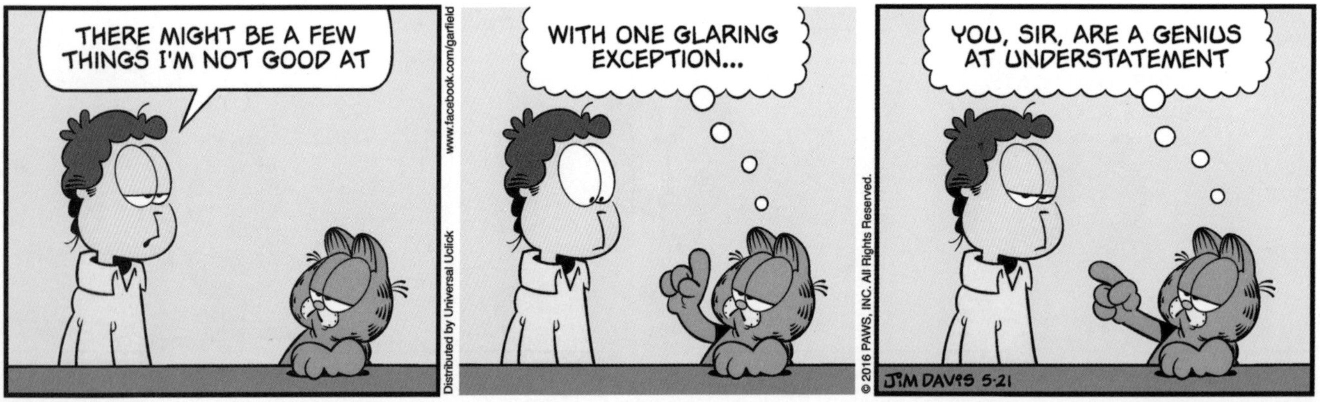
THERE MIGHT BE A FEW THINGS I'M NOT GOOD AT
www.facebook.com/garfield
Distributed by Universal Uclick
WITH ONE GLARING EXCEPTION...
YOU, SIR, ARE A GENIUS AT UNDERSTATEMENT
JIM DAVIS 5-21
© 2016 PAWS, INC. All Rights Reserved.

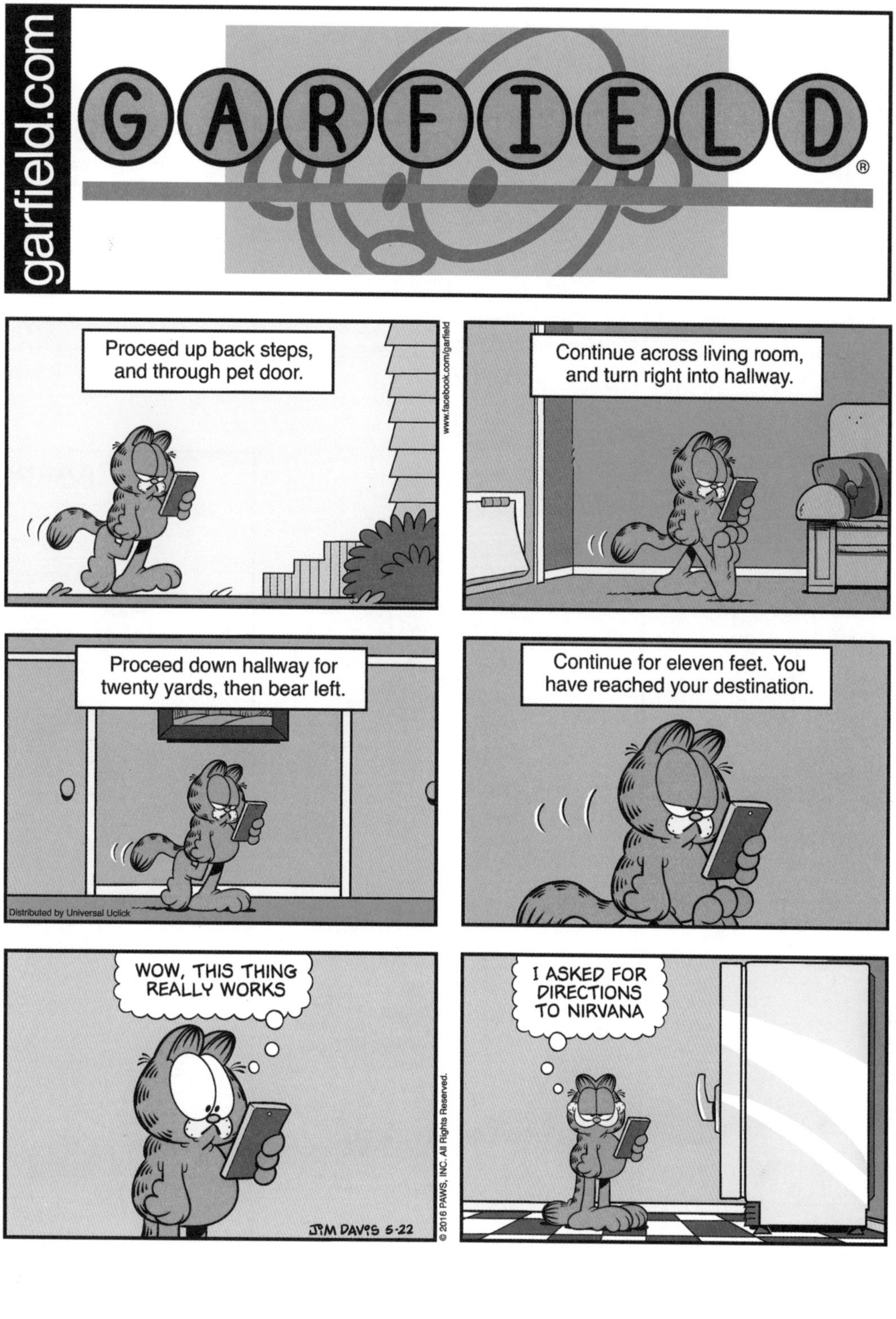
garfield.com
GARFIELD®
Proceed up back steps, and through pet door.
www.facebook.com/garfield
Continue across living room, and turn right into hallway.
Proceed down hallway for twenty yards, then bear left.
Distributed by Universal Uclick
Continue for eleven feet. You have reached your destination.
WOW, THIS THING REALLY WORKS
JIM DAVIS 5-22
© 2016 PAWS, INC. All Rights Reserved.
I ASKED FOR DIRECTIONS TO NIRVANA

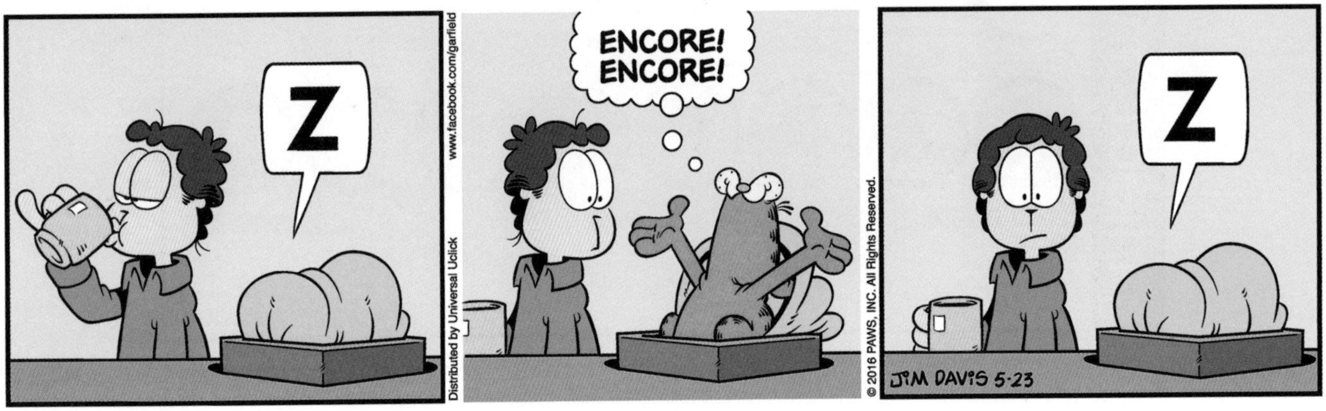
Z
ENCORE! ENCORE!
Z
www.facebook.com/garfield
Distributed by Universal Uclick
© 2016 PAWS, INC. All Rights Reserved.
JIM DAVIS 5-23

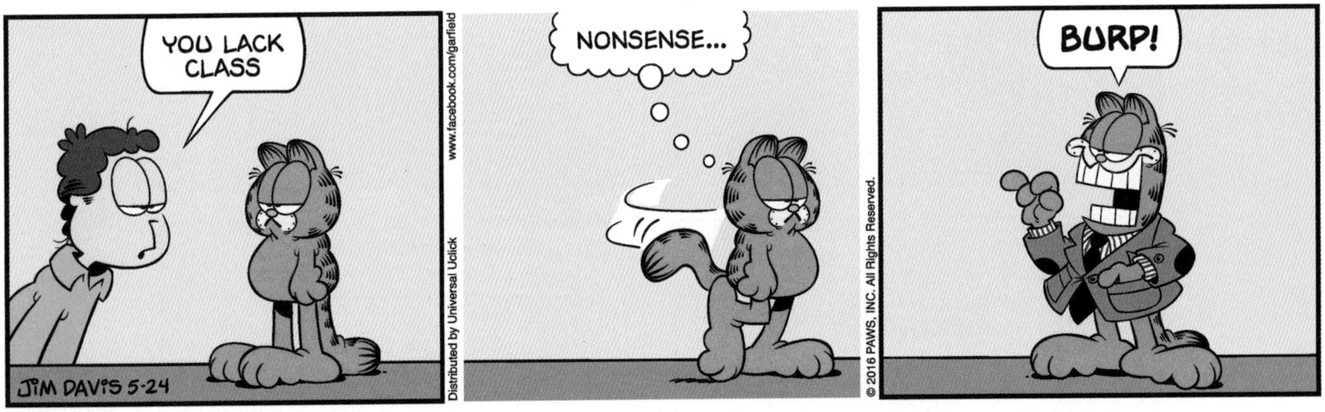
YOU LACK CLASS
NONSENSE...
BURP!
JIM DAVIS 5-24
www.facebook.com/garfield
Distributed by Universal Uclick
© 2016 PAWS, INC. All Rights Reserved.

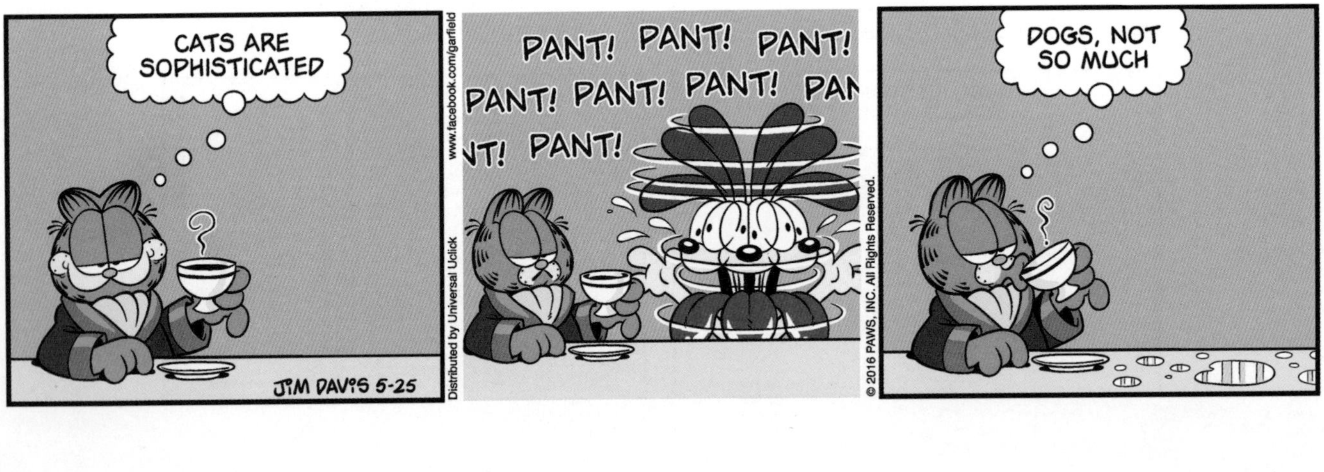
CATS ARE SOPHISTICATED
PANT! PANT! PANT!
PANT! PANT! PANT!
PANT!
DOGS, NOT SO MUCH
JIM DAVIS 5-25
www.facebook.com/garfield
Distributed by Universal Uclick
© 2016 PAWS, INC. All Rights Reserved.

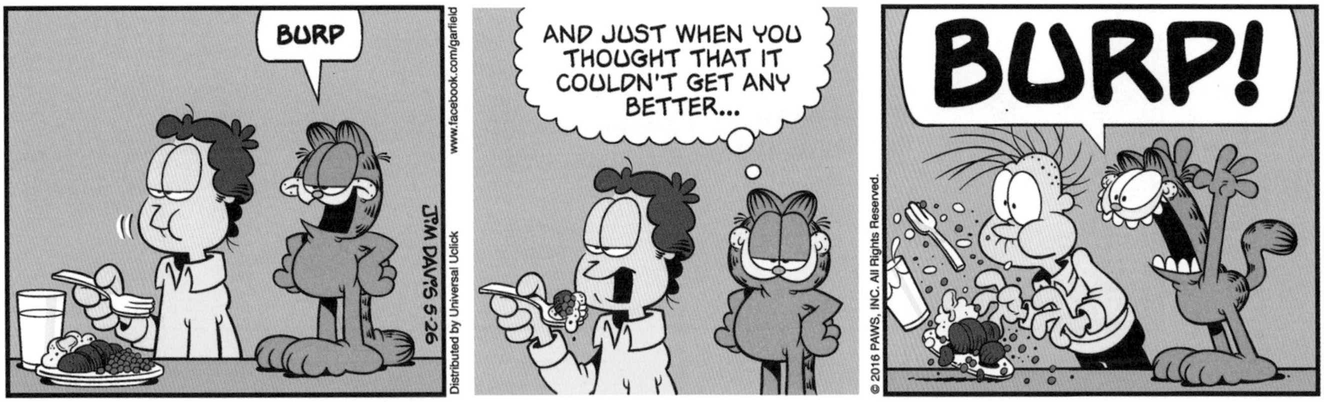
BURP
JIM DAVIS 5-26
www.facebook.com/garfield
Distributed by Universal Uclick
AND JUST WHEN YOU THOUGHT THAT IT COULDN'T GET ANY BETTER...
© 2016 PAWS, INC. All Rights Reserved.
BURP!

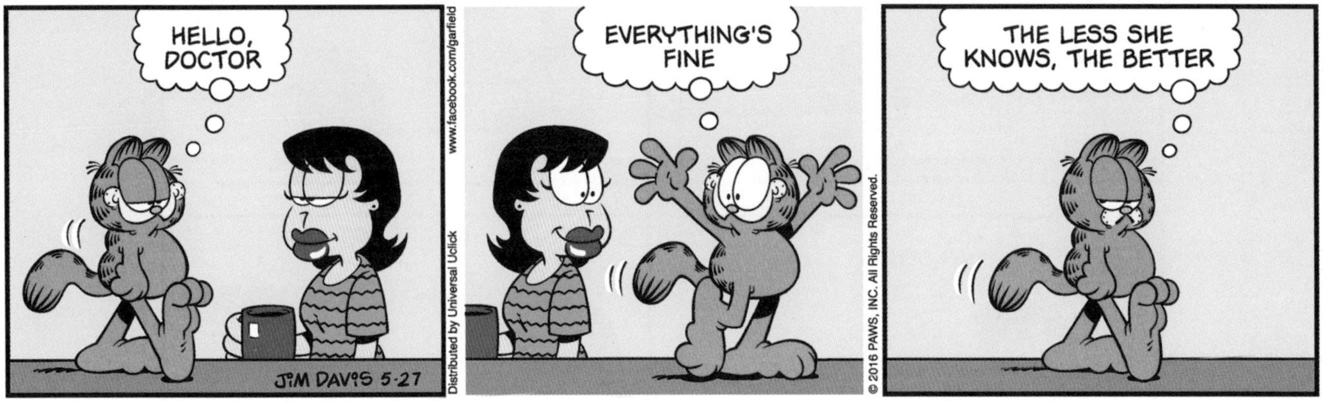
HELLO, DOCTOR
JIM DAVIS 5-27
www.facebook.com/garfield
Distributed by Universal Uclick
EVERYTHING'S FINE
© 2016 PAWS, INC. All Rights Reserved.
THE LESS SHE KNOWS, THE BETTER

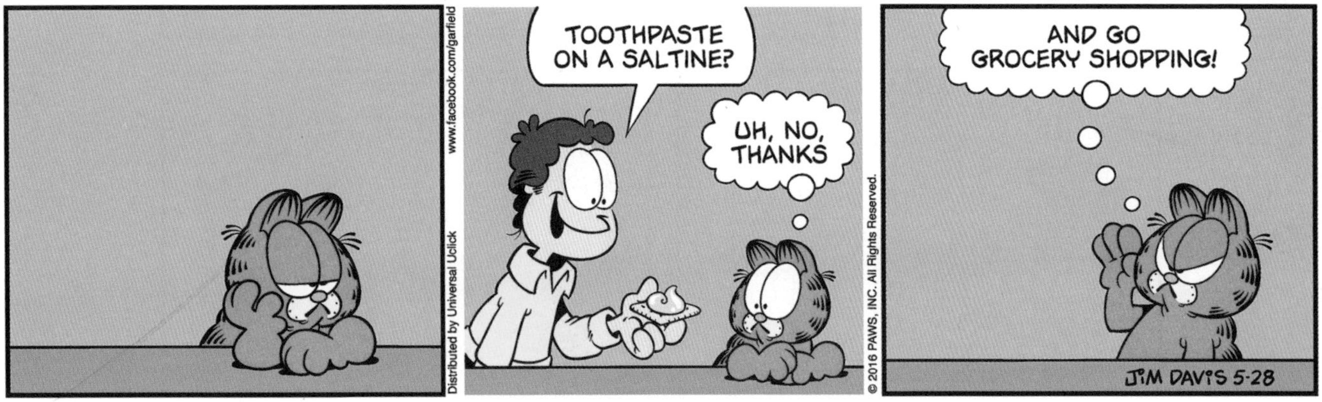
www.facebook.com/garfield
Distributed by Universal Uclick
TOOTHPASTE ON A SALTINE?
UH, NO, THANKS
© 2016 PAWS, INC. All Rights Reserved.
AND GO GROCERY SHOPPING!
JIM DAVIS 5-28

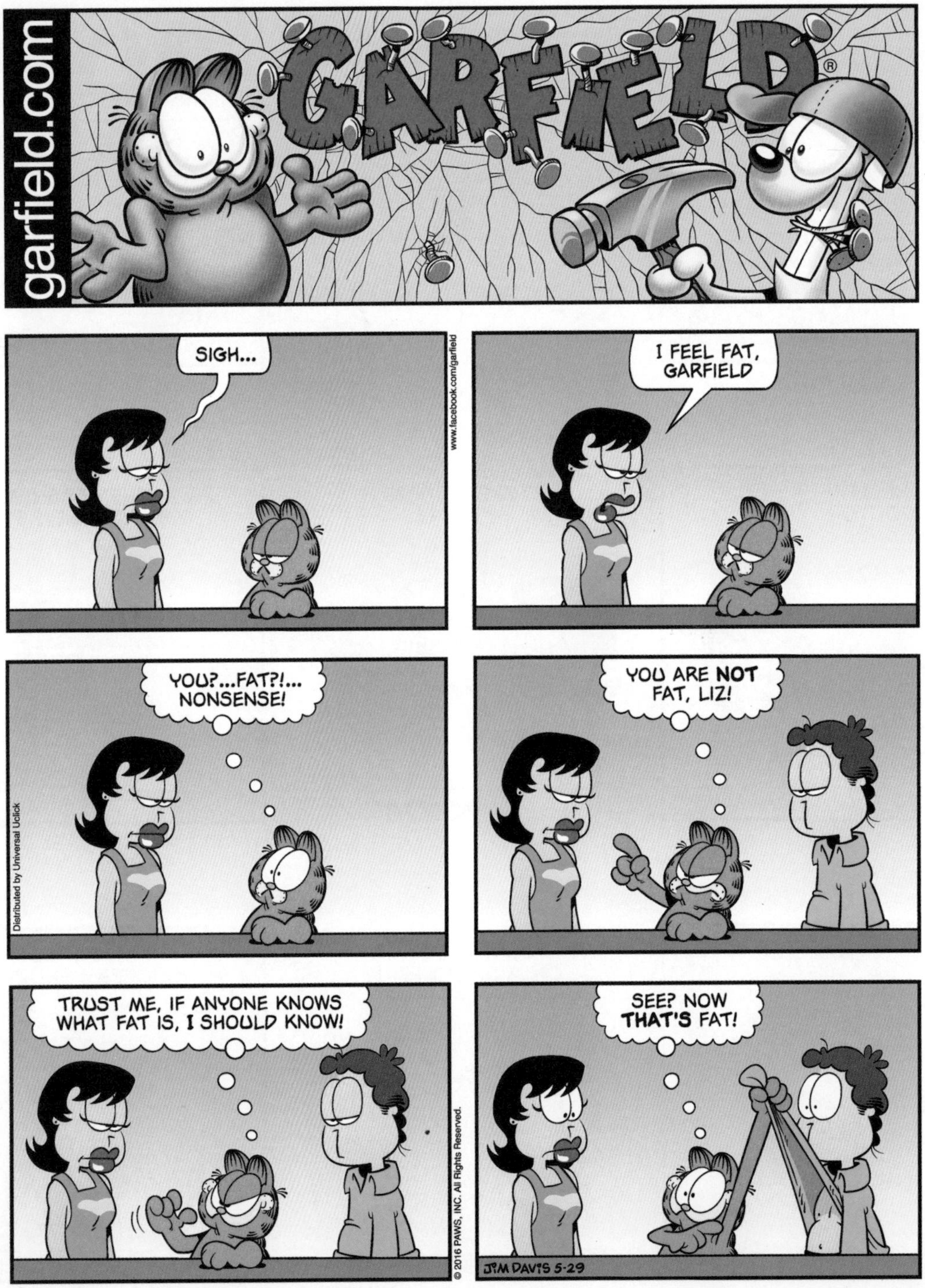
garfield.com
GARFIELD®
SIGH...
I FEEL FAT, GARFIELD
YOU?...FAT?!... NONSENSE!
YOU ARE NOT FAT, LIZ!
TRUST ME, IF ANYONE KNOWS WHAT FAT IS, I SHOULD KNOW!
SEE? NOW THAT'S FAT!
www.facebook.com/garfield
Distributed by Universal Uclick
© 2016 PAWS, INC. All Rights Reserved.
JIM DAVIS 5-29

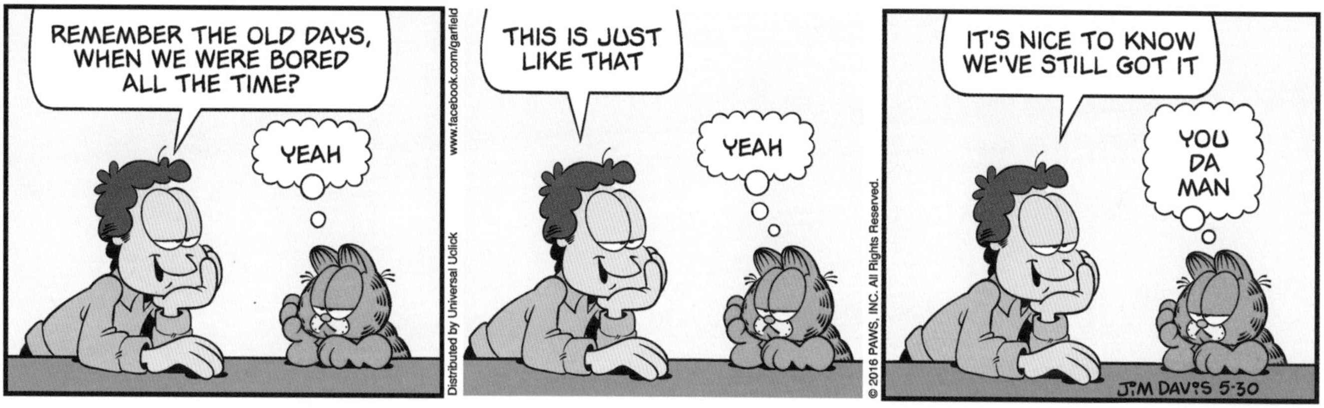
REMEMBER THE OLD DAYS, WHEN WE WERE BORED ALL THE TIME?
YEAH
THIS IS JUST LIKE THAT
YEAH
IT'S NICE TO KNOW WE'VE STILL GOT IT
YOU DA MAN
JIM DAVIS 5-30
www.facebook.com/garfield
Distributed by Universal Uclick
© 2016 PAWS, INC. All Rights Reserved.

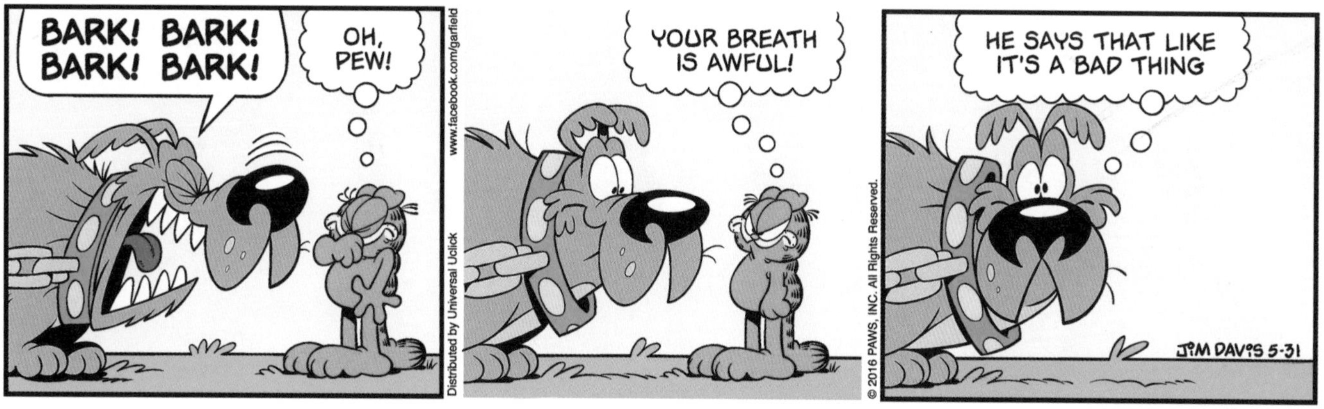
BARK! BARK! BARK! BARK!
OH, PEW!
YOUR BREATH IS AWFUL!
HE SAYS THAT LIKE IT'S A BAD THING
JIM DAVIS 5-31
www.facebook.com/garfield
Distributed by Universal Uclick
© 2016 PAWS, INC. All Rights Reserved.

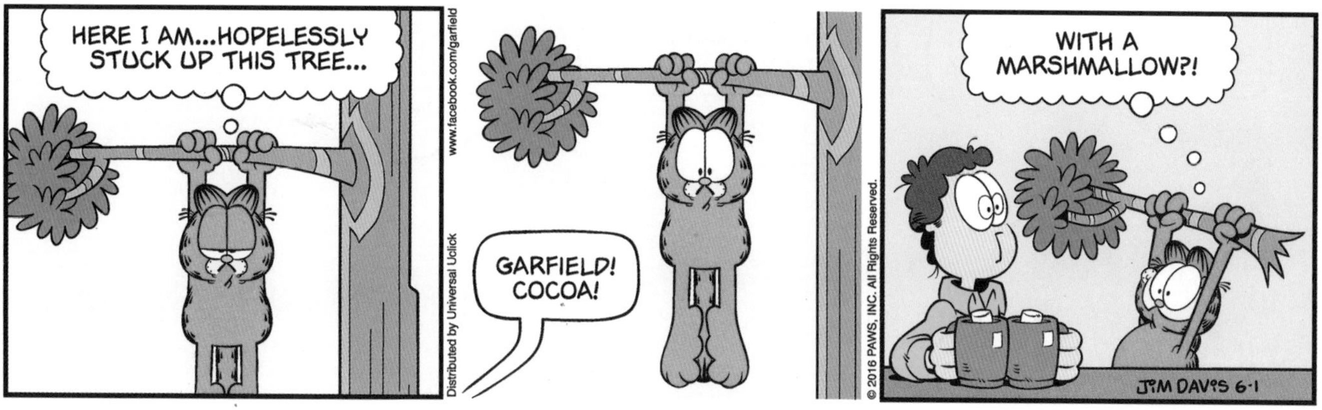
HERE I AM...HOPELESSLY STUCK UP THIS TREE...
GARFIELD! COCOA!
WITH A MARSHMALLOW?!
JIM DAVIS 6-1
www.facebook.com/garfield
Distributed by Universal Uclick
© 2016 PAWS, INC. All Rights Reserved.

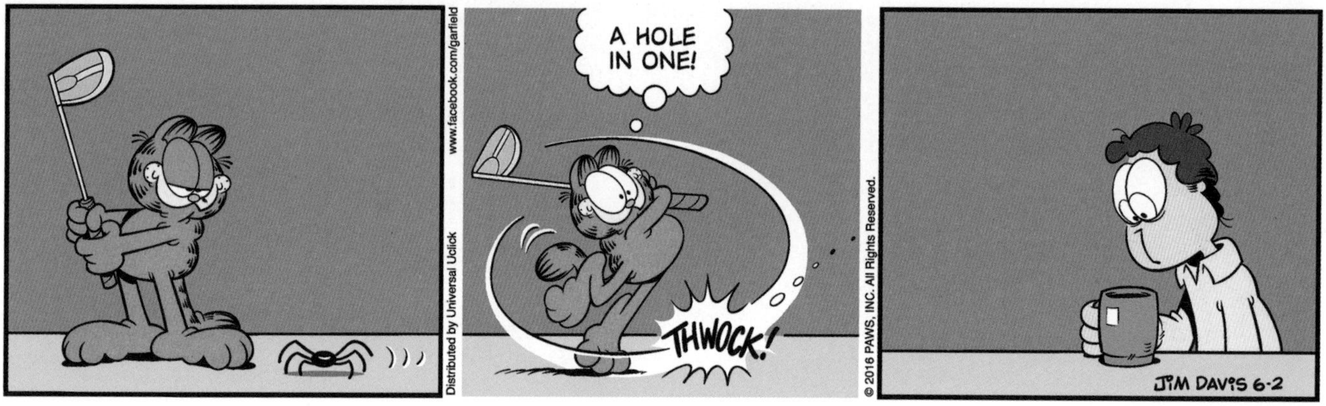
Distributed by Universal Uclick
www.facebook.com/garfield
A HOLE IN ONE!
THWOCK!
© 2016 PAWS, INC. All Rights Reserved.
JIM DAVIS 6-2

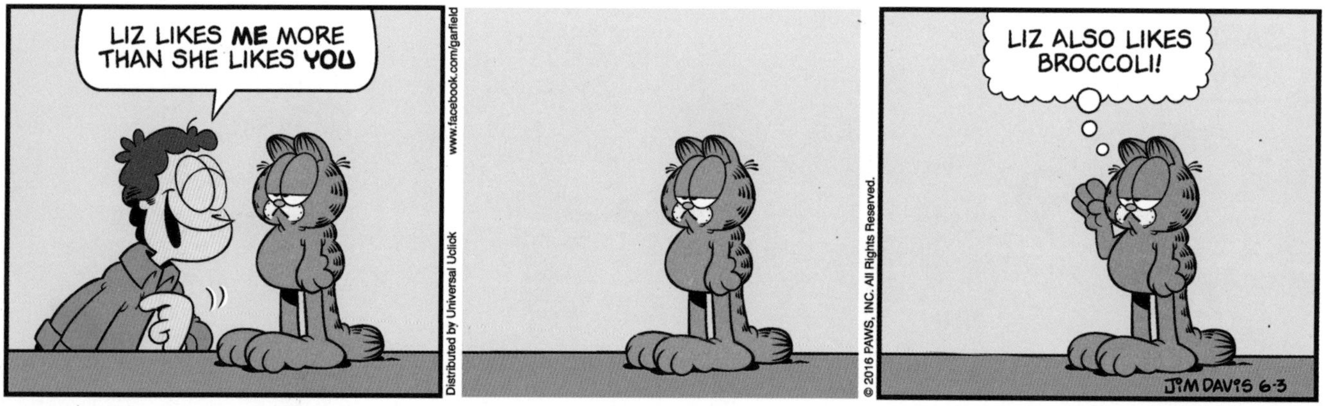
LIZ LIKES **ME** MORE THAN SHE LIKES **YOU**
Distributed by Universal Uclick
www.facebook.com/garfield
© 2016 PAWS, INC. All Rights Reserved.
LIZ ALSO LIKES BROCCOLI!
JIM DAVIS 6-3

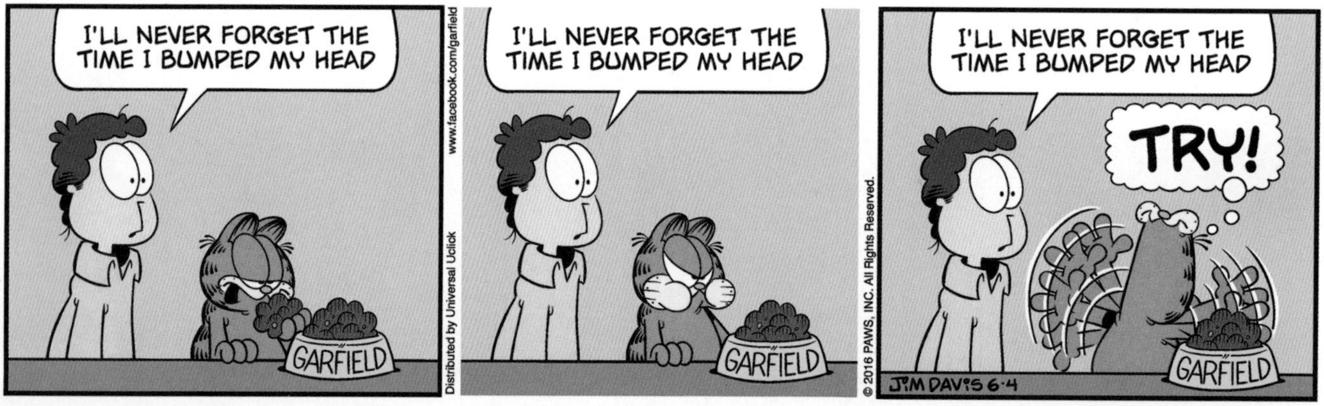
I'LL NEVER FORGET THE TIME I BUMPED MY HEAD
GARFIELD
Distributed by Universal Uclick
www.facebook.com/garfield
I'LL NEVER FORGET THE TIME I BUMPED MY HEAD
GARFIELD
© 2016 PAWS, INC. All Rights Reserved.
I'LL NEVER FORGET THE TIME I BUMPED MY HEAD
TRY!
GARFIELD
JIM DAVIS 6-4

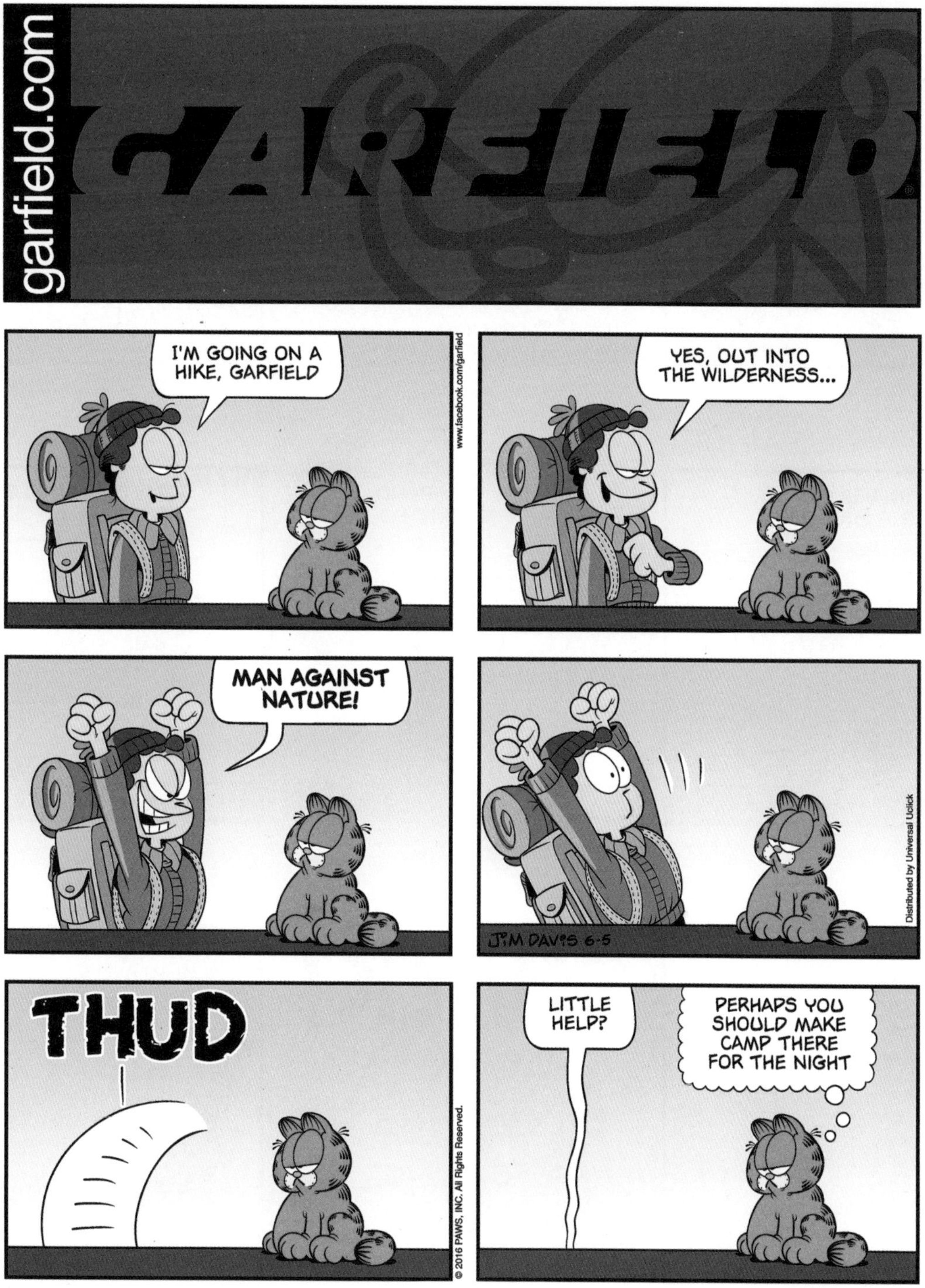
garfield.com
GARFIELD
I'M GOING ON A HIKE, GARFIELD
www.facebook.com/garfield
YES, OUT INTO THE WILDERNESS...
MAN AGAINST NATURE!
JIM DAVIS 6-5
Distributed by Universal Uclick
THUD
© 2016 PAWS, INC. All Rights Reserved.
LITTLE HELP?
PERHAPS YOU SHOULD MAKE CAMP THERE FOR THE NIGHT

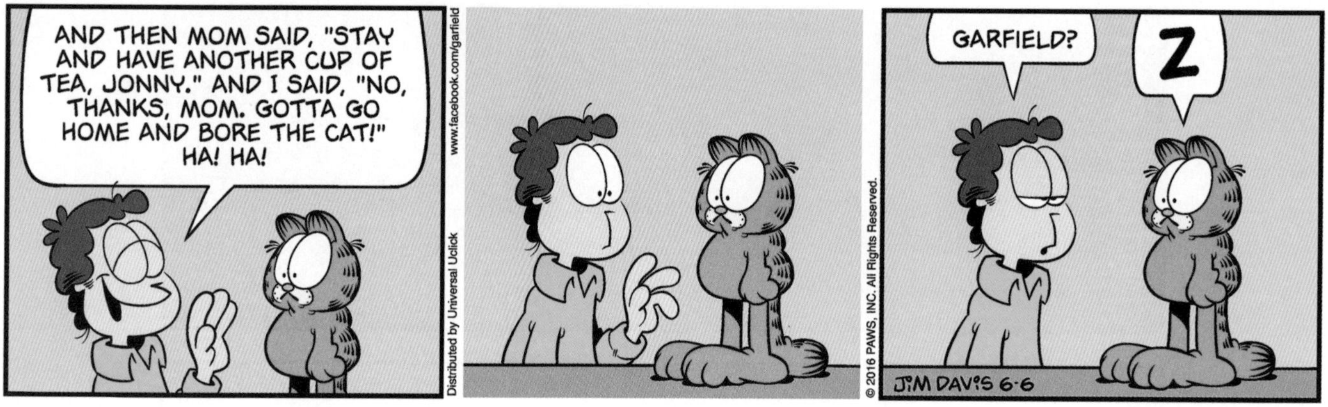
AND THEN MOM SAID, "STAY AND HAVE ANOTHER CUP OF TEA, JONNY." AND I SAID, "NO, THANKS, MOM. GOTTA GO HOME AND BORE THE CAT!" HA! HA!
www.facebook.com/garfield
Distributed by Universal Uclick
GARFIELD?
Z
© 2016 PAWS, INC. All Rights Reserved.
JIM DAVIS 6-6

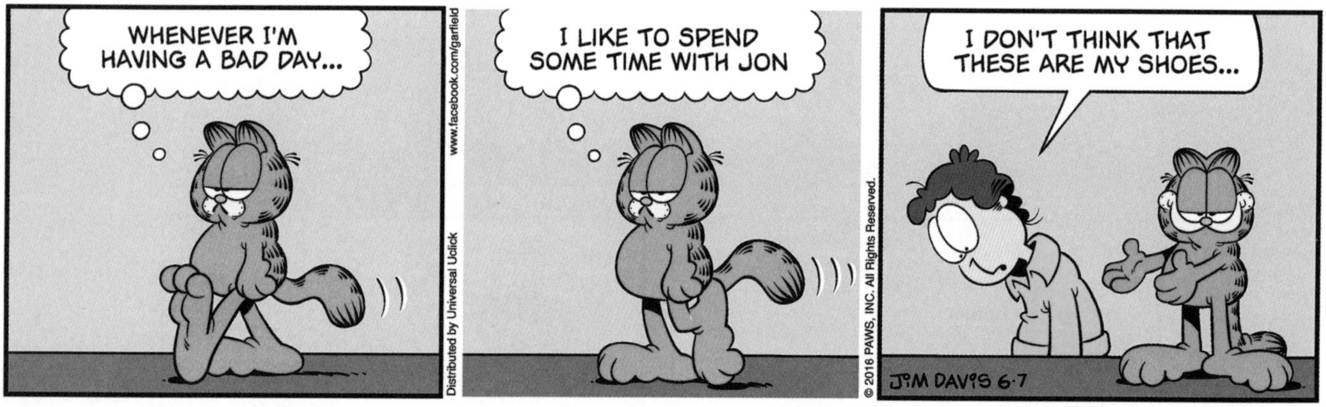
WHENEVER I'M HAVING A BAD DAY...
www.facebook.com/garfield
Distributed by Universal Uclick
I LIKE TO SPEND SOME TIME WITH JON
I DON'T THINK THAT THESE ARE MY SHOES...
© 2016 PAWS, INC. All Rights Reserved.
JIM DAVIS 6-7

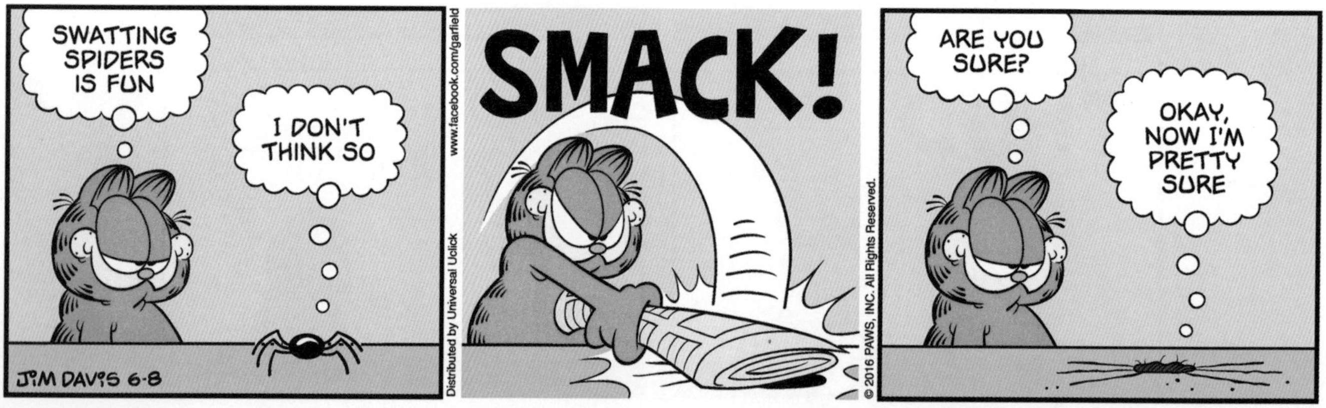
SWATTING SPIDERS IS FUN
I DON'T THINK SO
JIM DAVIS 6-8
www.facebook.com/garfield
Distributed by Universal Uclick
SMACK!
ARE YOU SURE?
OKAY, NOW I'M PRETTY SURE
© 2016 PAWS, INC. All Rights Reserved.

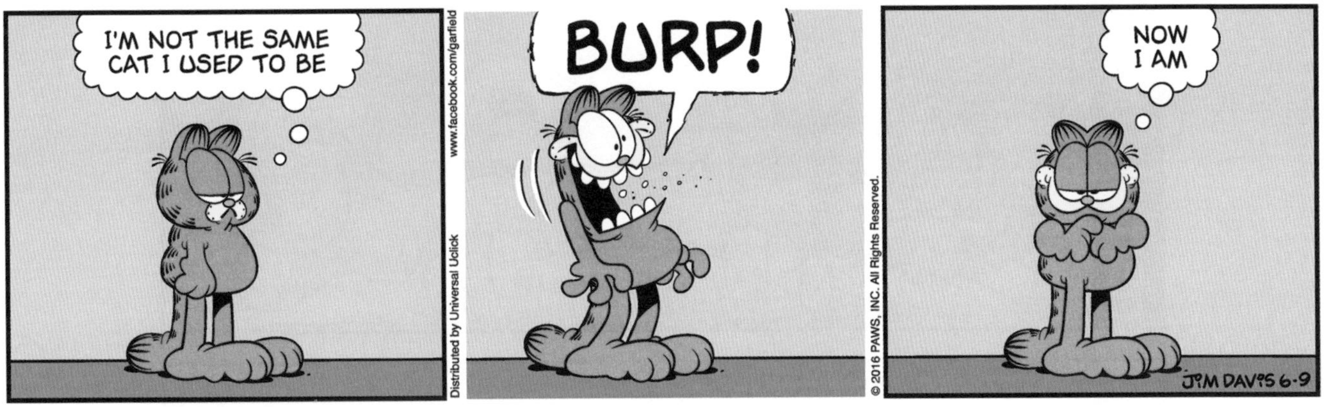
I'M NOT THE SAME CAT I USED TO BE
Distributed by Universal Uclick www.facebook.com/garfield
BURP!
© 2016 PAWS, INC. All Rights Reserved.
NOW I AM
JIM DAVIS 6-9

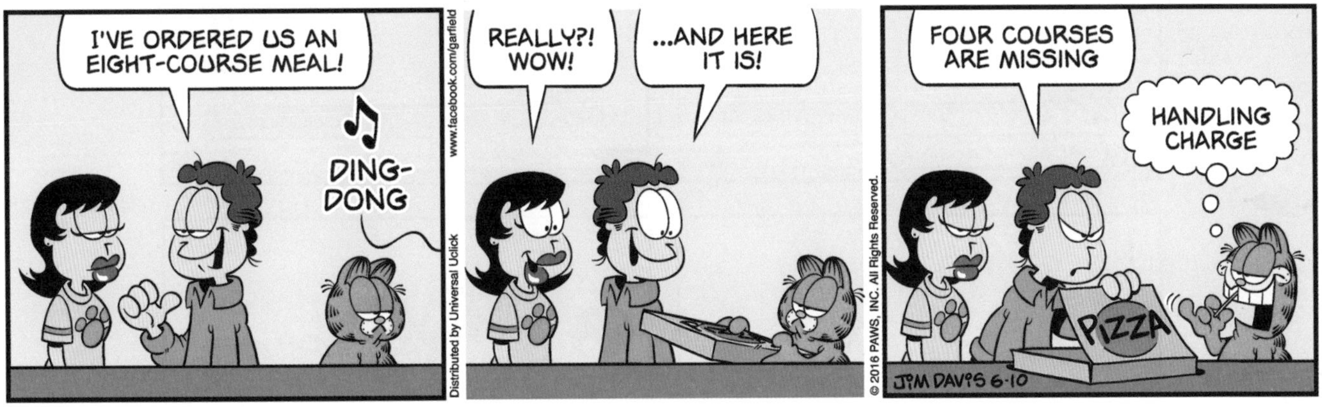
I'VE ORDERED US AN EIGHT-COURSE MEAL!
DING-DONG
Distributed by Universal Uclick www.facebook.com/garfield
REALLY?! WOW!
...AND HERE IT IS!
© 2016 PAWS, INC. All Rights Reserved.
FOUR COURSES ARE MISSING
HANDLING CHARGE
PIZZA
JIM DAVIS 6-10

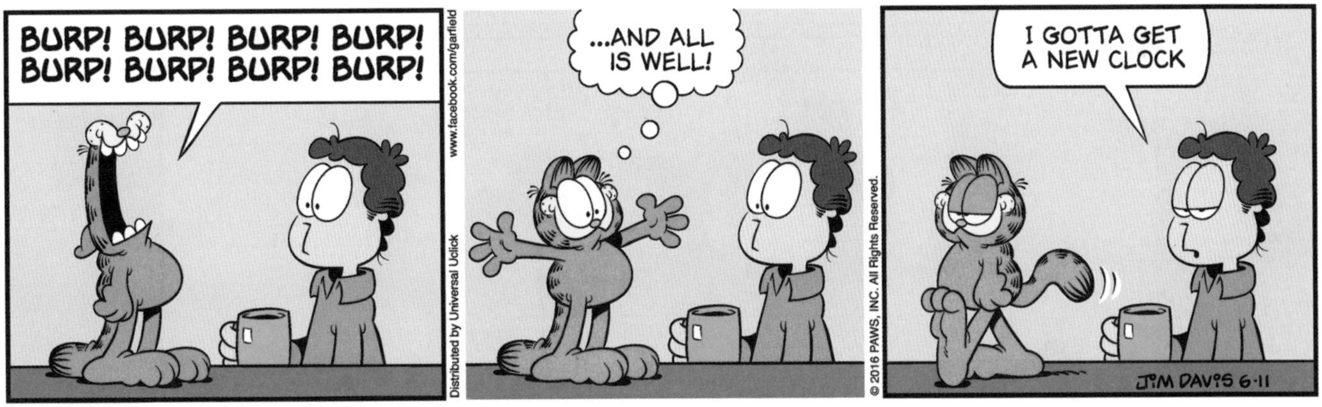
BURP! BURP! BURP! BURP! BURP! BURP! BURP! BURP!
Distributed by Universal Uclick www.facebook.com/garfield
...AND ALL IS WELL!
© 2016 PAWS, INC. All Rights Reserved.
I GOTTA GET A NEW CLOCK
JIM DAVIS 6-11

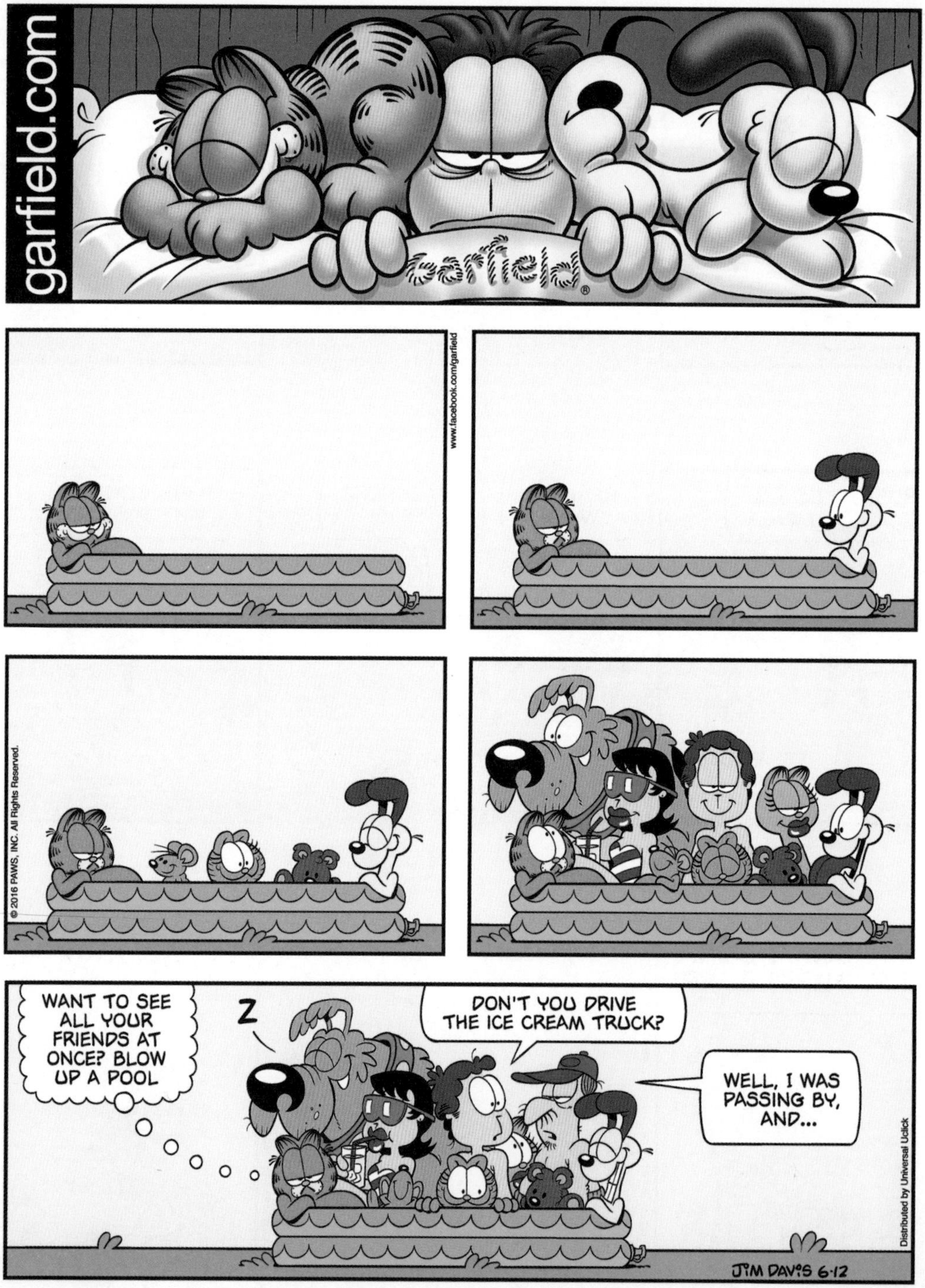
garfield.com
garfield®
www.facebook.com/garfield
© 2016 PAWS, INC. All Rights Reserved.
WANT TO SEE ALL YOUR FRIENDS AT ONCE? BLOW UP A POOL
Z
DON'T YOU DRIVE THE ICE CREAM TRUCK?
WELL, I WAS PASSING BY, AND...
JIM DAVIS 6·12
Distributed by Universal Uclick

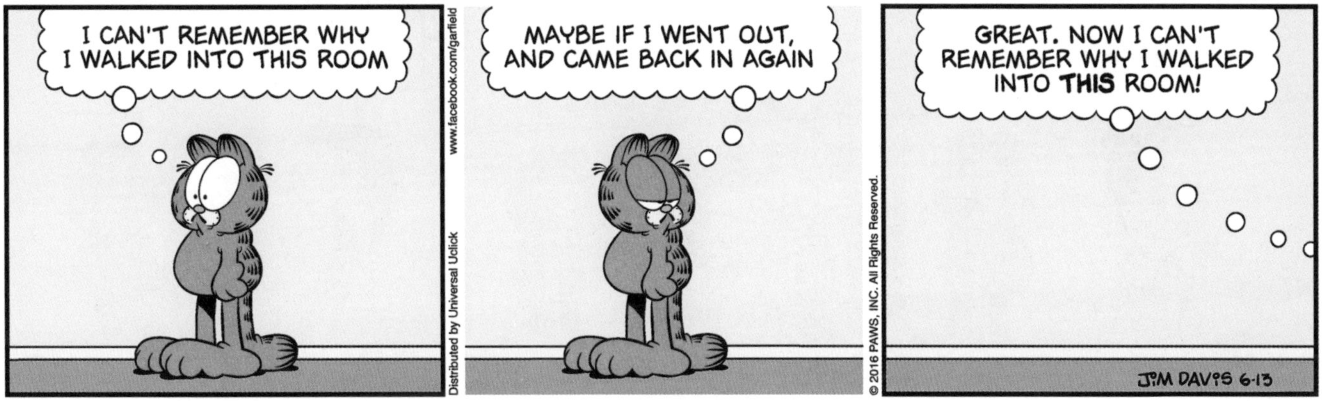
I CAN'T REMEMBER WHY I WALKED INTO THIS ROOM
www.facebook.com/garfield
Distributed by Universal Uclick
MAYBE IF I WENT OUT, AND CAME BACK IN AGAIN
© 2016 PAWS, INC. All Rights Reserved.
GREAT. NOW I CAN'T REMEMBER WHY I WALKED INTO **THIS** ROOM!
JIM DAVIS 6-13

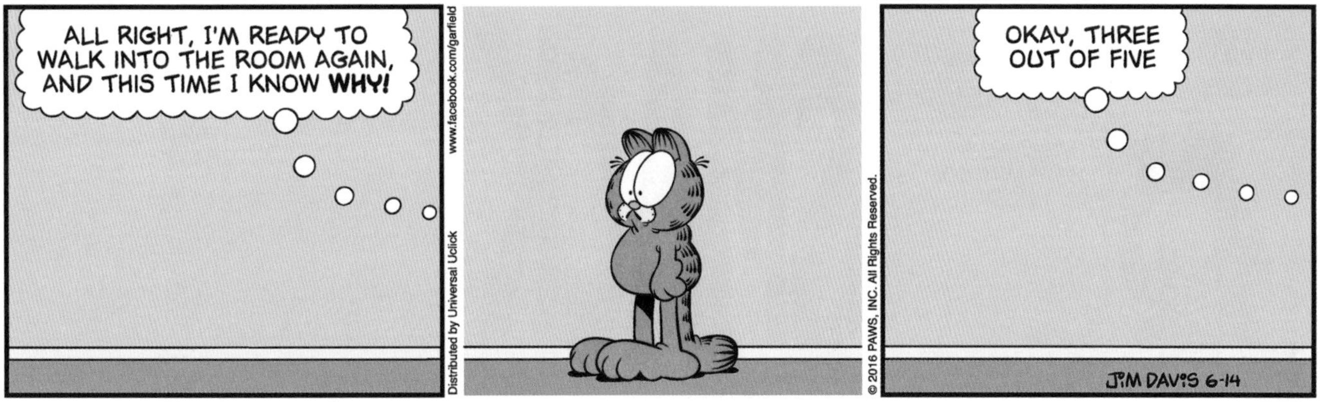
ALL RIGHT, I'M READY TO WALK INTO THE ROOM AGAIN, AND THIS TIME I KNOW **WHY!**
www.facebook.com/garfield
Distributed by Universal Uclick
© 2016 PAWS, INC. All Rights Reserved.
OKAY, THREE OUT OF FIVE
JIM DAVIS 6-14

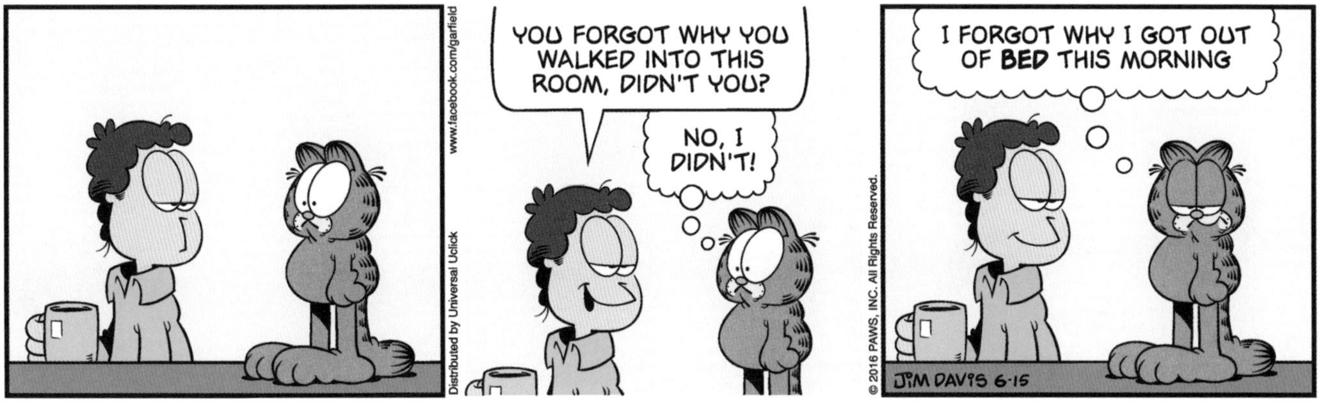
www.facebook.com/garfield
Distributed by Universal Uclick
YOU FORGOT WHY YOU WALKED INTO THIS ROOM, DIDN'T YOU?
NO, I DIDN'T!
© 2016 PAWS, INC. All Rights Reserved.
I FORGOT WHY I GOT OUT OF **BED** THIS MORNING
JIM DAVIS 6-15

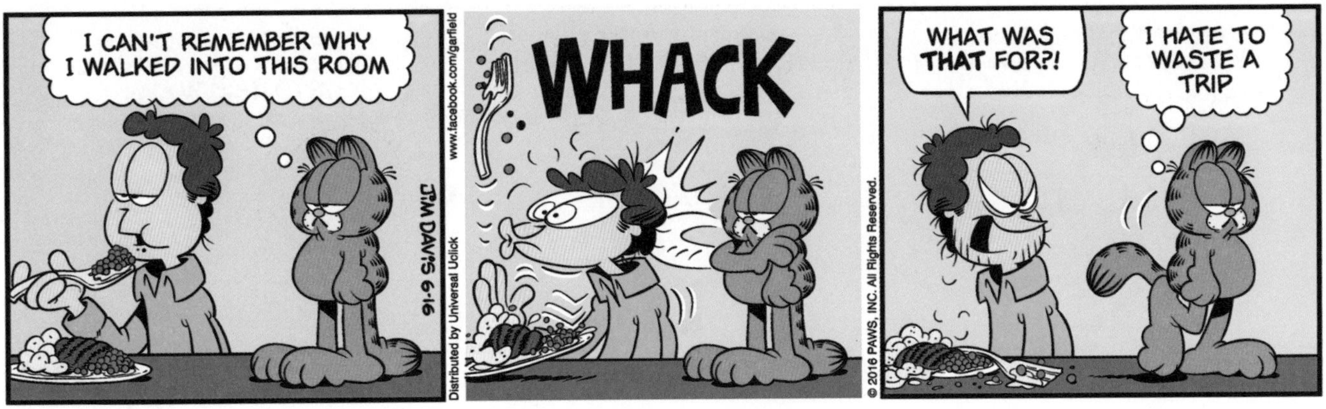
I CAN'T REMEMBER WHY I WALKED INTO THIS ROOM
JIM DAVIS 6-16
www.facebook.com/garfield
Distributed by Universal Uclick
WHACK
© 2016 PAWS, INC. All Rights Reserved.
WHAT WAS THAT FOR?!
I HATE TO WASTE A TRIP

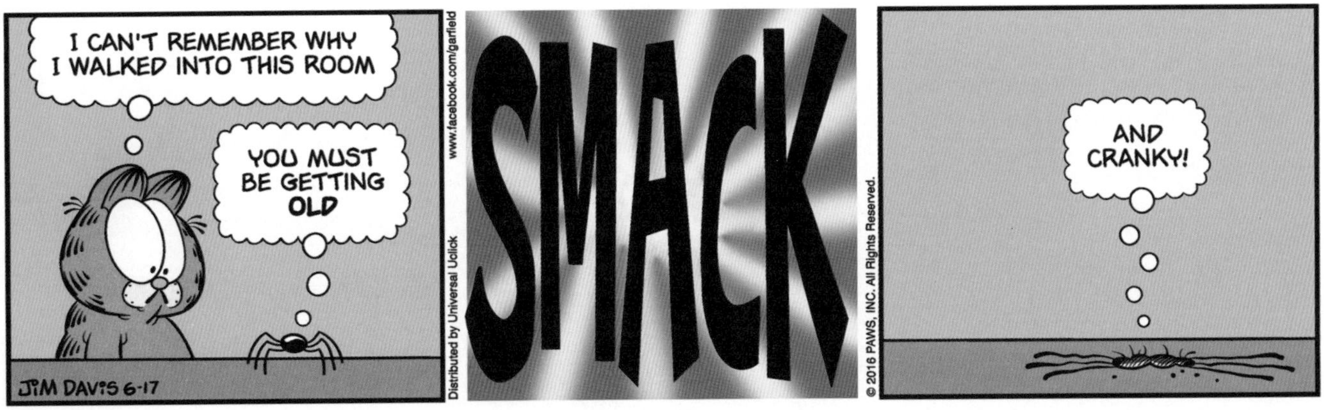
I CAN'T REMEMBER WHY I WALKED INTO THIS ROOM
YOU MUST BE GETTING OLD
JIM DAVIS 6-17
www.facebook.com/garfield
Distributed by Universal Uclick
SMACK
© 2016 PAWS, INC. All Rights Reserved.
AND CRANKY!

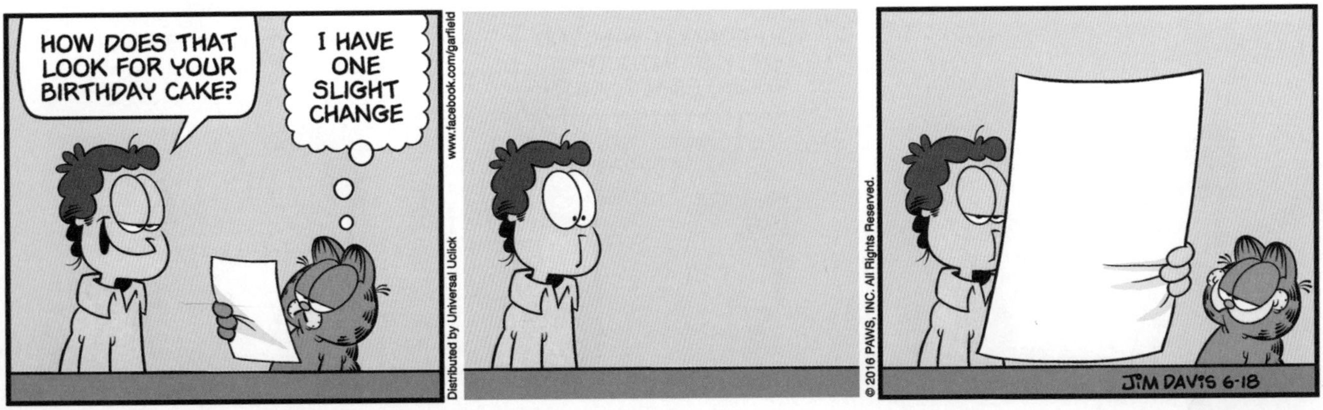
HOW DOES THAT LOOK FOR YOUR BIRTHDAY CAKE?
I HAVE ONE SLIGHT CHANGE
www.facebook.com/garfield
Distributed by Universal Uclick
© 2016 PAWS, INC. All Rights Reserved.
JIM DAVIS 6-18

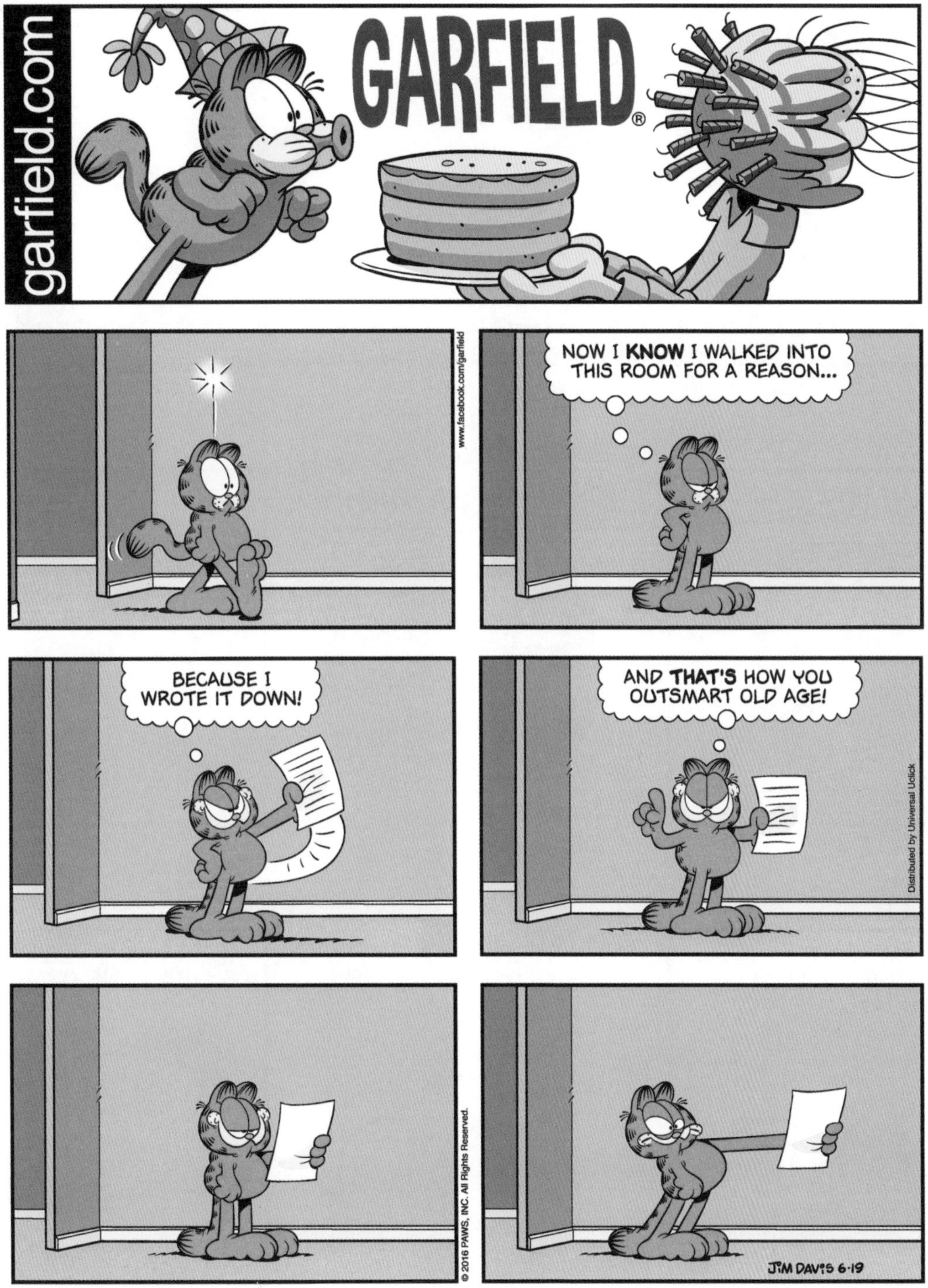
garfield.com
GARFIELD®
www.facebook.com/garfield
NOW I KNOW I WALKED INTO THIS ROOM FOR A REASON...
BECAUSE I WROTE IT DOWN!
AND THAT'S HOW YOU OUTSMART OLD AGE!
Distributed by Universal Uclick
© 2016 PAWS, INC. All Rights Reserved.
JIM DAVIS 6-19

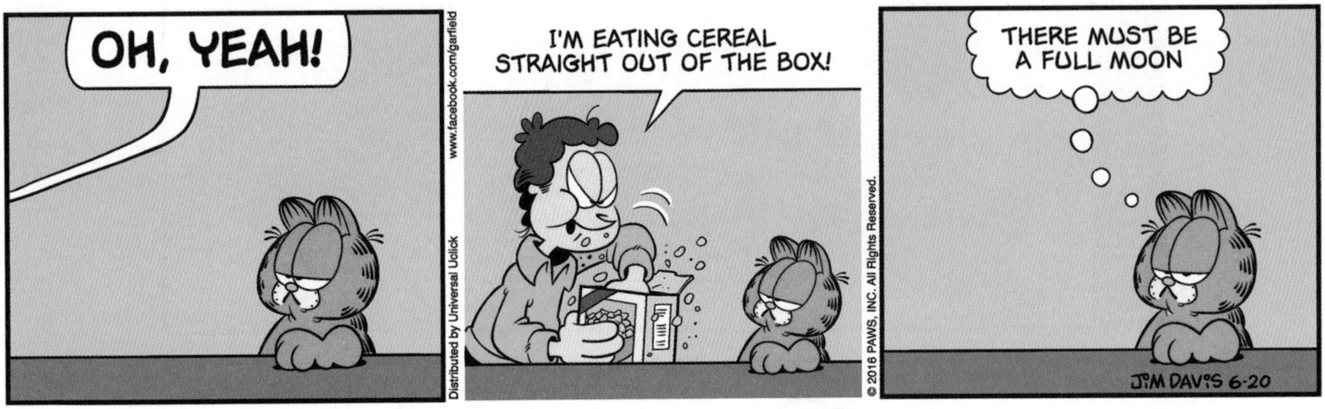
OH, YEAH!
Distributed by Universal Uclick www.facebook.com/garfield
I'M EATING CEREAL STRAIGHT OUT OF THE BOX!
© 2016 PAWS, INC. All Rights Reserved.
THERE MUST BE A FULL MOON
JIM DAVIS 6-20

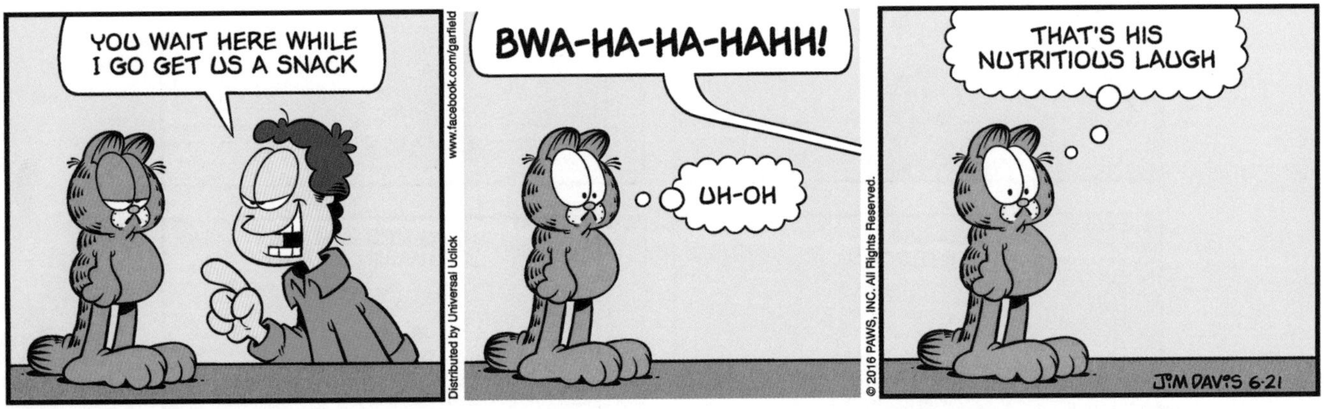
YOU WAIT HERE WHILE I GO GET US A SNACK
Distributed by Universal Uclick www.facebook.com/garfield
BWA-HA-HA-HAHH!
UH-OH
© 2016 PAWS, INC. All Rights Reserved.
THAT'S HIS NUTRITIOUS LAUGH
JIM DAVIS 6-21

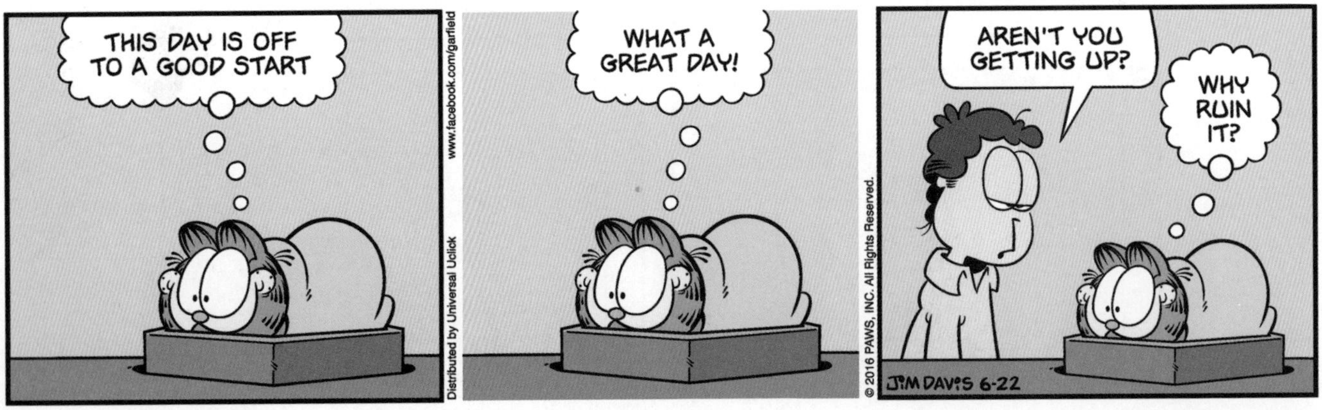
THIS DAY IS OFF TO A GOOD START
Distributed by Universal Uclick www.facebook.com/garfield
WHAT A GREAT DAY!
© 2016 PAWS, INC. All Rights Reserved.
AREN'T YOU GETTING UP?
WHY RUIN IT?
JIM DAVIS 6-22

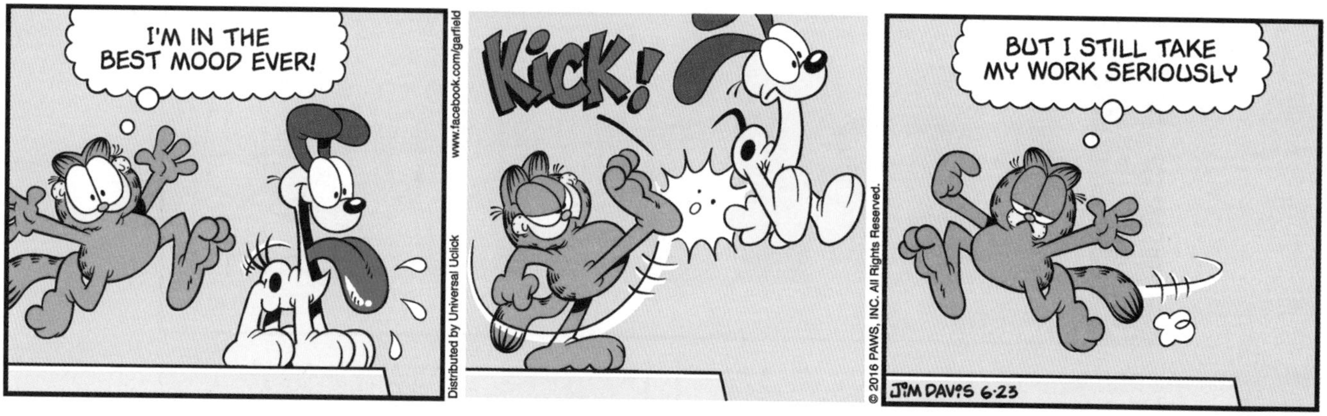
I'M IN THE BEST MOOD EVER!
KICK!
BUT I STILL TAKE MY WORK SERIOUSLY
JIM DAVIS 6-23
Distributed by Universal Uclick
www.facebook.com/garfield
© 2016 PAWS, INC. All Rights Reserved.

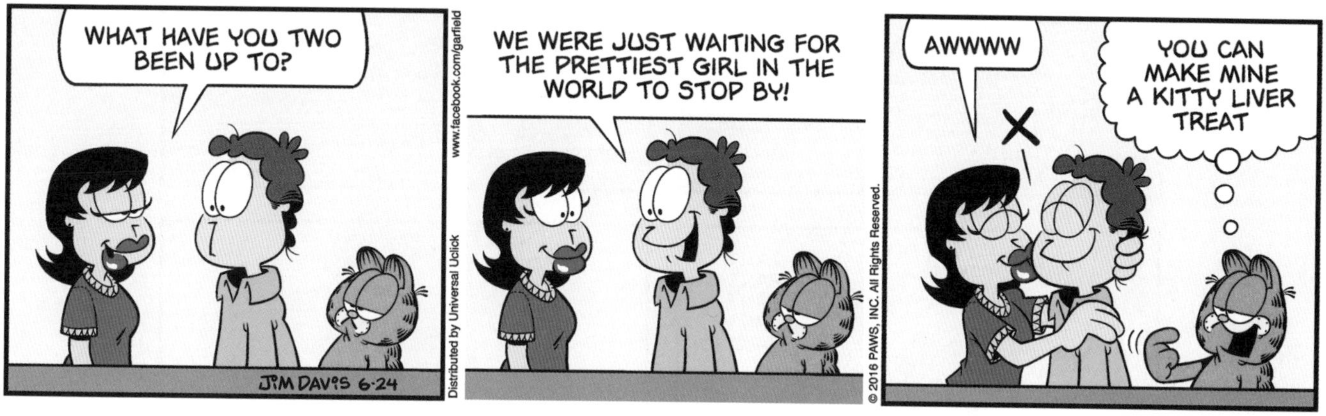
WHAT HAVE YOU TWO BEEN UP TO?
JIM DAVIS 6-24
WE WERE JUST WAITING FOR THE PRETTIEST GIRL IN THE WORLD TO STOP BY!
AWWWW
YOU CAN MAKE MINE A KITTY LIVER TREAT
Distributed by Universal Uclick
www.facebook.com/garfield
© 2016 PAWS, INC. All Rights Reserved.

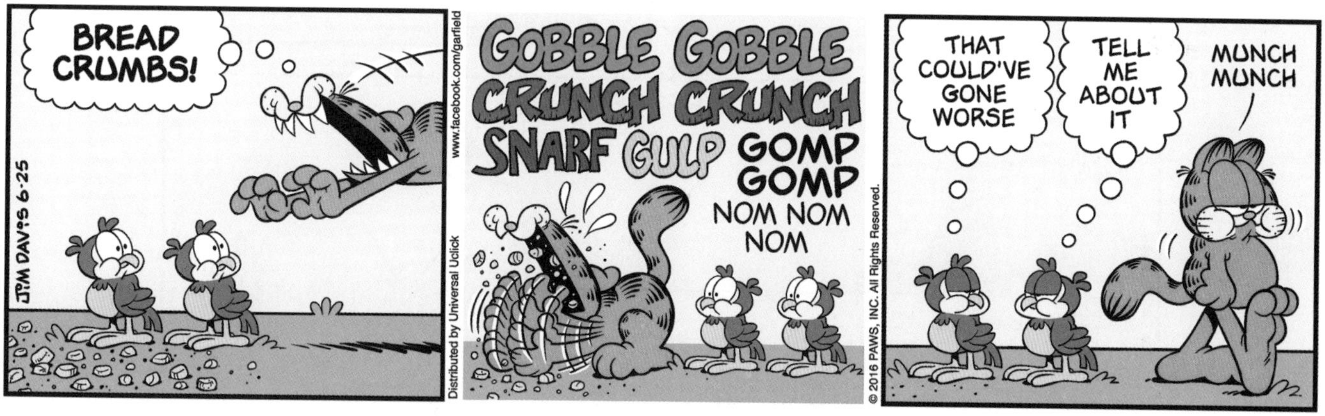
BREAD CRUMBS!
JIM DAVIS 6-25
GOBBLE GOBBLE
CRUNCH CRUNCH
SNARF GULP GOMP GOMP
NOM NOM NOM
THAT COULD'VE GONE WORSE
TELL ME ABOUT IT
MUNCH MUNCH
Distributed by Universal Uclick
www.facebook.com/garfield
© 2016 PAWS, INC. All Rights Reserved.

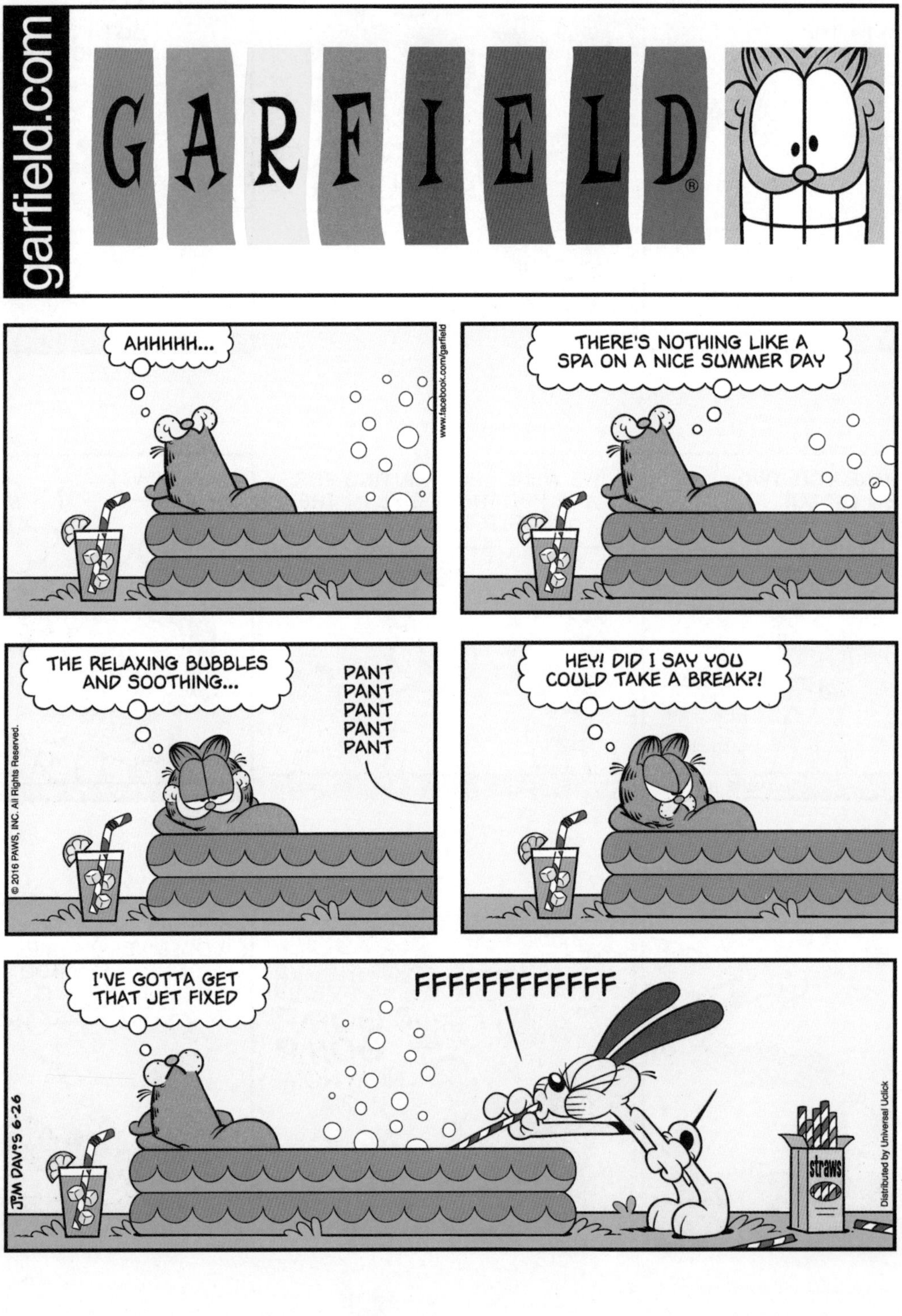
garfield.com
GARFIELD®
AHHHHH...
www.facebook.com/garfield
THERE'S NOTHING LIKE A SPA ON A NICE SUMMER DAY
THE RELAXING BUBBLES AND SOOTHING...
PANT PANT PANT PANT PANT
© 2016 PAWS, INC. All Rights Reserved.
HEY! DID I SAY YOU COULD TAKE A BREAK?!
I'VE GOTTA GET THAT JET FIXED
FFFFFFFFFFFF
JIM DAVIS 6-26
straws
Distributed by Universal Uclick

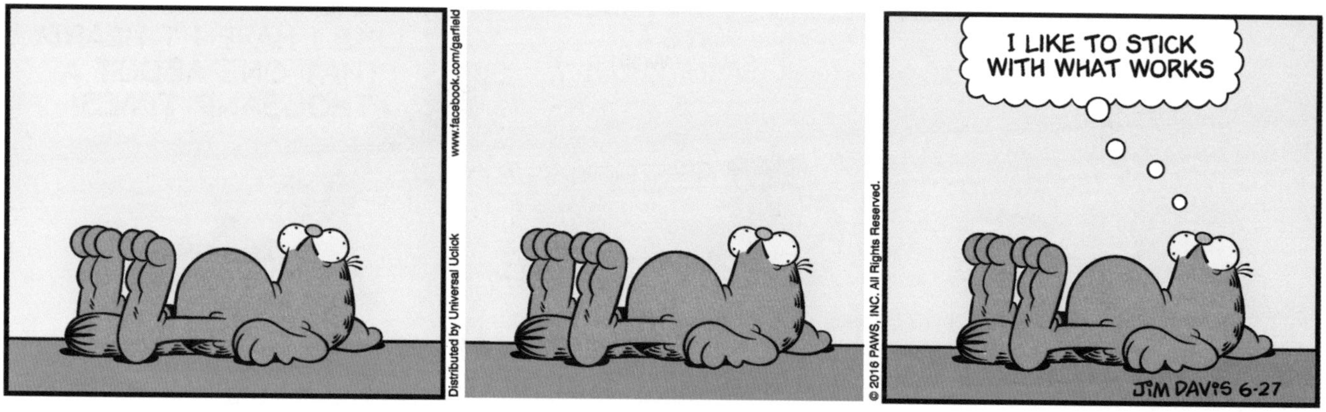
I LIKE TO STICK WITH WHAT WORKS
JIM DAVIS 6-27
Distributed by Universal Uclick www.facebook.com/garfield
© 2016 PAWS, INC. All Rights Reserved.

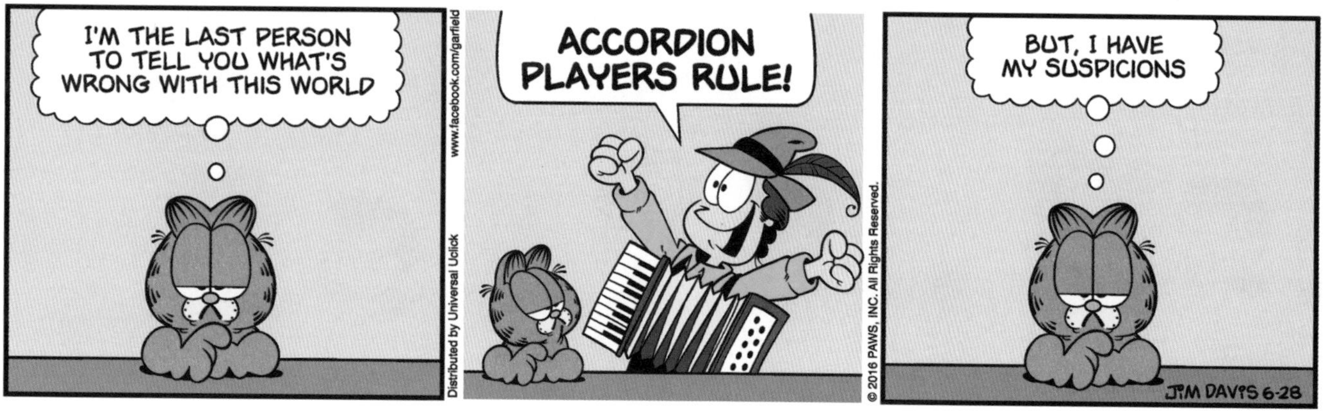
I'M THE LAST PERSON TO TELL YOU WHAT'S WRONG WITH THIS WORLD
ACCORDION PLAYERS RULE!
BUT, I HAVE MY SUSPICIONS
JIM DAVIS 6-28
Distributed by Universal Uclick www.facebook.com/garfield
© 2016 PAWS, INC. All Rights Reserved.

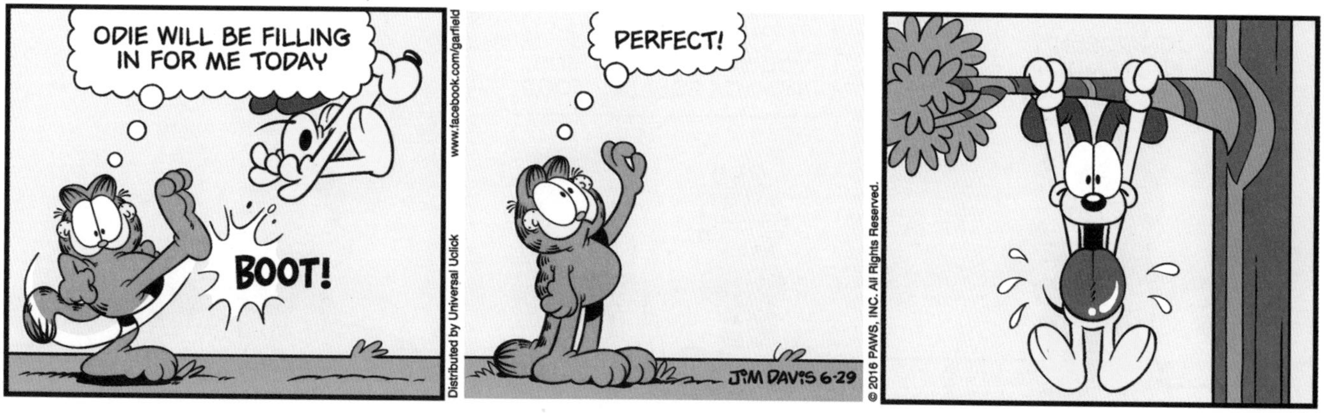
ODIE WILL BE FILLING IN FOR ME TODAY
BOOT!
PERFECT!
JIM DAVIS 6-29
Distributed by Universal Uclick www.facebook.com/garfield
© 2016 PAWS, INC. All Rights Reserved.

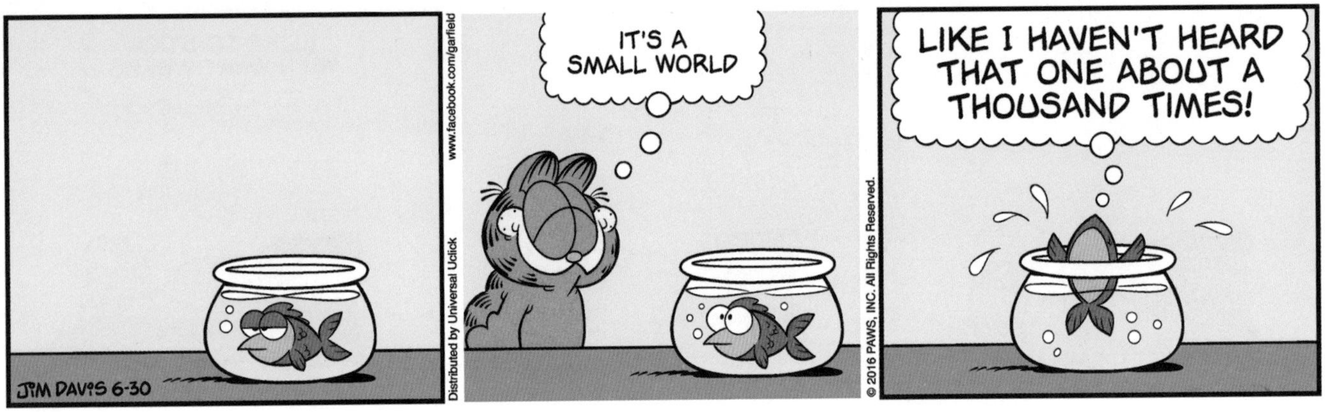
JIM DAVIS 6-30
IT'S A SMALL WORLD
LIKE I HAVEN'T HEARD THAT ONE ABOUT A THOUSAND TIMES!
www.facebook.com/garfield
Distributed by Universal Uclick
© 2016 PAWS, INC. All Rights Reserved.

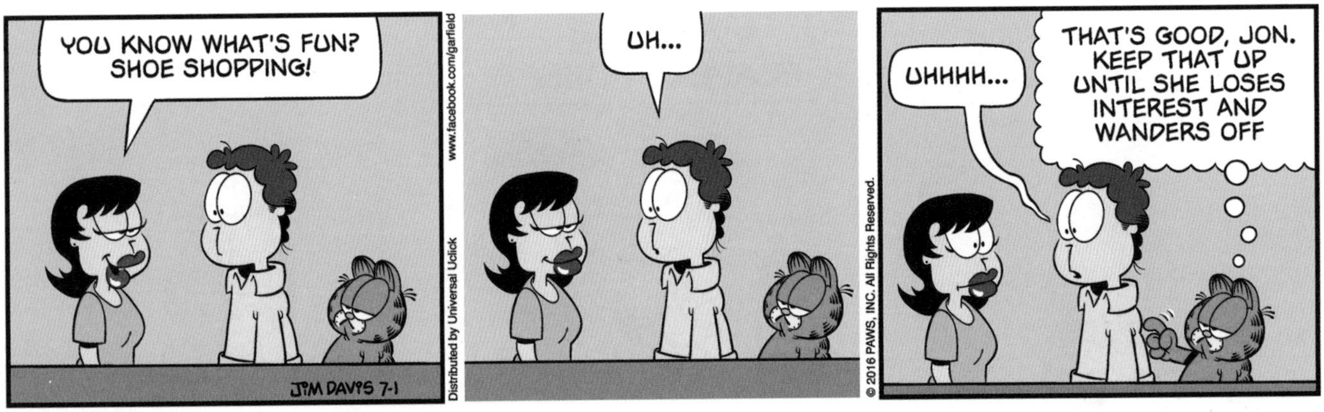
YOU KNOW WHAT'S FUN? SHOE SHOPPING!
JIM DAVIS 7-1
UH...
UHHHH...
THAT'S GOOD, JON. KEEP THAT UP UNTIL SHE LOSES INTEREST AND WANDERS OFF
www.facebook.com/garfield
Distributed by Universal Uclick
© 2016 PAWS, INC. All Rights Reserved.

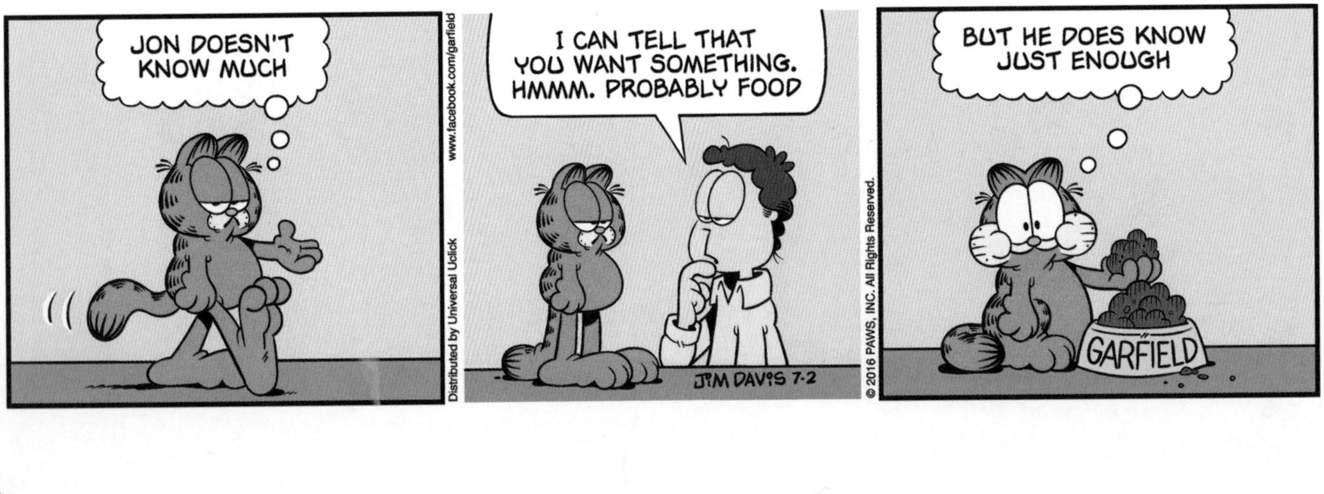
JON DOESN'T KNOW MUCH
I CAN TELL THAT YOU WANT SOMETHING. HMMM. PROBABLY FOOD
JIM DAVIS 7-2
BUT HE DOES KNOW JUST ENOUGH
GARFIELD
www.facebook.com/garfield
Distributed by Universal Uclick
© 2016 PAWS, INC. All Rights Reserved.

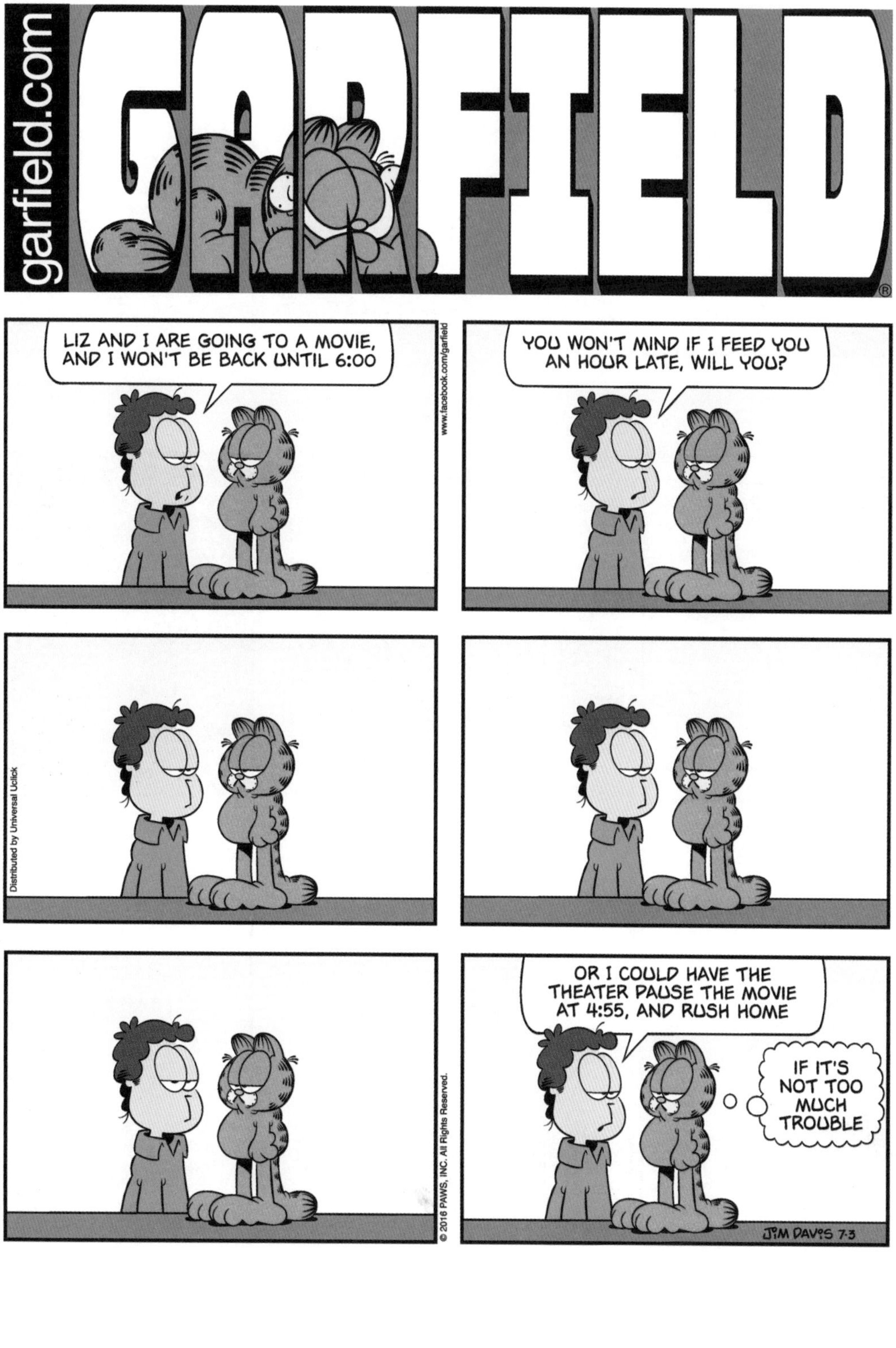
garfield.com
GARFIELD
LIZ AND I ARE GOING TO A MOVIE, AND I WON'T BE BACK UNTIL 6:00
www.facebook.com/garfield
YOU WON'T MIND IF I FEED YOU AN HOUR LATE, WILL YOU?
Distributed by Universal Uclick
OR I COULD HAVE THE THEATER PAUSE THE MOVIE AT 4:55, AND RUSH HOME
IF IT'S NOT TOO MUCH TROUBLE
© 2016 PAWS, INC. All Rights Reserved.
JIM DAVIS 7-3

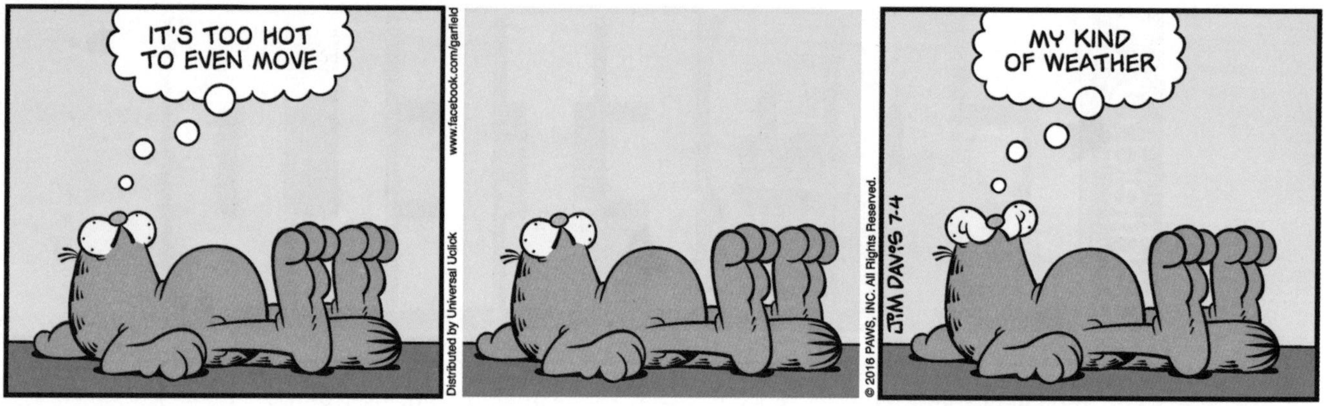
IT'S TOO HOT TO EVEN MOVE
Distributed by Universal Uclick www.facebook.com/garfield
© 2016 PAWS, INC. All Rights Reserved.
JIM DAVIS 7-4
MY KIND OF WEATHER

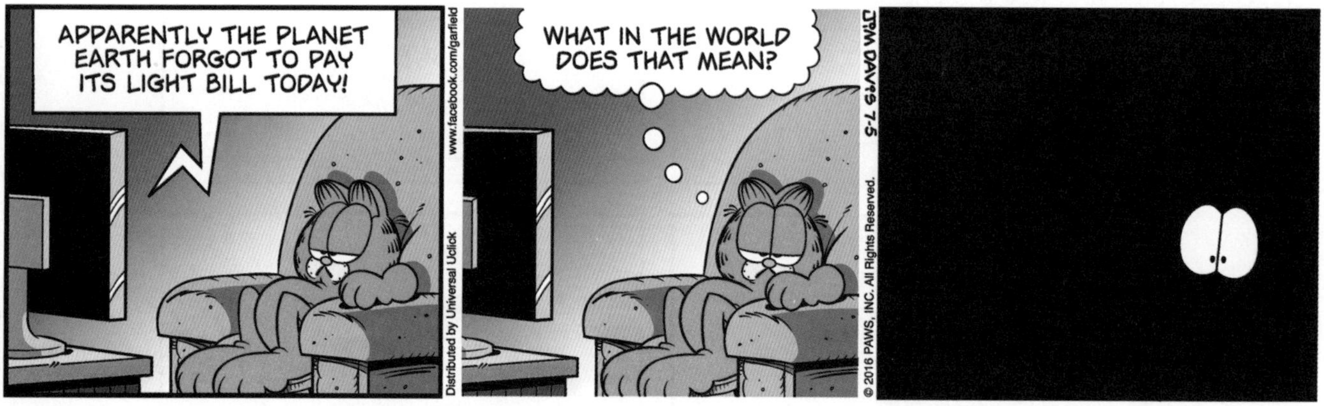
APPARENTLY THE PLANET EARTH FORGOT TO PAY ITS LIGHT BILL TODAY!
Distributed by Universal Uclick www.facebook.com/garfield
WHAT IN THE WORLD DOES THAT MEAN?
© 2016 PAWS, INC. All Rights Reserved.
JIM DAVIS 7-5

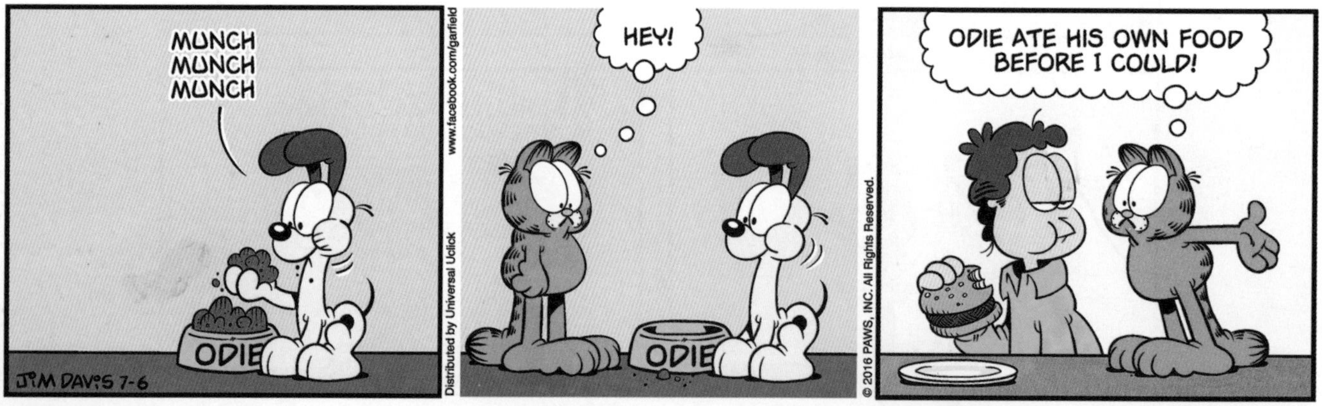
MUNCH
MUNCH
MUNCH
ODIE
JIM DAVIS 7-6
Distributed by Universal Uclick www.facebook.com/garfield
HEY!
ODIE
© 2016 PAWS, INC. All Rights Reserved.
ODIE ATE HIS OWN FOOD BEFORE I COULD!

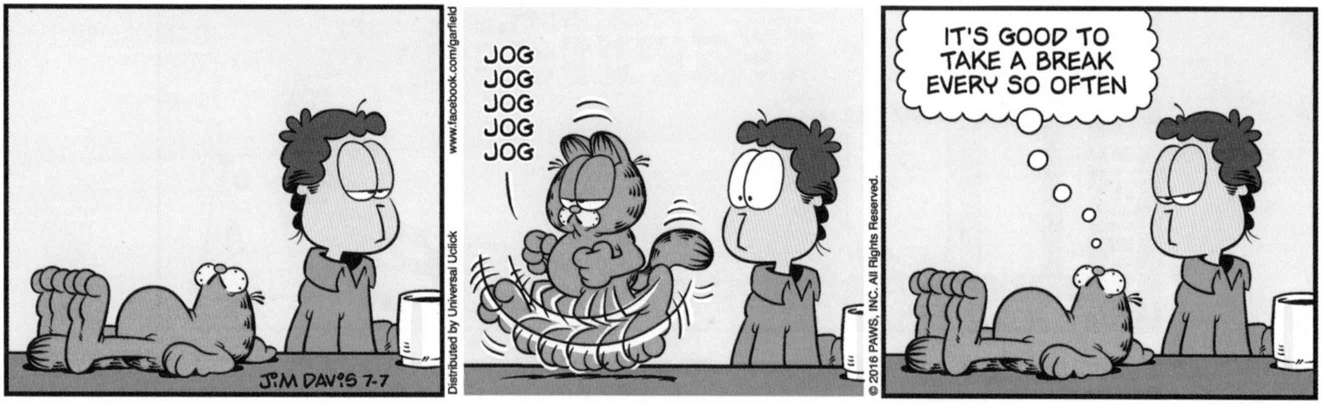
JIM DAVIS 7-7
Distributed by Universal Uclick
www.facebook.com/garfield
JOG JOG JOG JOG JOG
© 2016 PAWS, INC. All Rights Reserved.
IT'S GOOD TO TAKE A BREAK EVERY SO OFTEN

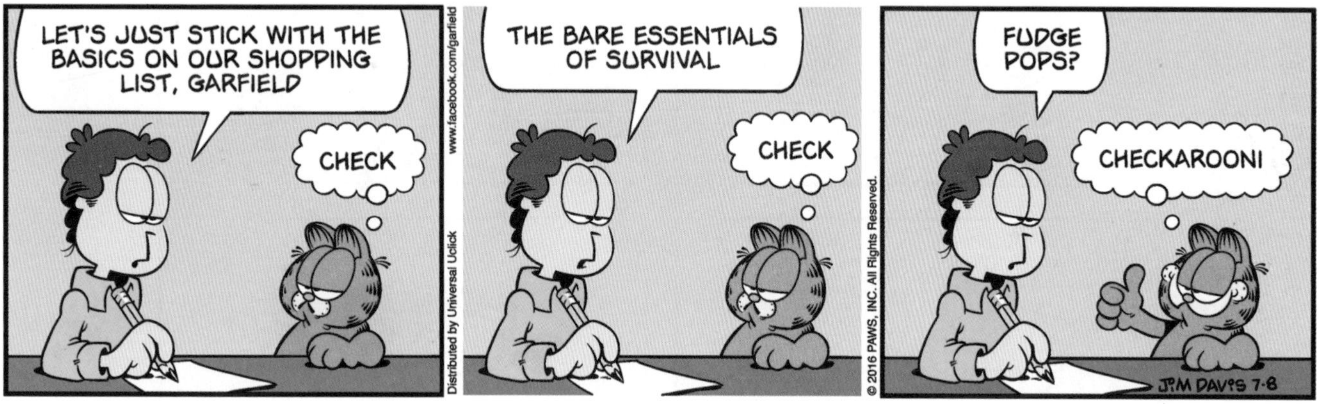
LET'S JUST STICK WITH THE BASICS ON OUR SHOPPING LIST, GARFIELD
CHECK
Distributed by Universal Uclick
www.facebook.com/garfield
THE BARE ESSENTIALS OF SURVIVAL
CHECK
© 2016 PAWS, INC. All Rights Reserved.
FUDGE POPS?
CHECKAROONI
JIM DAVIS 7-8

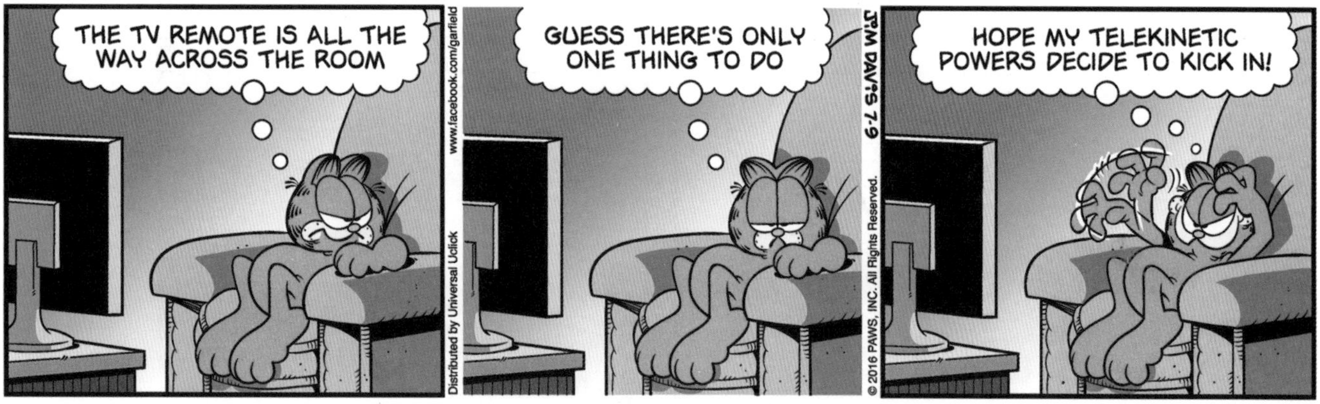
THE TV REMOTE IS ALL THE WAY ACROSS THE ROOM
Distributed by Universal Uclick
www.facebook.com/garfield
GUESS THERE'S ONLY ONE THING TO DO
JIM DAVIS 7-9
© 2016 PAWS, INC. All Rights Reserved.
HOPE MY TELEKINETIC POWERS DECIDE TO KICK IN!

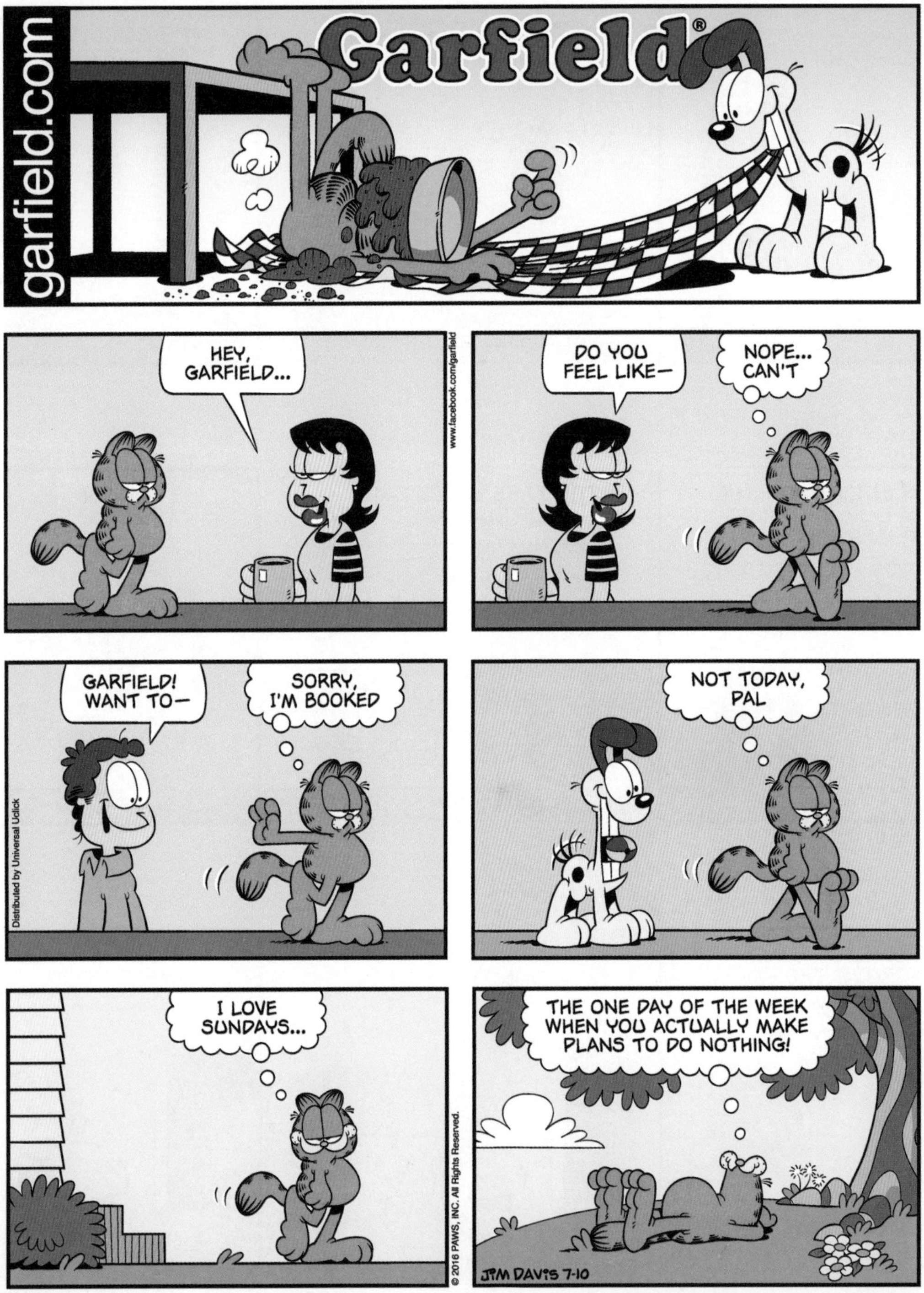
garfield.com
Garfield®
HEY, GARFIELD...
www.facebook.com/garfield
DO YOU FEEL LIKE—
NOPE... CAN'T
GARFIELD! WANT TO—
SORRY, I'M BOOKED
Distributed by Universal Uclick
NOT TODAY, PAL
I LOVE SUNDAYS...
© 2016 PAWS, INC. All Rights Reserved.
THE ONE DAY OF THE WEEK WHEN YOU ACTUALLY MAKE PLANS TO DO NOTHING!
JIM DAVIS 7-10

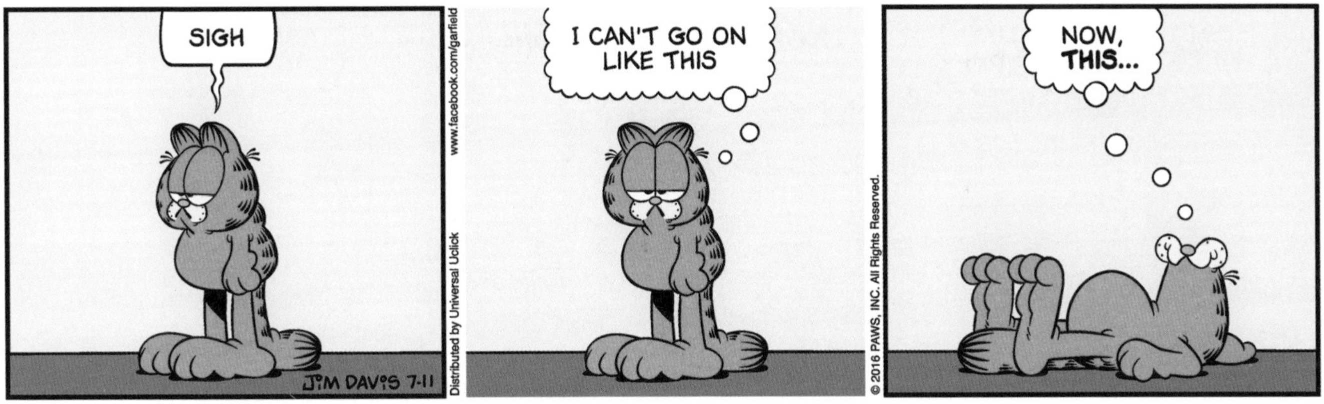
SIGH
JIM DAVIS 7-11
Distributed by Universal Uclick www.facebook.com/garfield
I CAN'T GO ON LIKE THIS
© 2016 PAWS, INC. All Rights Reserved.
NOW, **THIS...**

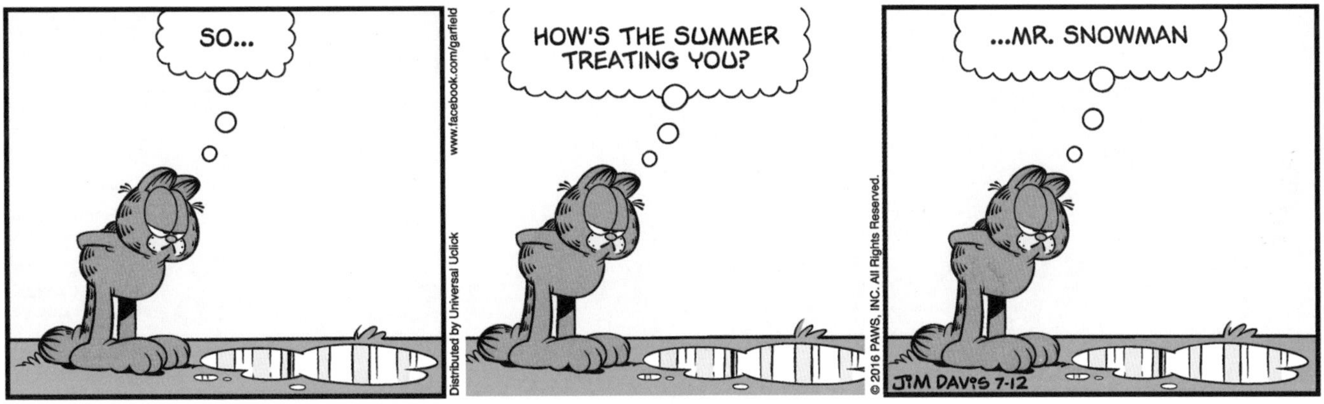
SO...
Distributed by Universal Uclick www.facebook.com/garfield
HOW'S THE SUMMER TREATING YOU?
© 2016 PAWS, INC. All Rights Reserved.
...MR. SNOWMAN
JIM DAVIS 7-12

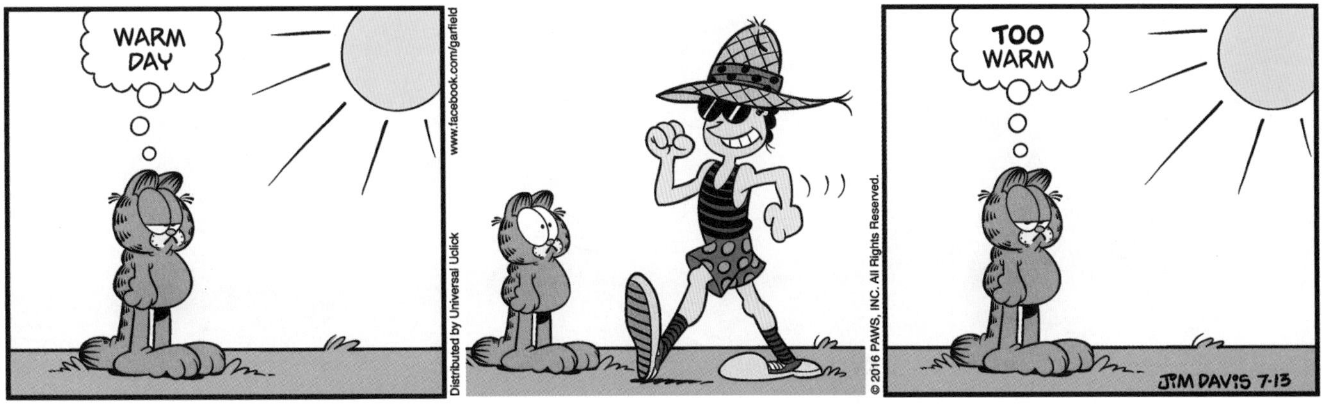
WARM DAY
Distributed by Universal Uclick www.facebook.com/garfield
© 2016 PAWS, INC. All Rights Reserved.
TOO WARM
JIM DAVIS 7-13

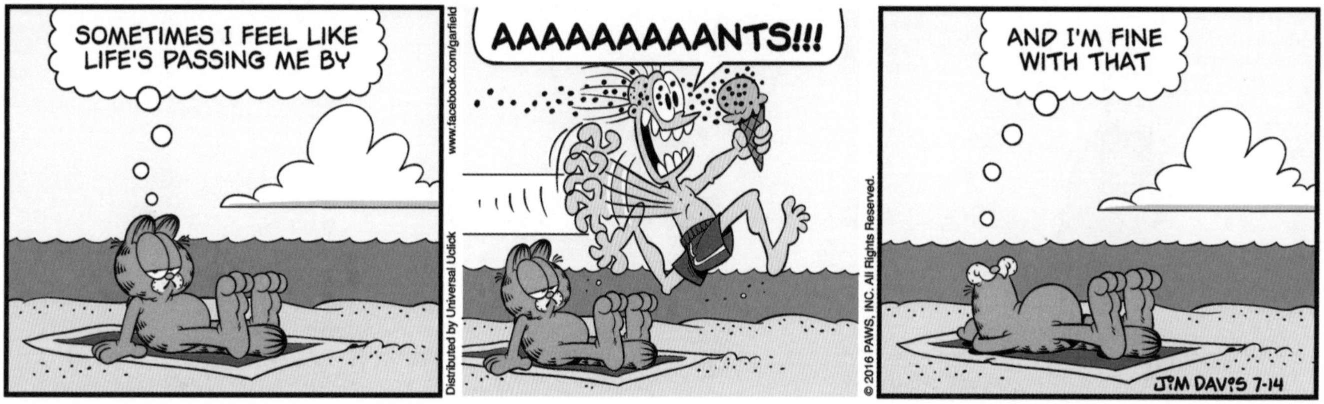
SOMETIMES I FEEL LIKE LIFE'S PASSING ME BY
AAAAAAAAANTS!!!
AND I'M FINE WITH THAT
JIM DAVIS 7-14
Distributed by Universal Uclick www.facebook.com/garfield
© 2016 PAWS, INC. All Rights Reserved.

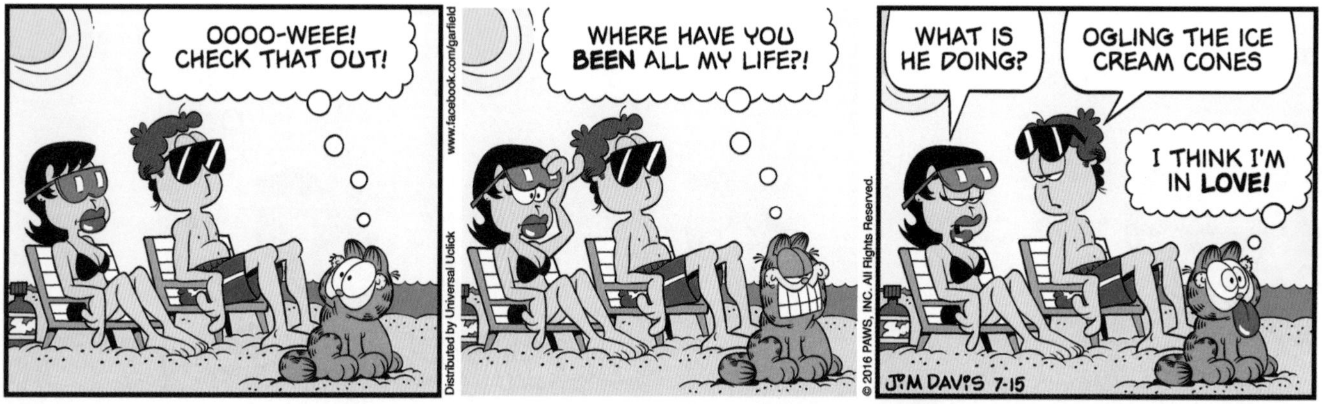
OOOO-WEEE! CHECK THAT OUT!
WHERE HAVE YOU **BEEN** ALL MY LIFE?!
WHAT IS HE DOING?
OGLING THE ICE CREAM CONES
I THINK I'M IN **LOVE!**
JIM DAVIS 7-15
Distributed by Universal Uclick www.facebook.com/garfield
© 2016 PAWS, INC. All Rights Reserved.

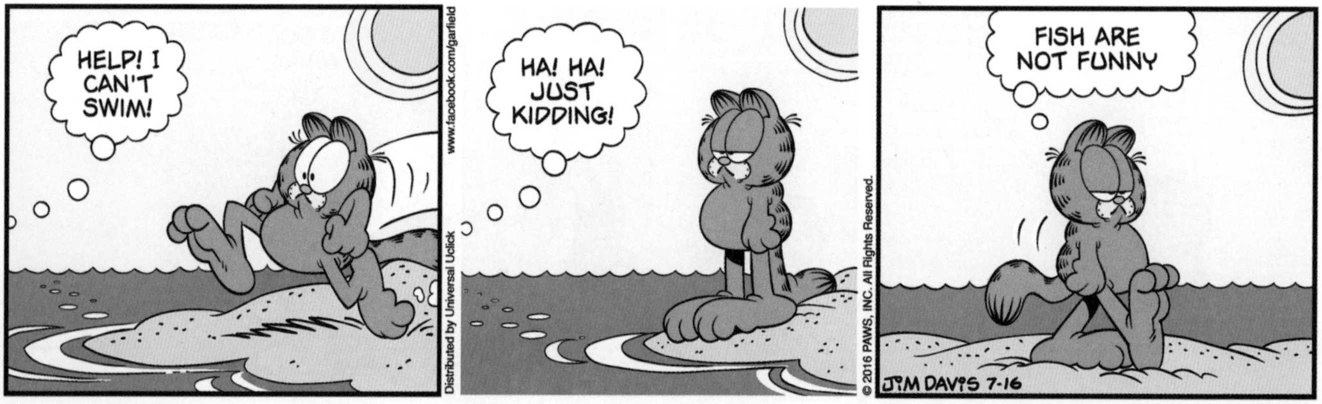
HELP! I CAN'T SWIM!
HA! HA! JUST KIDDING!
FISH ARE NOT FUNNY
JIM DAVIS 7-16
Distributed by Universal Uclick www.facebook.com/garfield
© 2016 PAWS, INC. All Rights Reserved.

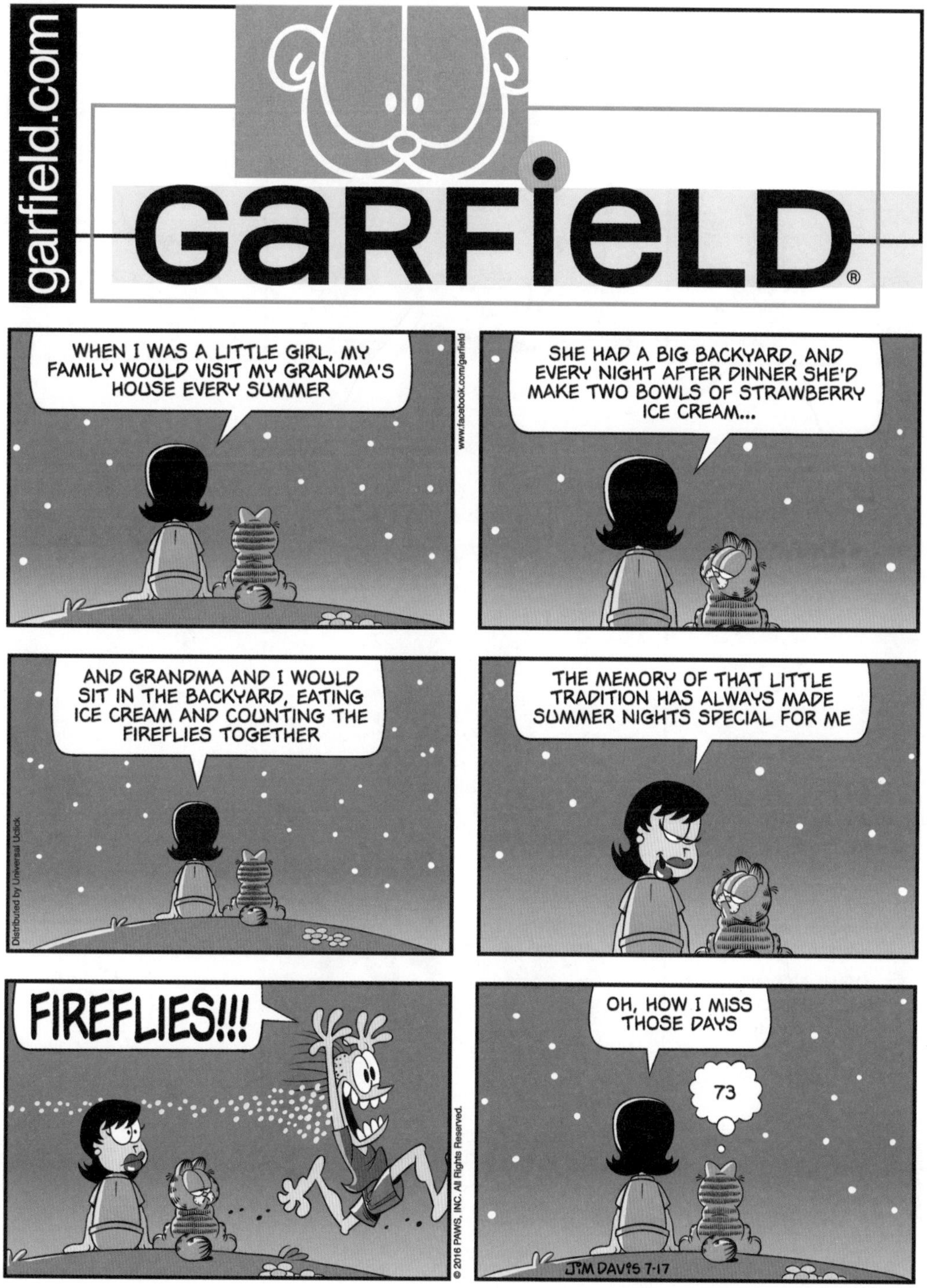
garfield.com
GARFIELD®
WHEN I WAS A LITTLE GIRL, MY FAMILY WOULD VISIT MY GRANDMA'S HOUSE EVERY SUMMER
www.facebook.com/garfield
SHE HAD A BIG BACKYARD, AND EVERY NIGHT AFTER DINNER SHE'D MAKE TWO BOWLS OF STRAWBERRY ICE CREAM...
AND GRANDMA AND I WOULD SIT IN THE BACKYARD, EATING ICE CREAM AND COUNTING THE FIREFLIES TOGETHER
Distributed by Universal Uclick
THE MEMORY OF THAT LITTLE TRADITION HAS ALWAYS MADE SUMMER NIGHTS SPECIAL FOR ME
FIREFLIES!!!
© 2016 PAWS, INC. All Rights Reserved.
OH, HOW I MISS THOSE DAYS
73
JIM DAVIS 7-17

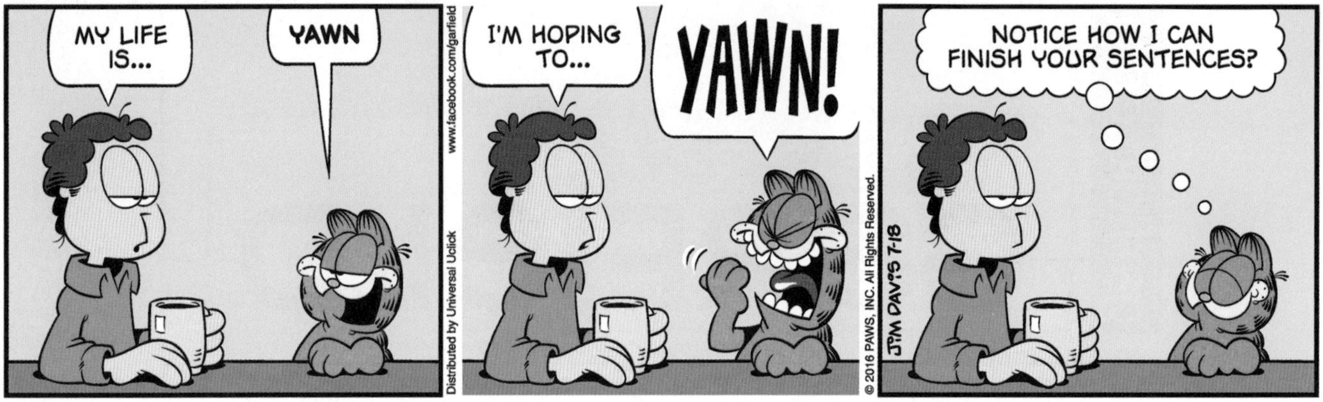
MY LIFE IS...
YAWN
I'M HOPING TO...
YAWN!
NOTICE HOW I CAN FINISH YOUR SENTENCES?
Distributed by Universal Uclick www.facebook.com/garfield
© 2016 PAWS, INC. All Rights Reserved.
JIM DAVIS 7-18

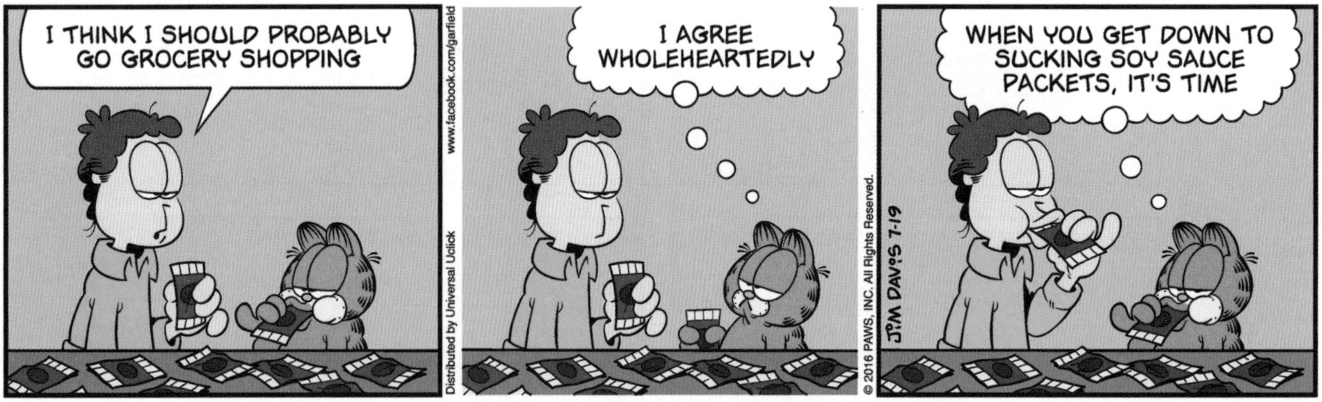
I THINK I SHOULD PROBABLY GO GROCERY SHOPPING
I AGREE WHOLEHEARTEDLY
WHEN YOU GET DOWN TO SUCKING SOY SAUCE PACKETS, IT'S TIME
Distributed by Universal Uclick www.facebook.com/garfield
© 2016 PAWS, INC. All Rights Reserved.
JIM DAVIS 7-19

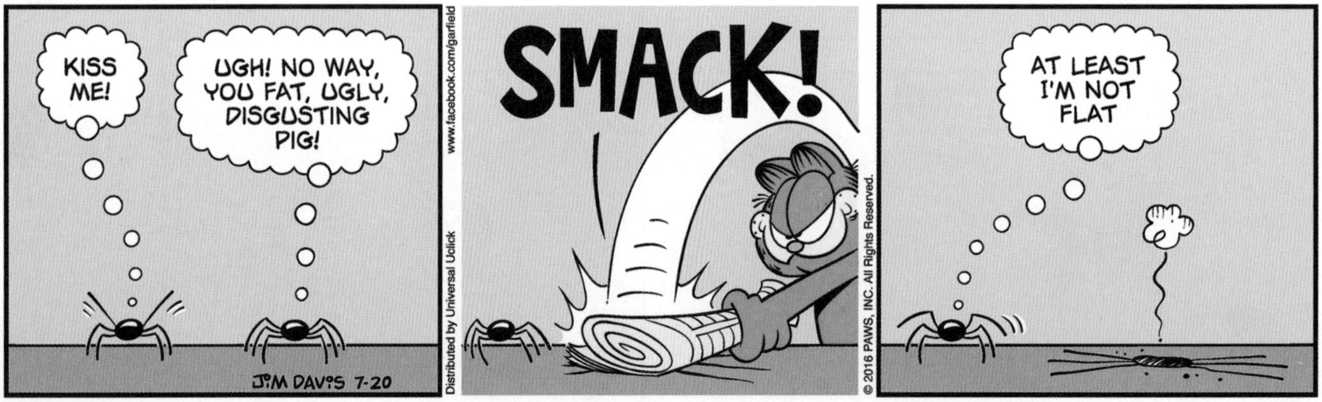
KISS ME!
UGH! NO WAY, YOU FAT, UGLY, DISGUSTING PIG!
JIM DAVIS 7-20
SMACK!
AT LEAST I'M NOT FLAT
Distributed by Universal Uclick www.facebook.com/garfield
© 2016 PAWS, INC. All Rights Reserved.

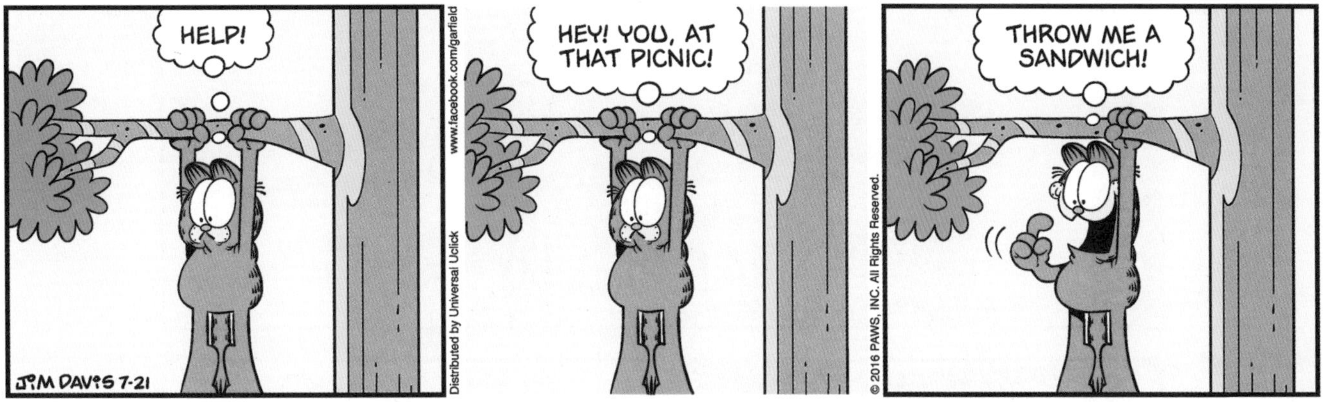
HELP!
HEY! YOU, AT THAT PICNIC!
THROW ME A SANDWICH!
JIM DAVIS 7-21
Distributed by Universal Uclick www.facebook.com/garfield
© 2016 PAWS, INC. All Rights Reserved.

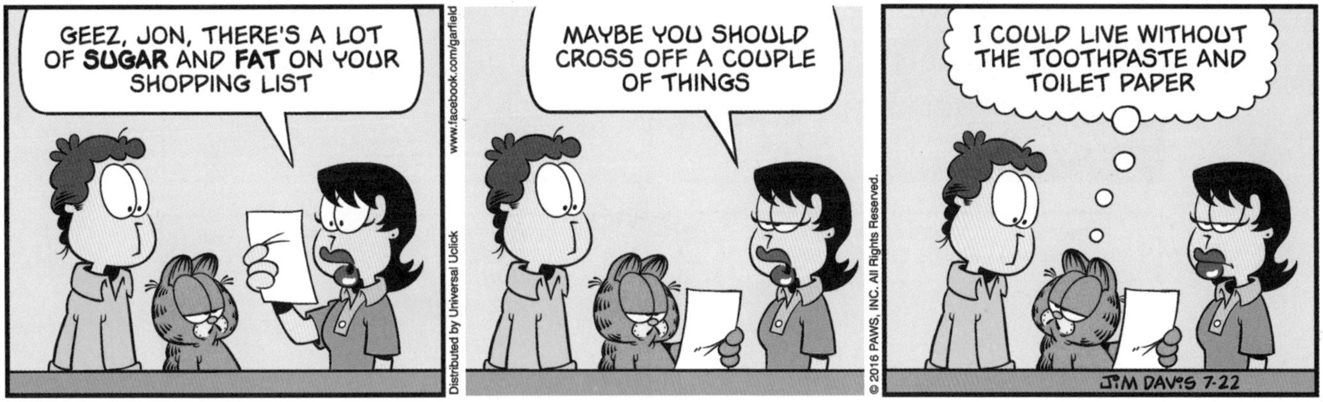
GEEZ, JON, THERE'S A LOT OF **SUGAR** AND **FAT** ON YOUR SHOPPING LIST
MAYBE YOU SHOULD CROSS OFF A COUPLE OF THINGS
I COULD LIVE WITHOUT THE TOOTHPASTE AND TOILET PAPER
JIM DAVIS 7-22
Distributed by Universal Uclick www.facebook.com/garfield
© 2016 PAWS, INC. All Rights Reserved.

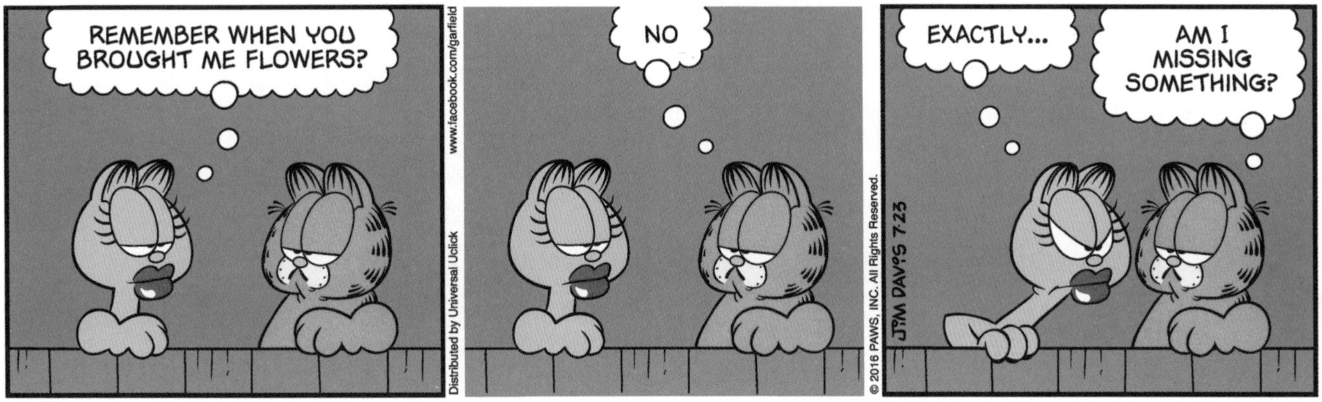
REMEMBER WHEN YOU BROUGHT ME FLOWERS?
NO
EXACTLY...
AM I MISSING SOMETHING?
JIM DAVIS 7-23
Distributed by Universal Uclick www.facebook.com/garfield
© 2016 PAWS, INC. All Rights Reserved.

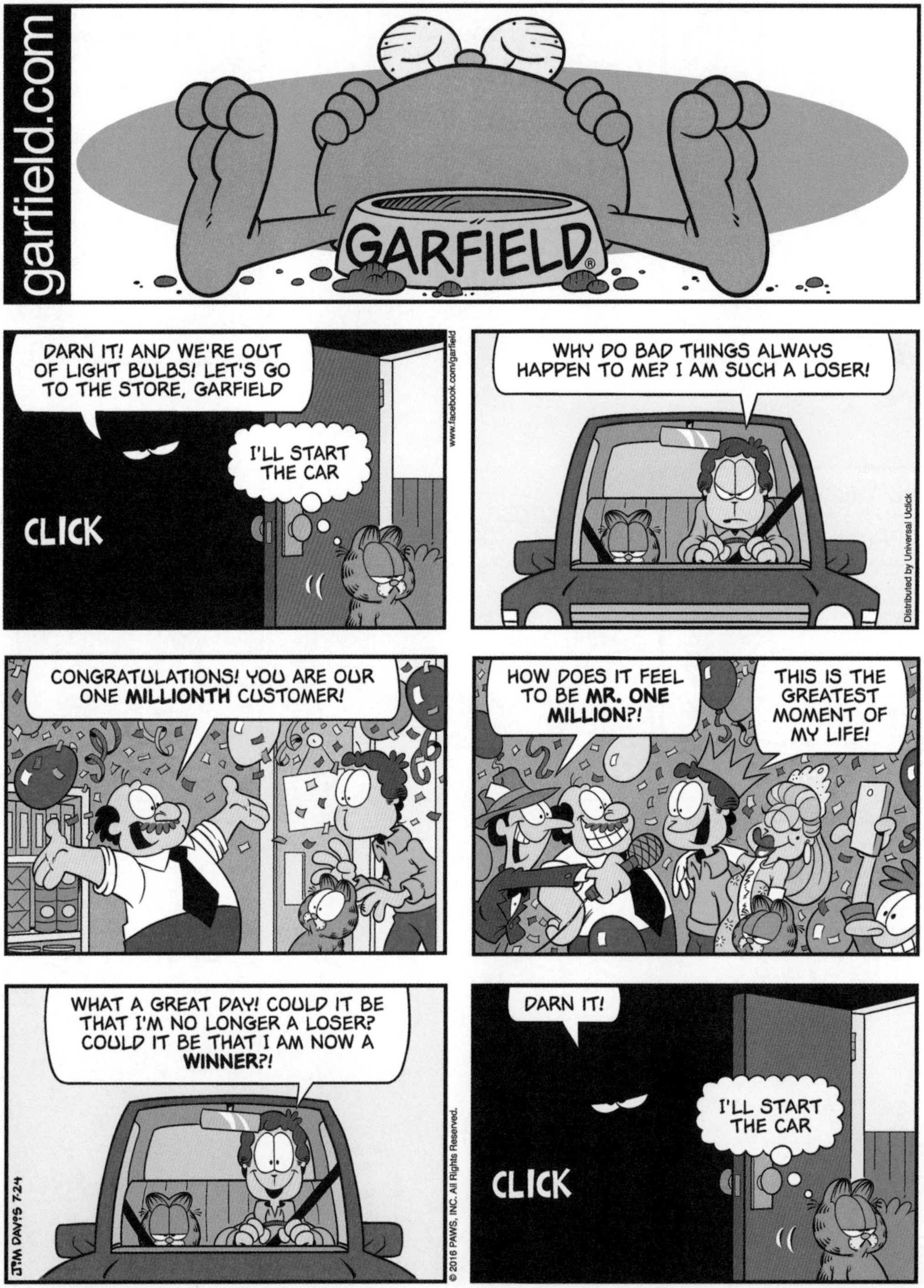
garfield.com
GARFIELD®
DARN IT! AND WE'RE OUT OF LIGHT BULBS! LET'S GO TO THE STORE, GARFIELD
I'LL START THE CAR
CLICK
www.facebook.com/garfield
WHY DO BAD THINGS ALWAYS HAPPEN TO ME? I AM SUCH A LOSER!
Distributed by Universal Uclick
CONGRATULATIONS! YOU ARE OUR ONE MILLIONTH CUSTOMER!
HOW DOES IT FEEL TO BE MR. ONE MILLION?!
THIS IS THE GREATEST MOMENT OF MY LIFE!
WHAT A GREAT DAY! COULD IT BE THAT I'M NO LONGER A LOSER? COULD IT BE THAT I AM NOW A WINNER?!
JIM DAVIS 7-24
© 2016 PAWS, INC. All Rights Reserved.
DARN IT!
I'LL START THE CAR
CLICK

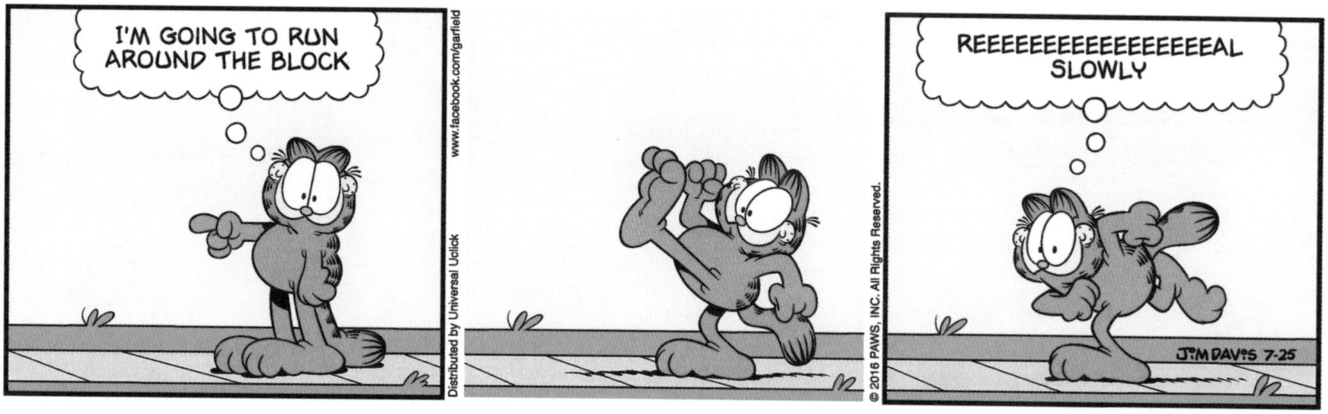
I'M GOING TO RUN AROUND THE BLOCK
REEEEEEEEEEEEEEEEEEAL SLOWLY
JIM DAVIS 7-25
www.facebook.com/garfield
Distributed by Universal Uclick
© 2016 PAWS, INC. All Rights Reserved.

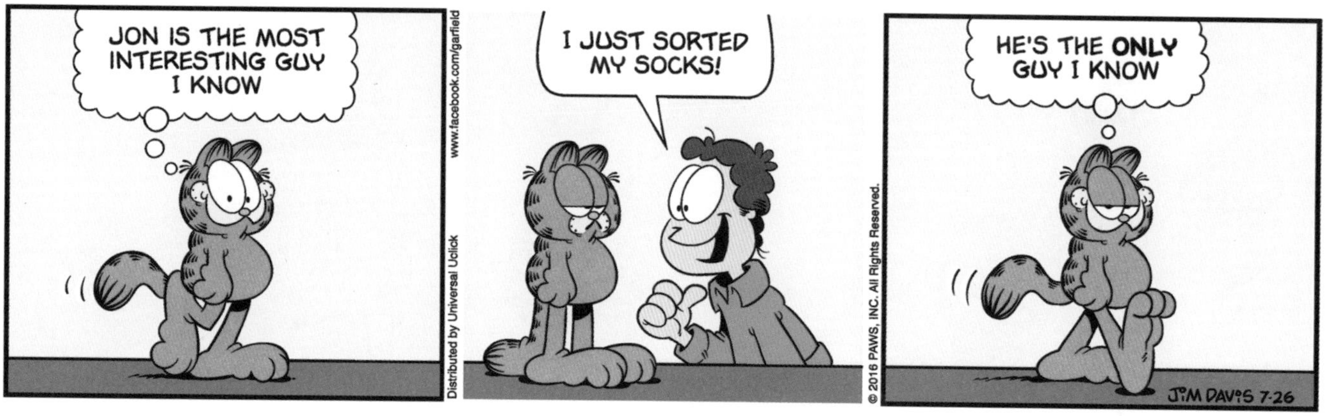
JON IS THE MOST INTERESTING GUY I KNOW
I JUST SORTED MY SOCKS!
HE'S THE **ONLY** GUY I KNOW
JIM DAVIS 7-26
www.facebook.com/garfield
Distributed by Universal Uclick
© 2016 PAWS, INC. All Rights Reserved.

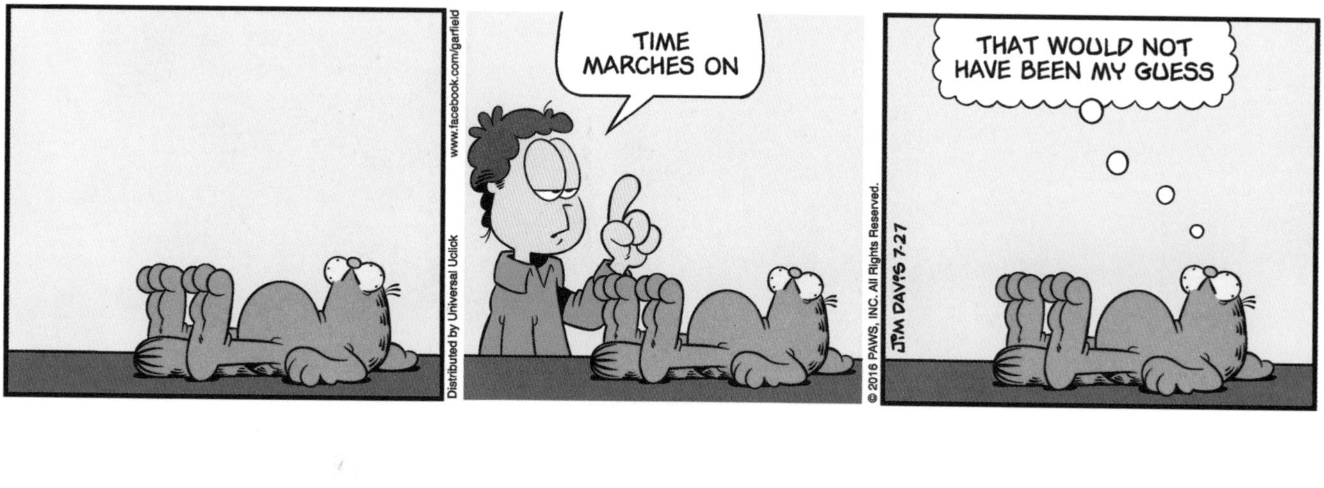
TIME MARCHES ON
THAT WOULD NOT HAVE BEEN MY GUESS
JIM DAVIS 7-27
www.facebook.com/garfield
Distributed by Universal Uclick
© 2016 PAWS, INC. All Rights Reserved.

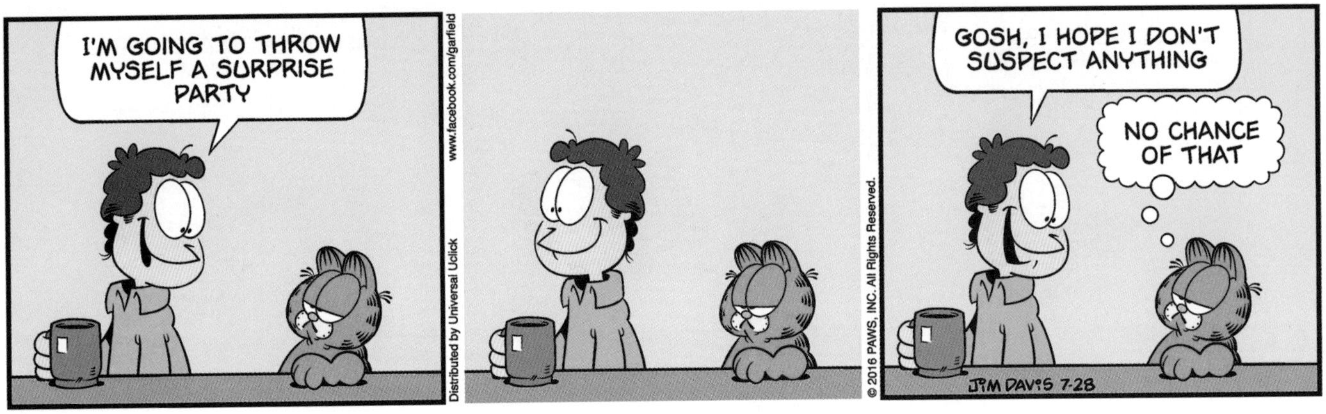
I'M GOING TO THROW MYSELF A SURPRISE PARTY
Distributed by Universal Uclick
www.facebook.com/garfield
GOSH, I HOPE I DON'T SUSPECT ANYTHING
NO CHANCE OF THAT
© 2016 PAWS, INC. All Rights Reserved.
JIM DAVIS 7-28

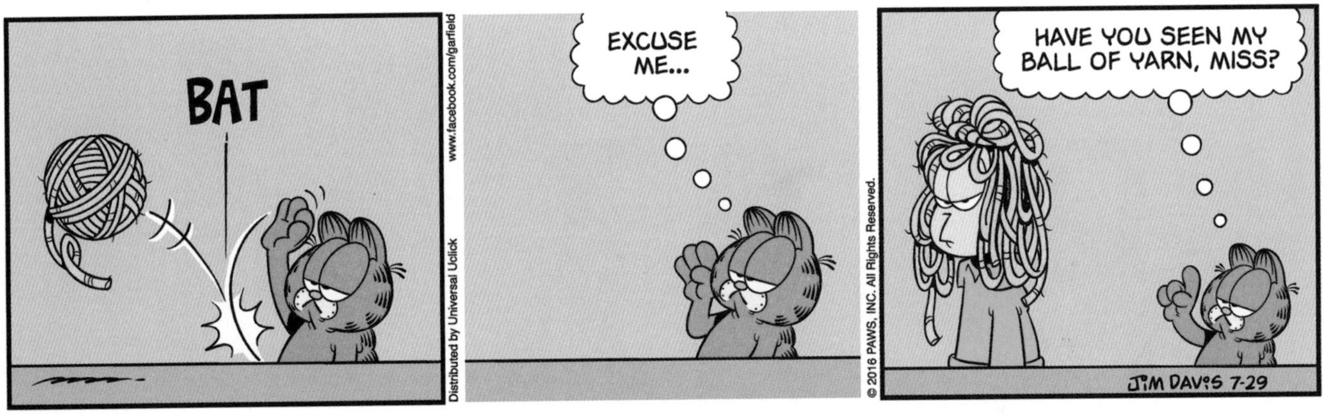
BAT
Distributed by Universal Uclick
www.facebook.com/garfield
EXCUSE ME...
HAVE YOU SEEN MY BALL OF YARN, MISS?
© 2016 PAWS, INC. All Rights Reserved.
JIM DAVIS 7-29

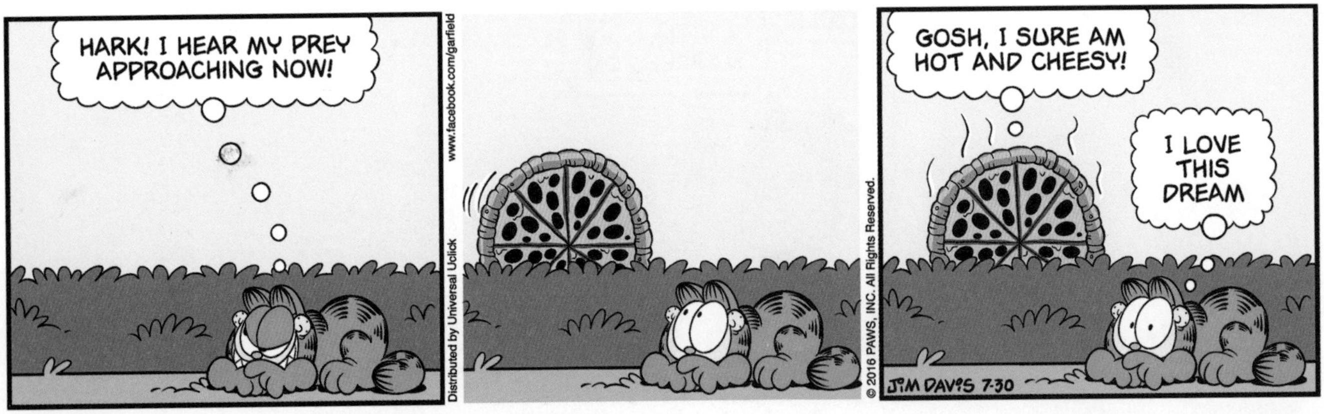
HARK! I HEAR MY PREY APPROACHING NOW!
Distributed by Universal Uclick
www.facebook.com/garfield
GOSH, I SURE AM HOT AND CHEESY!
I LOVE THIS DREAM
© 2016 PAWS, INC. All Rights Reserved.
JIM DAVIS 7-30

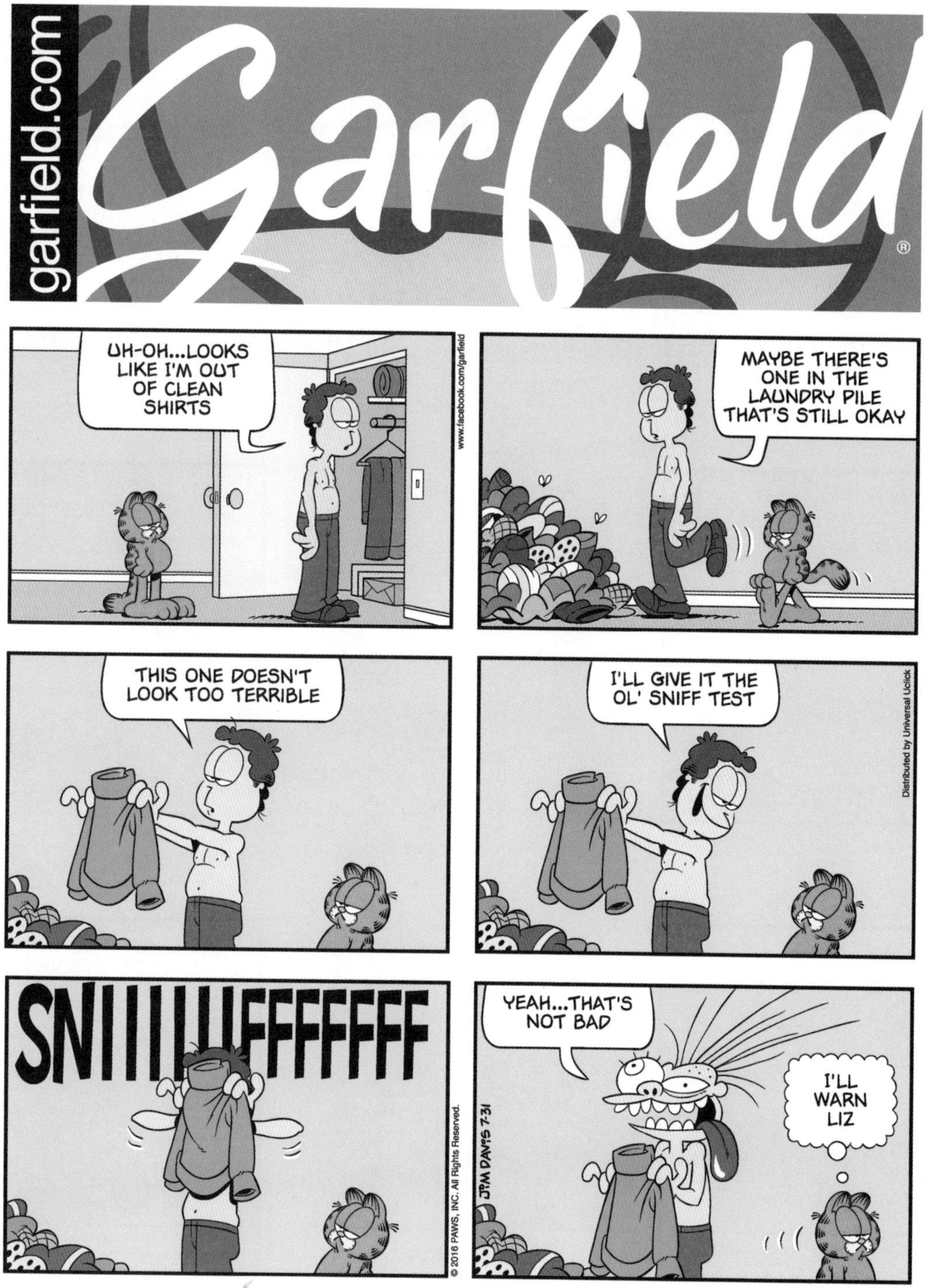
garfield.com
Garfield
UH-OH...LOOKS LIKE I'M OUT OF CLEAN SHIRTS
www.facebook.com/garfield
MAYBE THERE'S ONE IN THE LAUNDRY PILE THAT'S STILL OKAY
THIS ONE DOESN'T LOOK TOO TERRIBLE
I'LL GIVE IT THE OL' SNIFF TEST
Distributed by Universal Uclick
SNIIIIIIFFFFFFF
© 2016 PAWS, INC. All Rights Reserved.
JPM DAVIS 7-31
YEAH...THAT'S NOT BAD
I'LL WARN LIZ

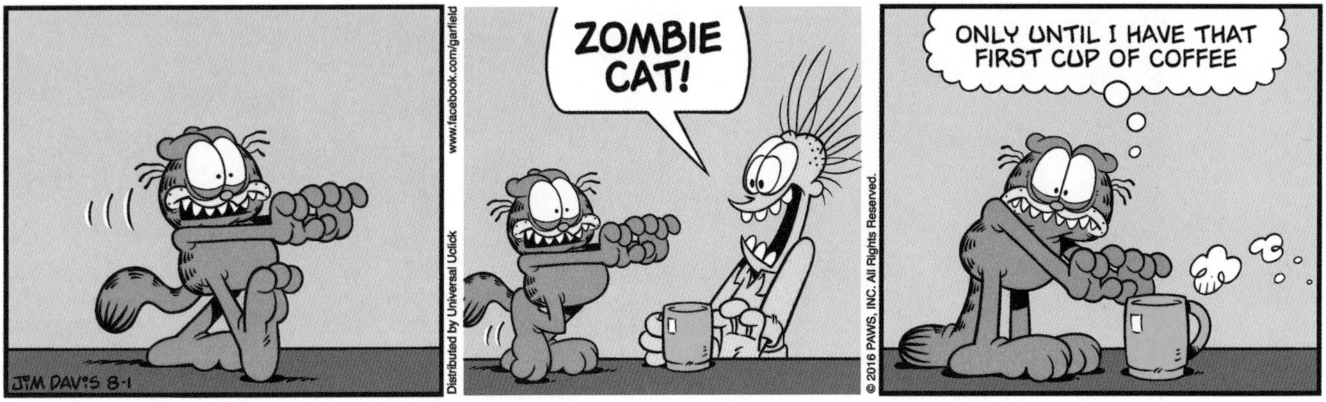
JIM DAVIS 8-1
Distributed by Universal Uclick
www.facebook.com/garfield
ZOMBIE CAT!
© 2016 PAWS, INC. All Rights Reserved.
ONLY UNTIL I HAVE THAT FIRST CUP OF COFFEE

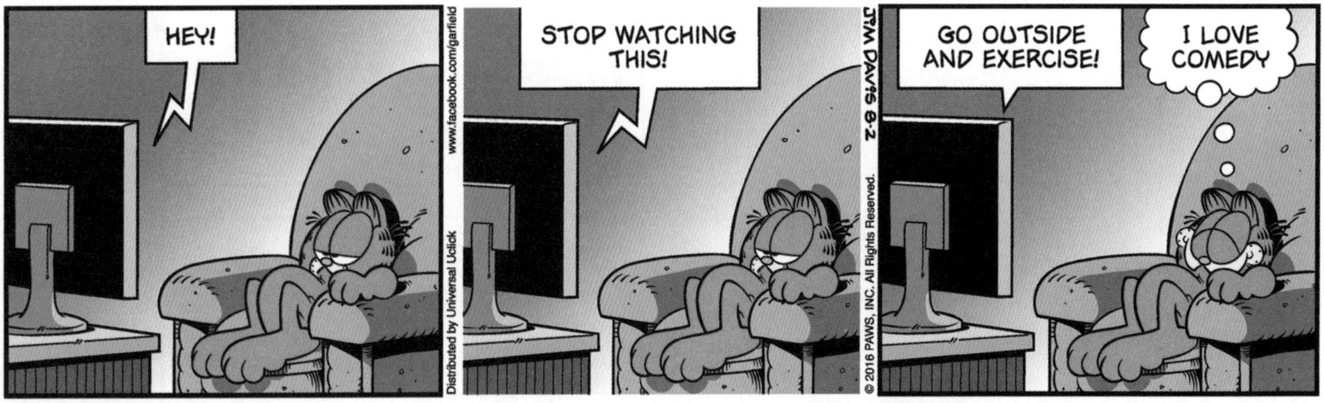
HEY!
Distributed by Universal Uclick
www.facebook.com/garfield
STOP WATCHING THIS!
JIM DAVIS 8-2
© 2016 PAWS, INC. All Rights Reserved.
GO OUTSIDE AND EXERCISE!
I LOVE COMEDY

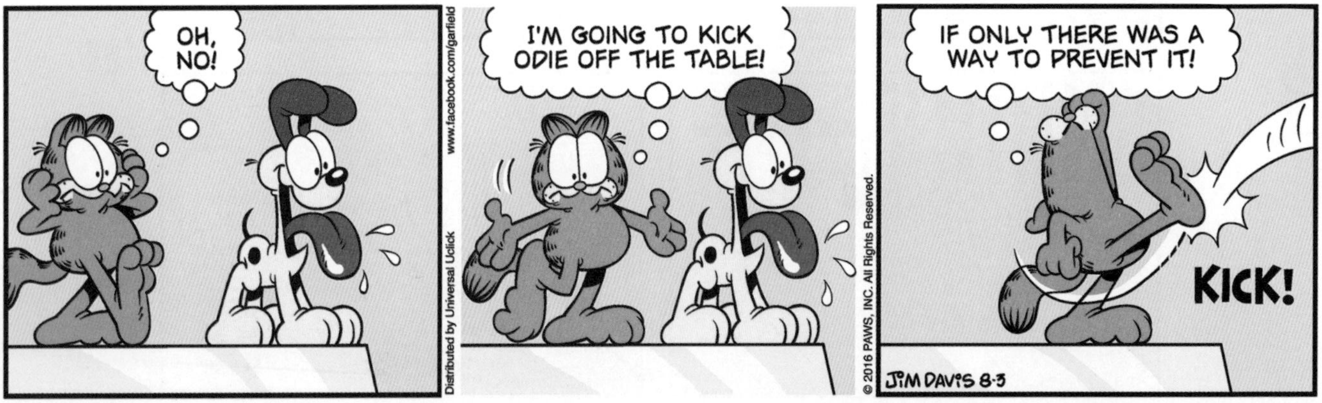
OH, NO!
Distributed by Universal Uclick
www.facebook.com/garfield
I'M GOING TO KICK ODIE OFF THE TABLE!
© 2016 PAWS, INC. All Rights Reserved.
IF ONLY THERE WAS A WAY TO PREVENT IT!
KICK!
JIM DAVIS 8-3

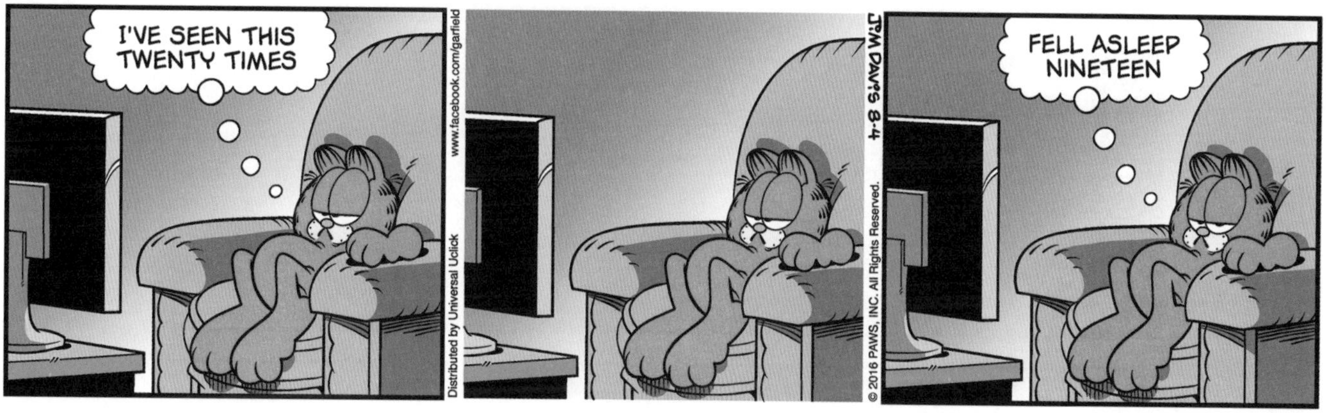
I'VE SEEN THIS TWENTY TIMES
JIM DAVIS 8-4
FELL ASLEEP NINETEEN

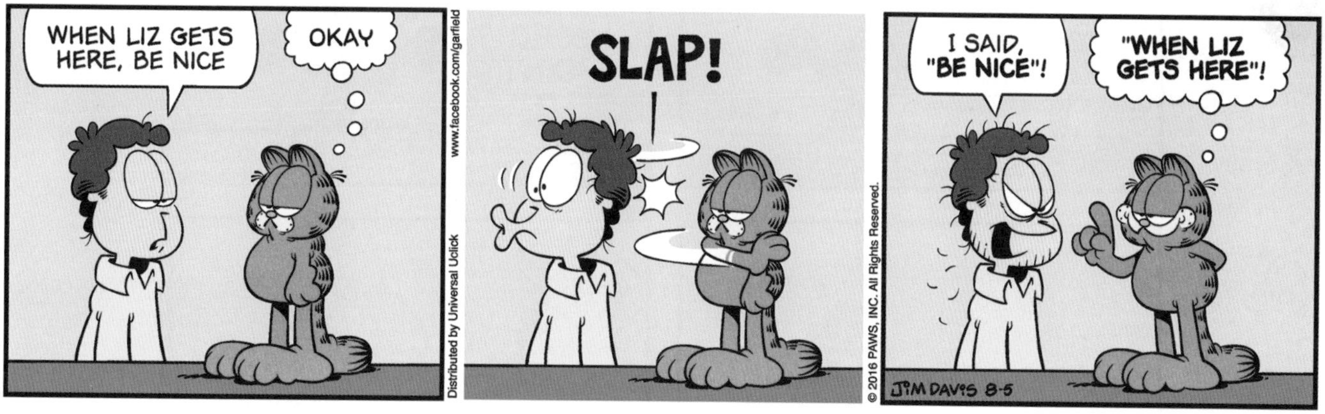
WHEN LIZ GETS HERE, BE NICE
OKAY
SLAP!
I SAID, "BE NICE"!
"WHEN LIZ GETS HERE"!
JIM DAVIS 8-5

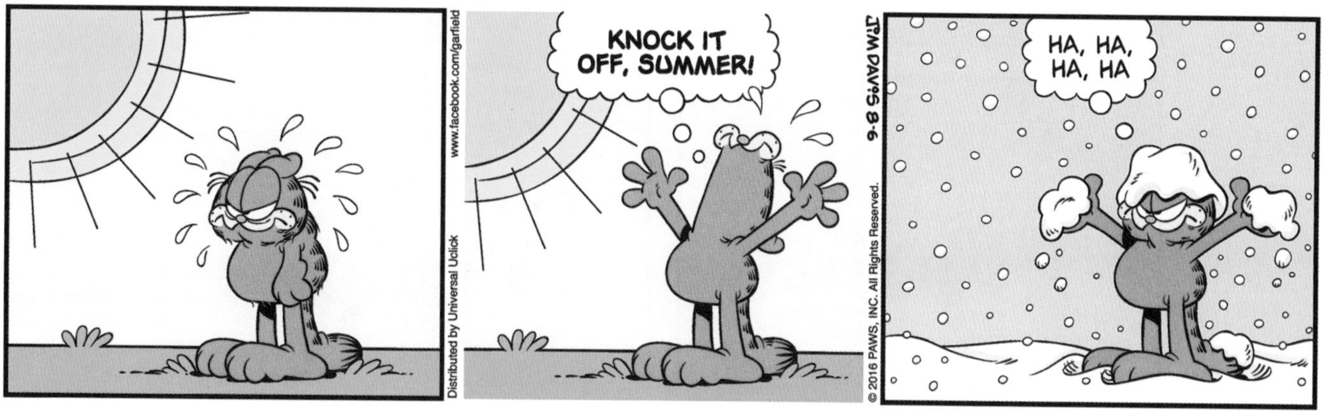
KNOCK IT OFF, SUMMER!
JIM DAVIS 8-6
HA, HA, HA, HA

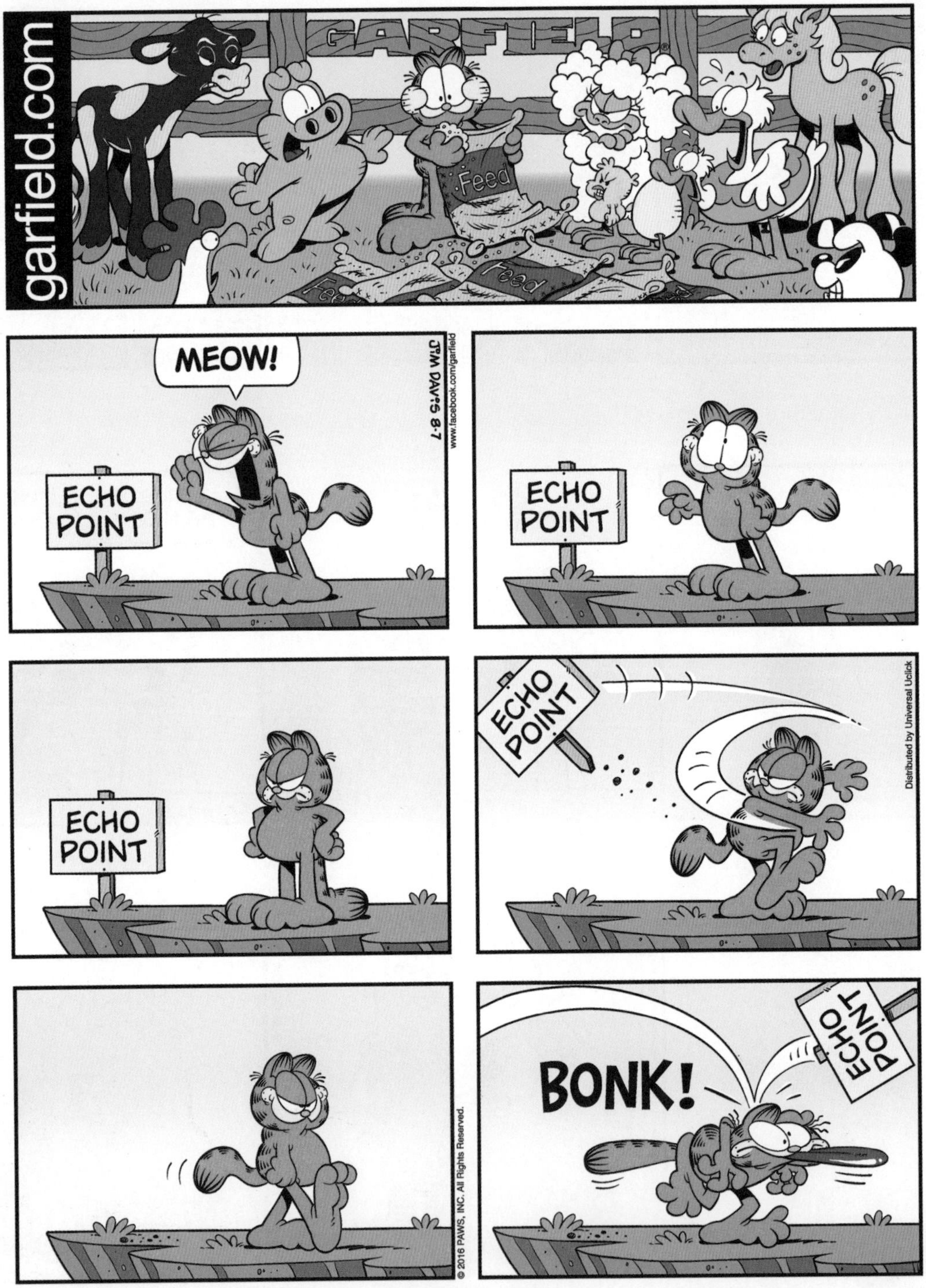
garfield.com
GARFIELD
Feed
Feed
Feed
MEOW!
JIM DAVIS 8-7
www.facebook.com/garfield
ECHO POINT
ECHO POINT
ECHO POINT
ECHO POINT
Distributed by Universal Uclick
© 2016 PAWS, INC. All Rights Reserved.
BONK!
ECHO POINT

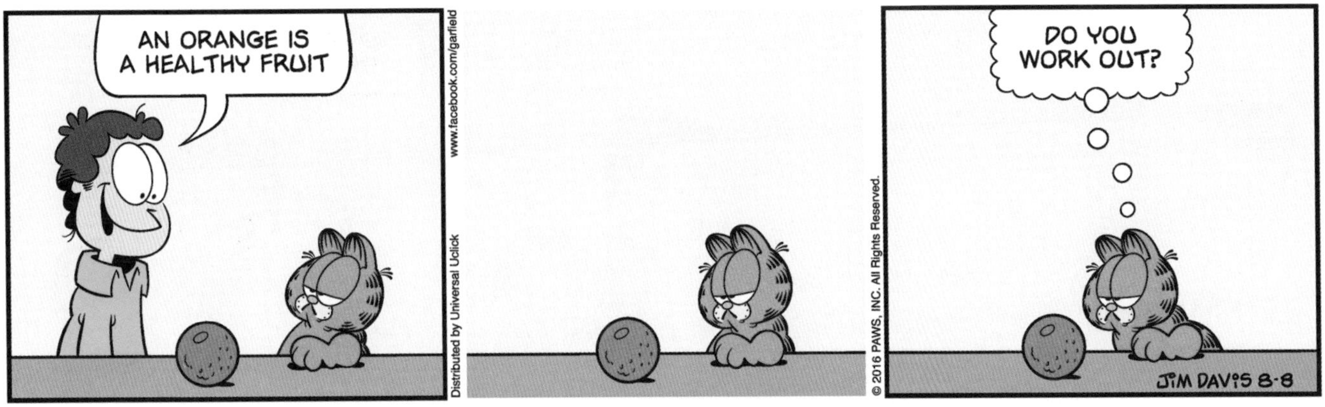
AN ORANGE IS A HEALTHY FRUIT
DO YOU WORK OUT?
JIM DAVIS 8-8
Distributed by Universal Uclick www.facebook.com/garfield
© 2016 PAWS, INC. All Rights Reserved.

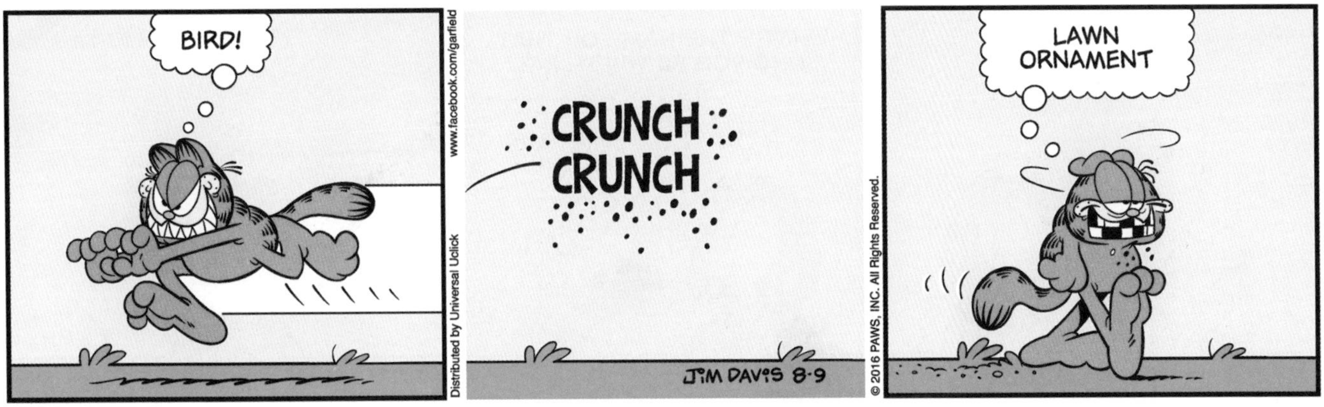
BIRD!
CRUNCH CRUNCH
JIM DAVIS 8-9
LAWN ORNAMENT
Distributed by Universal Uclick www.facebook.com/garfield
© 2016 PAWS, INC. All Rights Reserved.

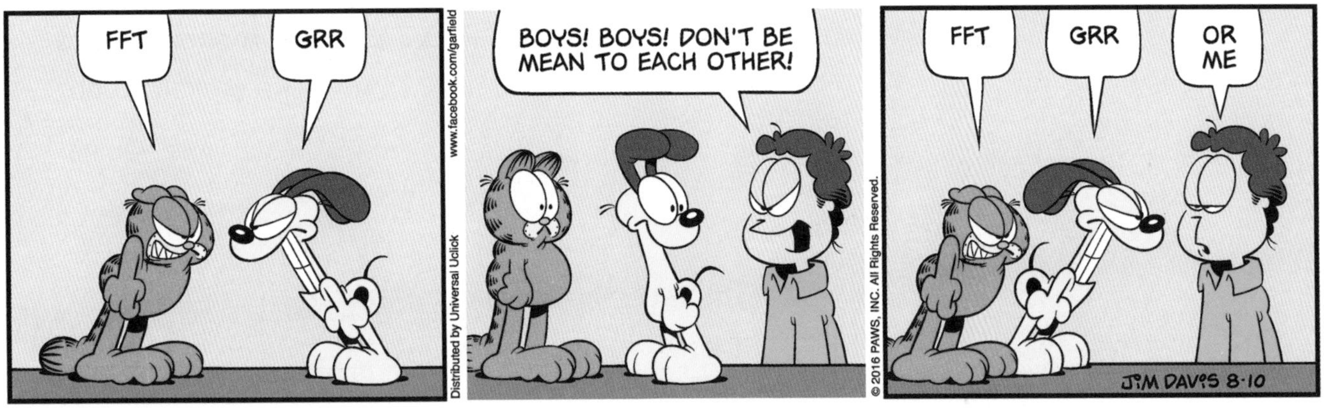
FFT
GRR
BOYS! BOYS! DON'T BE MEAN TO EACH OTHER!
FFT
GRR
OR ME
JIM DAVIS 8-10
Distributed by Universal Uclick www.facebook.com/garfield
© 2016 PAWS, INC. All Rights Reserved.

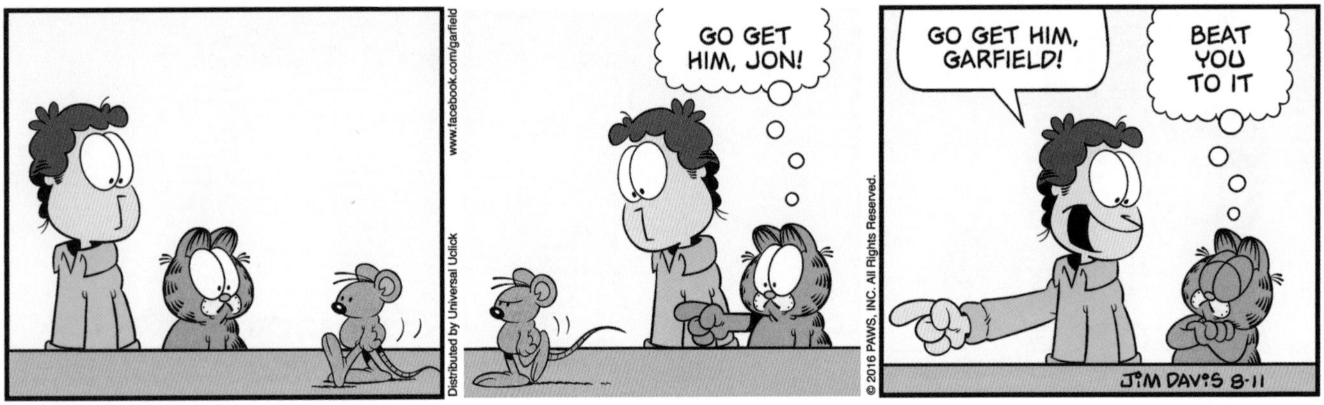
Distributed by Universal Uclick www.facebook.com/garfield
GO GET HIM, JON!
© 2016 PAWS, INC. All Rights Reserved.
GO GET HIM, GARFIELD!
BEAT YOU TO IT
JIM DAVIS 8-11

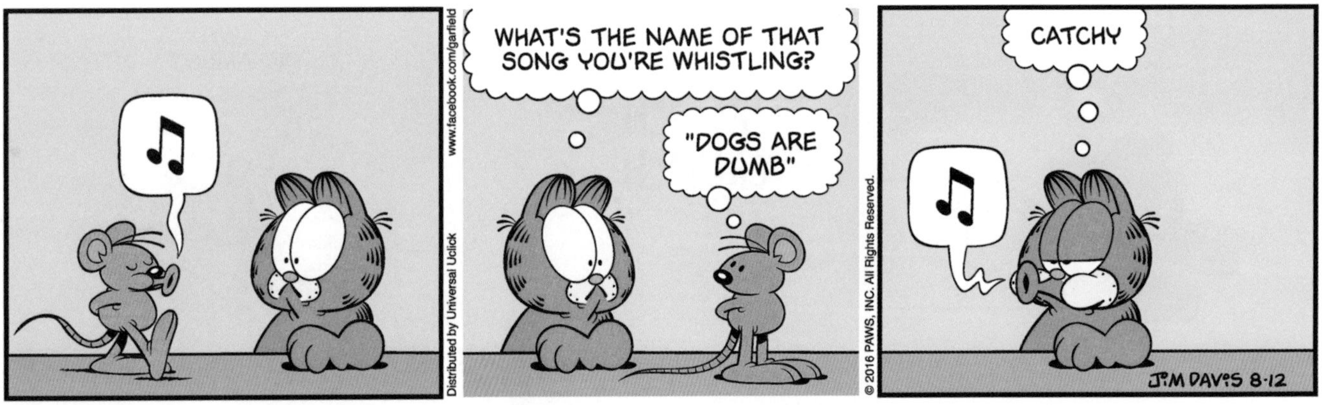
Distributed by Universal Uclick www.facebook.com/garfield
WHAT'S THE NAME OF THAT SONG YOU'RE WHISTLING?
"DOGS ARE DUMB"
© 2016 PAWS, INC. All Rights Reserved.
CATCHY
JIM DAVIS 8-12

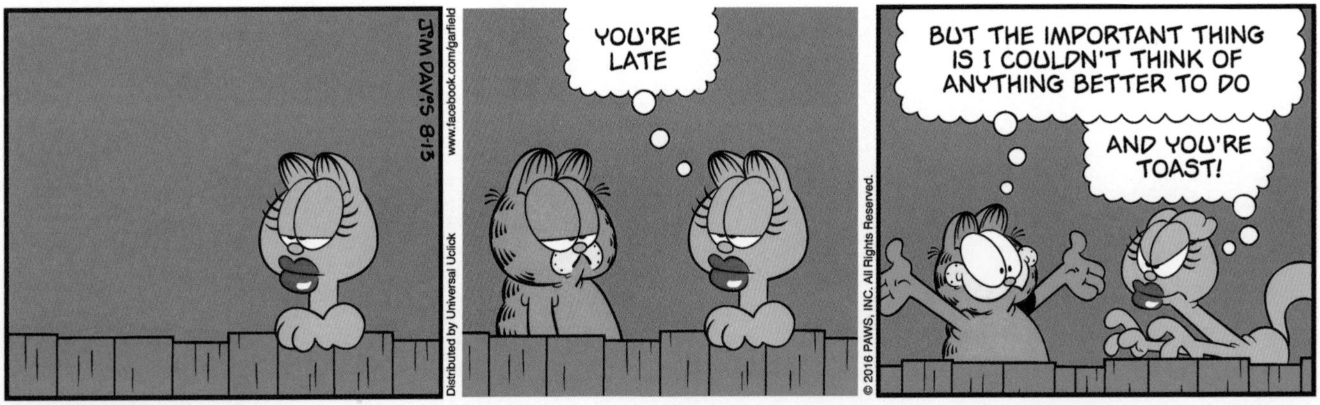
JIM DAVIS 8-13
Distributed by Universal Uclick www.facebook.com/garfield
YOU'RE LATE
© 2016 PAWS, INC. All Rights Reserved.
BUT THE IMPORTANT THING IS I COULDN'T THINK OF ANYTHING BETTER TO DO
AND YOU'RE TOAST!

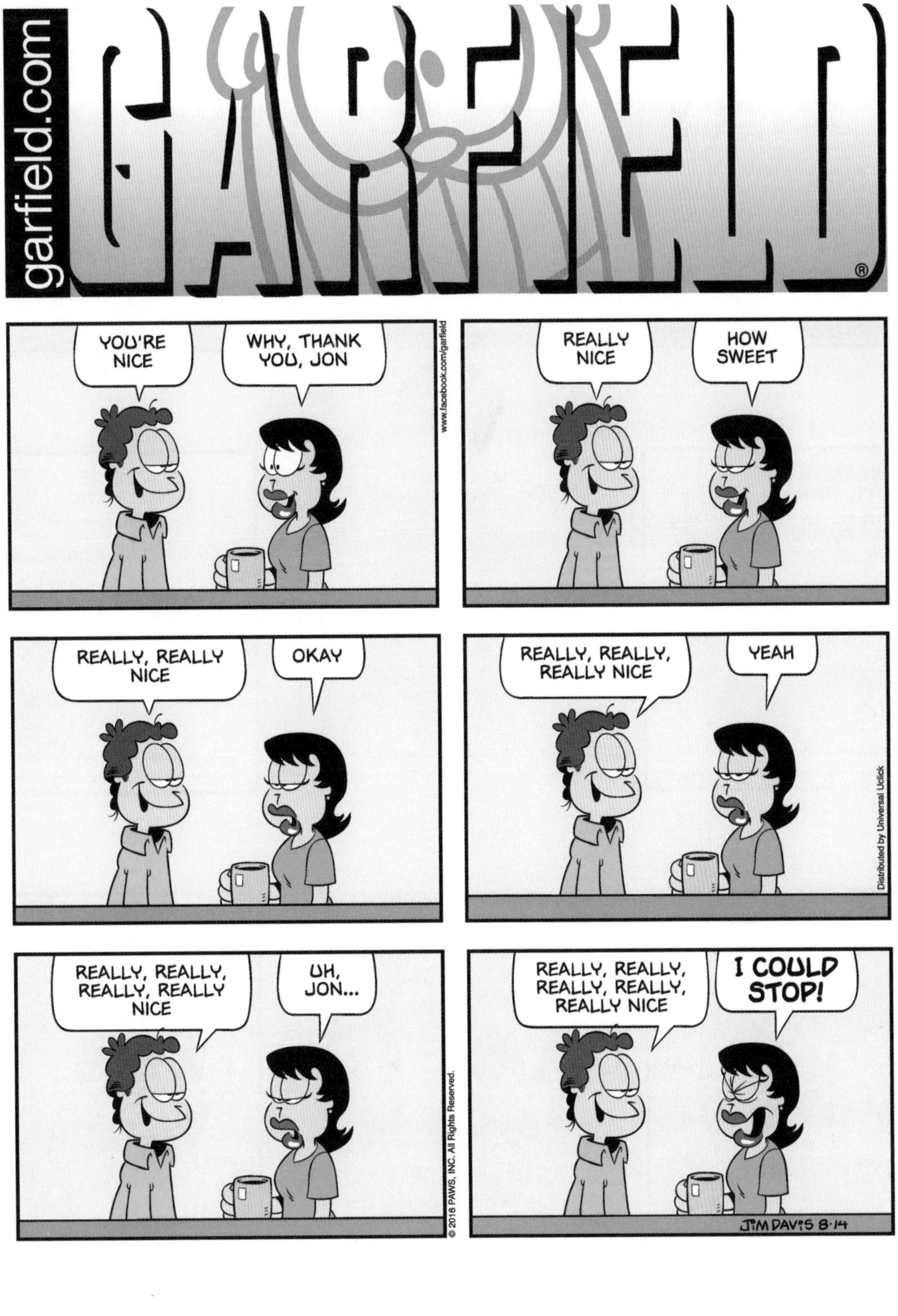
garfield.com
GARFIELD®
YOU'RE NICE
WHY, THANK YOU, JON
www.facebook.com/garfield
REALLY NICE
HOW SWEET
REALLY, REALLY NICE
OKAY
REALLY, REALLY, REALLY NICE
YEAH
Distributed by Universal Uclick
REALLY, REALLY, REALLY, REALLY NICE
UH, JON...
© 2016 PAWS, INC. All Rights Reserved.
REALLY, REALLY, REALLY, REALLY, REALLY NICE
I COULD STOP!
JIM DAVIS 8-14

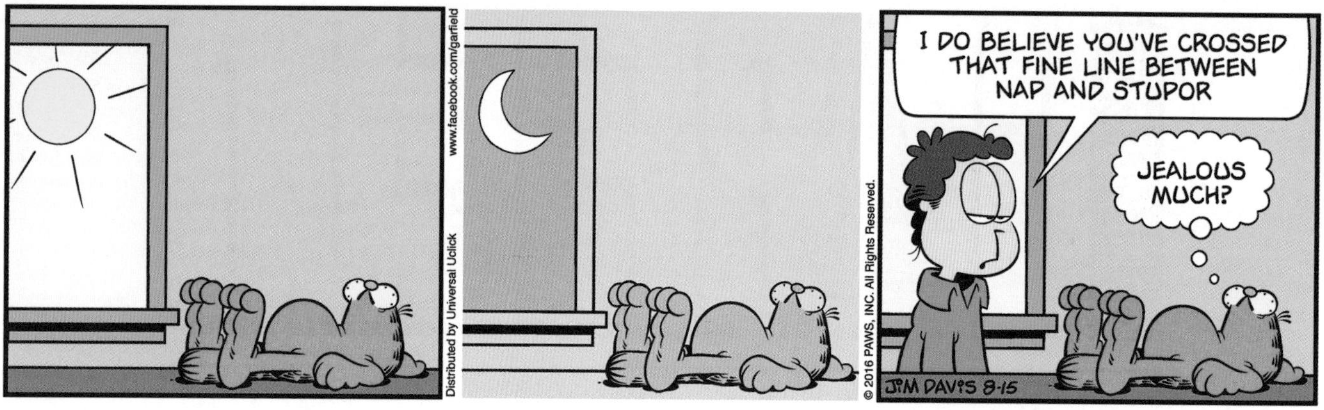
I DO BELIEVE YOU'VE CROSSED THAT FINE LINE BETWEEN NAP AND STUPOR
JEALOUS MUCH?
JIM DAVIS 8-15
Distributed by Universal Uclick www.facebook.com/garfield
© 2016 PAWS, INC. All Rights Reserved.

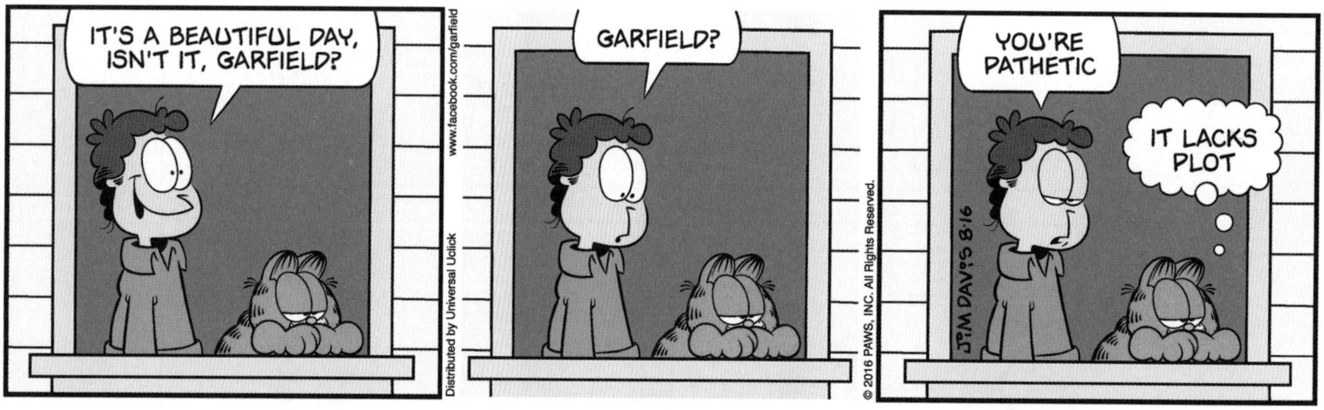
IT'S A BEAUTIFUL DAY, ISN'T IT, GARFIELD?
GARFIELD?
YOU'RE PATHETIC
IT LACKS PLOT
JIM DAVIS 8-16
Distributed by Universal Uclick www.facebook.com/garfield
© 2016 PAWS, INC. All Rights Reserved.

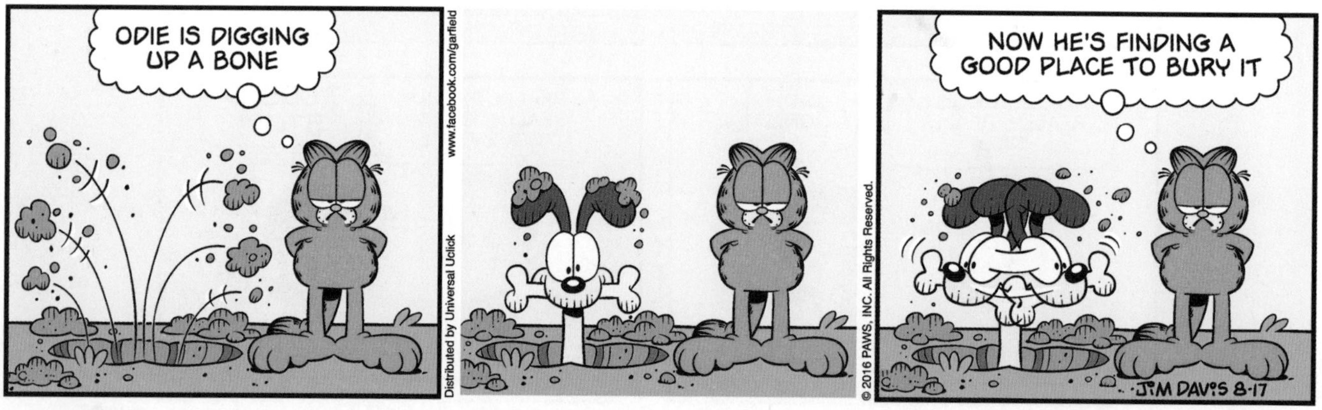
ODIE IS DIGGING UP A BONE
NOW HE'S FINDING A GOOD PLACE TO BURY IT
JIM DAVIS 8-17
Distributed by Universal Uclick www.facebook.com/garfield
© 2016 PAWS, INC. All Rights Reserved.

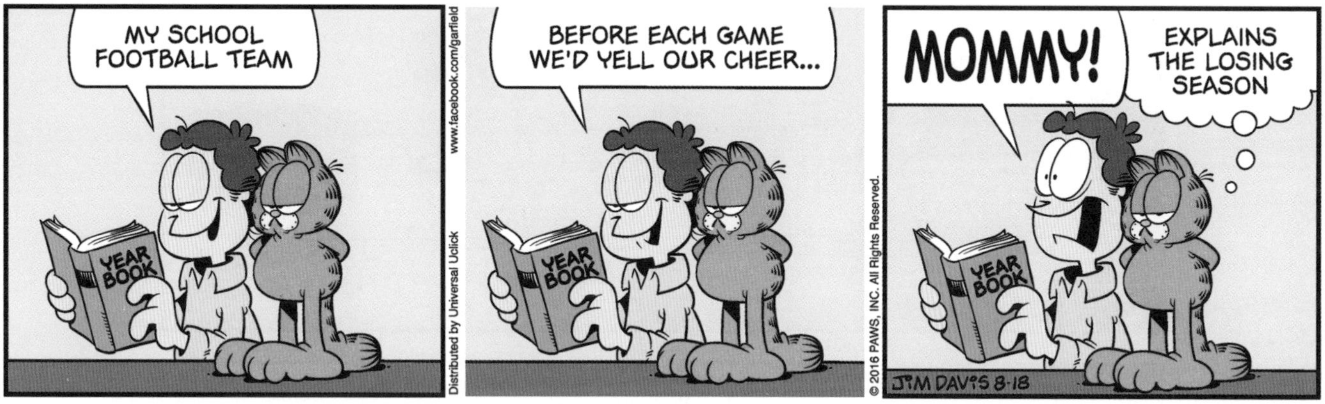
MY SCHOOL FOOTBALL TEAM
YEAR BOOK
Distributed by Universal Uclick
www.facebook.com/garfield
BEFORE EACH GAME WE'D YELL OUR CHEER...
© 2016 PAWS, INC. All Rights Reserved.
MOMMY!
EXPLAINS THE LOSING SEASON
JIM DAVIS 8-18

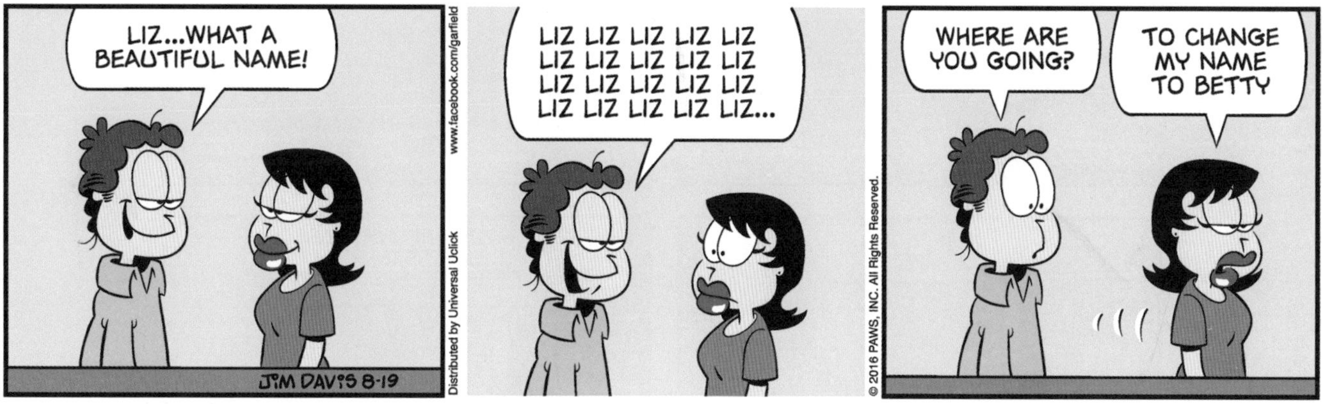
LIZ...WHAT A BEAUTIFUL NAME!
JIM DAVIS 8-19
Distributed by Universal Uclick
www.facebook.com/garfield
LIZ LIZ LIZ LIZ LIZ
LIZ LIZ LIZ LIZ LIZ
LIZ LIZ LIZ LIZ LIZ
LIZ LIZ LIZ LIZ LIZ...
© 2016 PAWS, INC. All Rights Reserved.
WHERE ARE YOU GOING?
TO CHANGE MY NAME TO BETTY

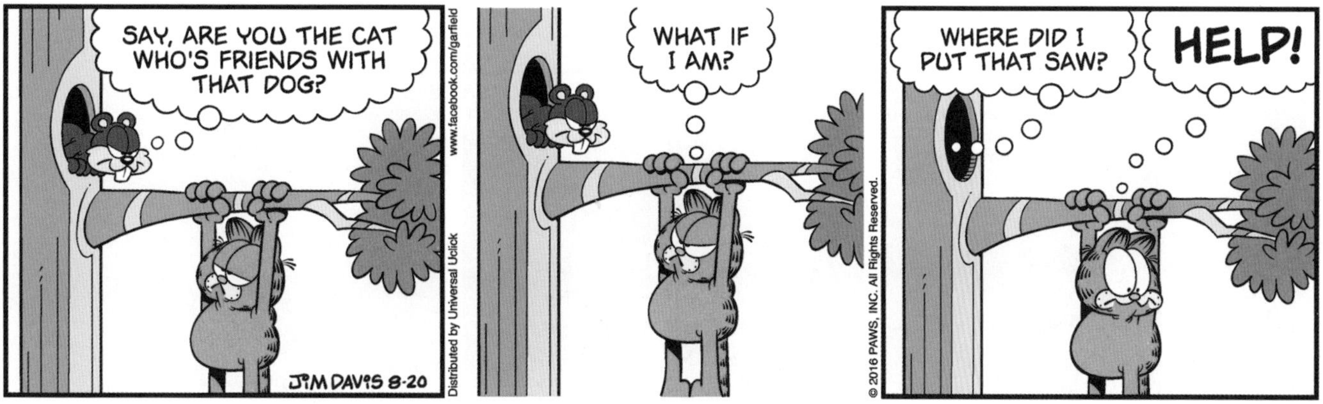
SAY, ARE YOU THE CAT WHO'S FRIENDS WITH THAT DOG?
JIM DAVIS 8-20
Distributed by Universal Uclick
www.facebook.com/garfield
WHAT IF I AM?
© 2016 PAWS, INC. All Rights Reserved.
WHERE DID I PUT THAT SAW?
HELP!

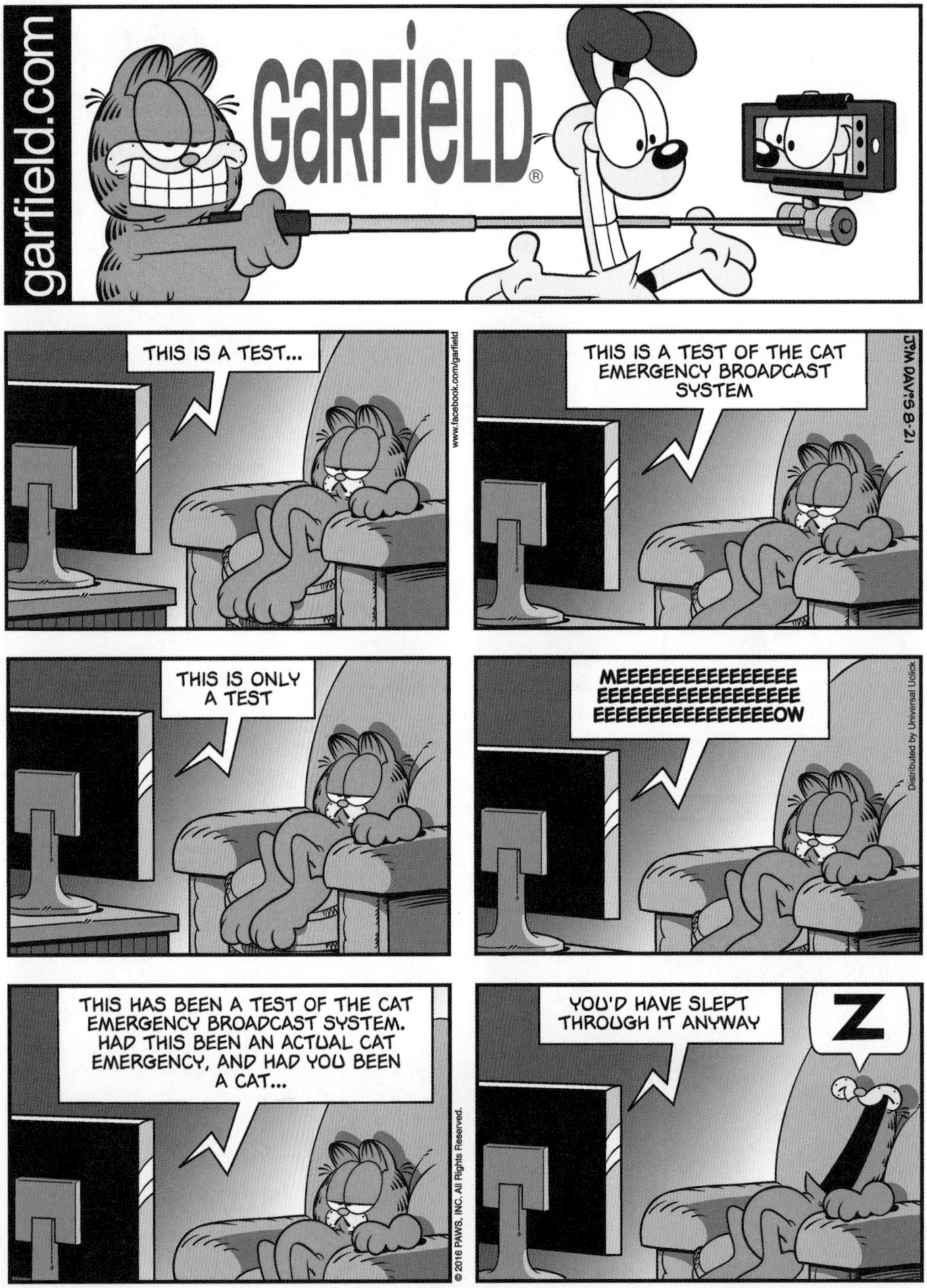
garfield.com
GARFIELD
THIS IS A TEST...
www.facebook.com/garfield
THIS IS A TEST OF THE CAT EMERGENCY BROADCAST SYSTEM
JIM DAVIS 8-21
THIS IS ONLY A TEST
MEEEEEEEEEEEEEEEE EEEEEEEEEEEEEEEEE EEEEEEEEEEEEEEEEOW
Distributed by Universal Uclick
THIS HAS BEEN A TEST OF THE CAT EMERGENCY BROADCAST SYSTEM. HAD THIS BEEN AN ACTUAL CAT EMERGENCY, AND HAD YOU BEEN A CAT...
© 2016 PAWS, INC. All Rights Reserved.
YOU'D HAVE SLEPT THROUGH IT ANYWAY
Z

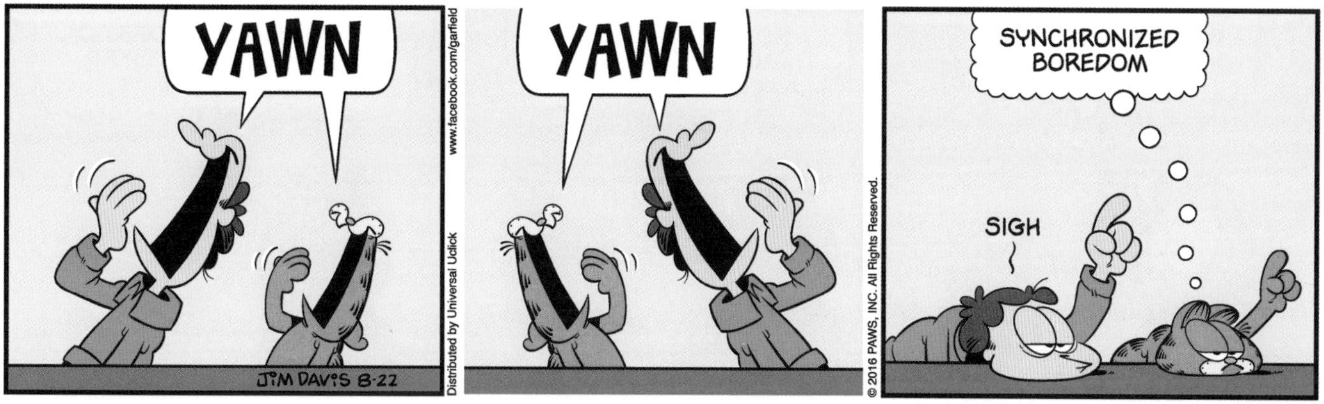
YAWN
JIM DAVIS 8-22
www.facebook.com/garfield
Distributed by Universal Uclick
YAWN
© 2016 PAWS, INC. All Rights Reserved.
SYNCHRONIZED BOREDOM
SIGH

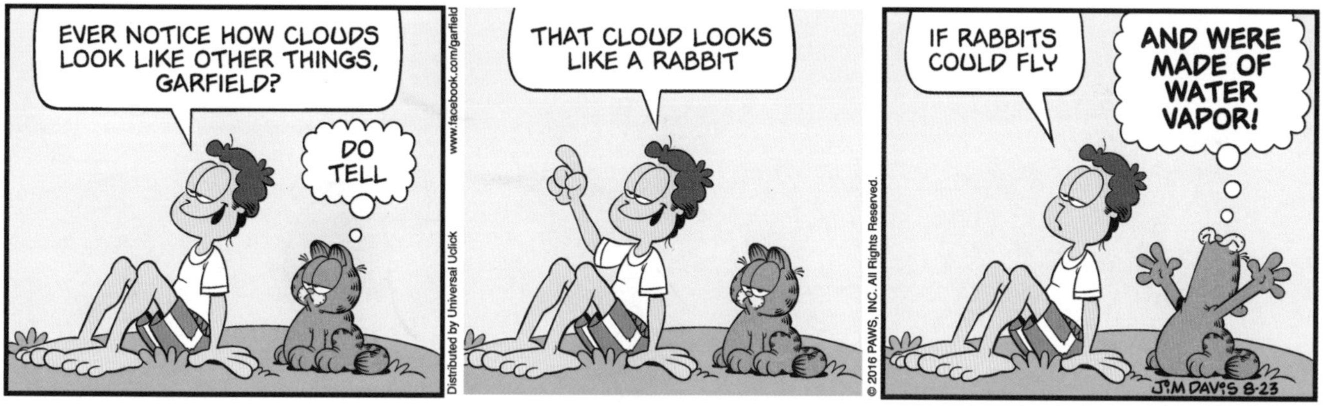
EVER NOTICE HOW CLOUDS LOOK LIKE OTHER THINGS, GARFIELD?
DO TELL
www.facebook.com/garfield
Distributed by Universal Uclick
THAT CLOUD LOOKS LIKE A RABBIT
© 2016 PAWS, INC. All Rights Reserved.
IF RABBITS COULD FLY
AND WERE MADE OF WATER VAPOR!
JIM DAVIS 8-23

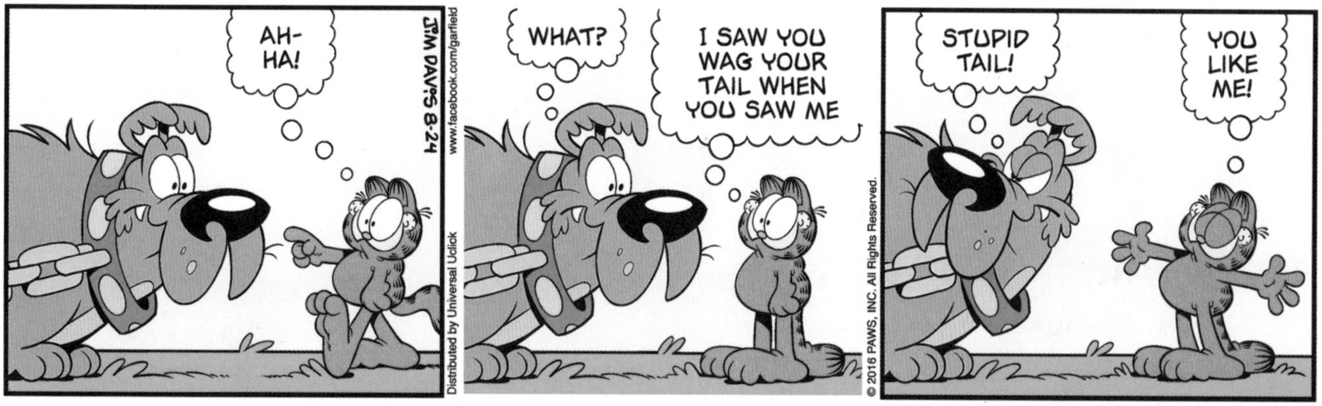
AH-HA!
JIM DAVIS 8-24
www.facebook.com/garfield
Distributed by Universal Uclick
WHAT?
I SAW YOU WAG YOUR TAIL WHEN YOU SAW ME
© 2016 PAWS, INC. All Rights Reserved.
STUPID TAIL!
YOU LIKE ME!

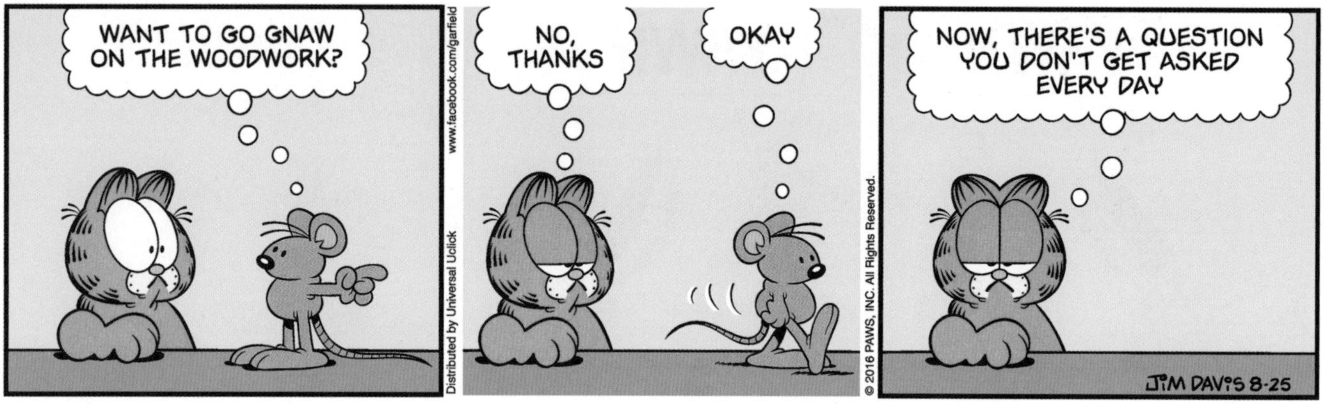
WANT TO GO GNAW ON THE WOODWORK?
www.facebook.com/garfield
Distributed by Universal Uclick
NO, THANKS
OKAY
© 2016 PAWS, INC. All Rights Reserved.
NOW, THERE'S A QUESTION YOU DON'T GET ASKED EVERY DAY
JIM DAVIS 8-25

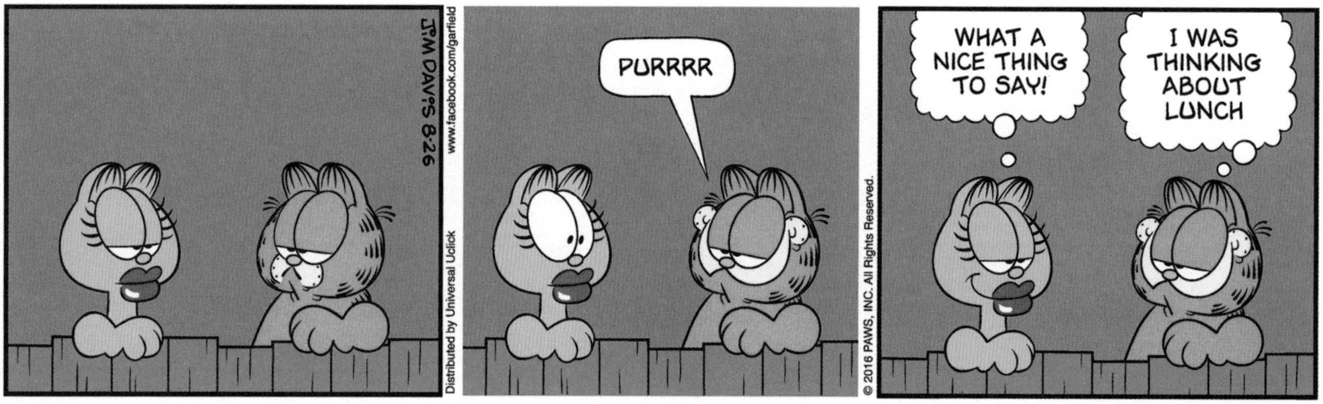
JIM DAVIS 8-26
www.facebook.com/garfield
Distributed by Universal Uclick
PURRRR
© 2016 PAWS, INC. All Rights Reserved.
WHAT A NICE THING TO SAY!
I WAS THINKING ABOUT LUNCH

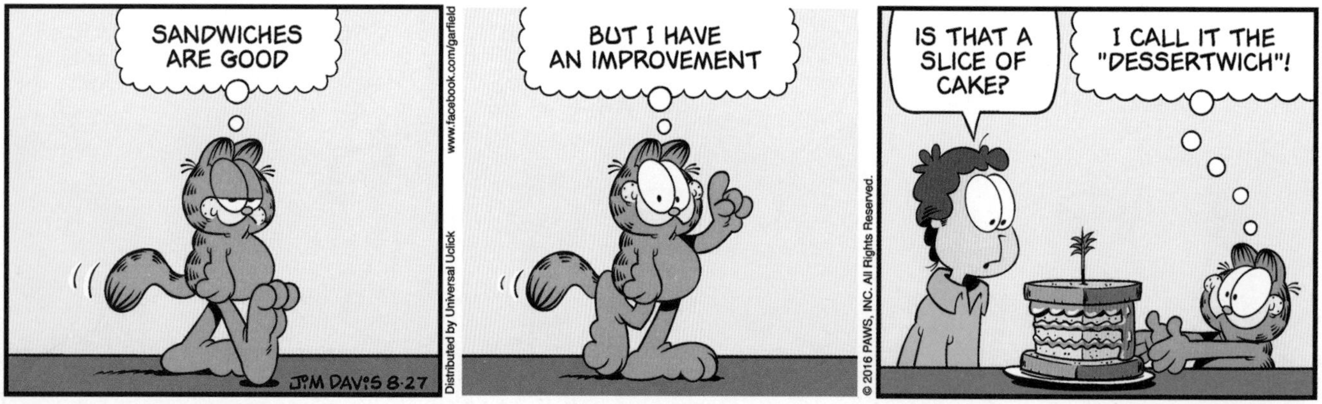
SANDWICHES ARE GOOD
JIM DAVIS 8-27
www.facebook.com/garfield
Distributed by Universal Uclick
BUT I HAVE AN IMPROVEMENT
© 2016 PAWS, INC. All Rights Reserved.
IS THAT A SLICE OF CAKE?
I CALL IT THE "DESSERTWICH"!

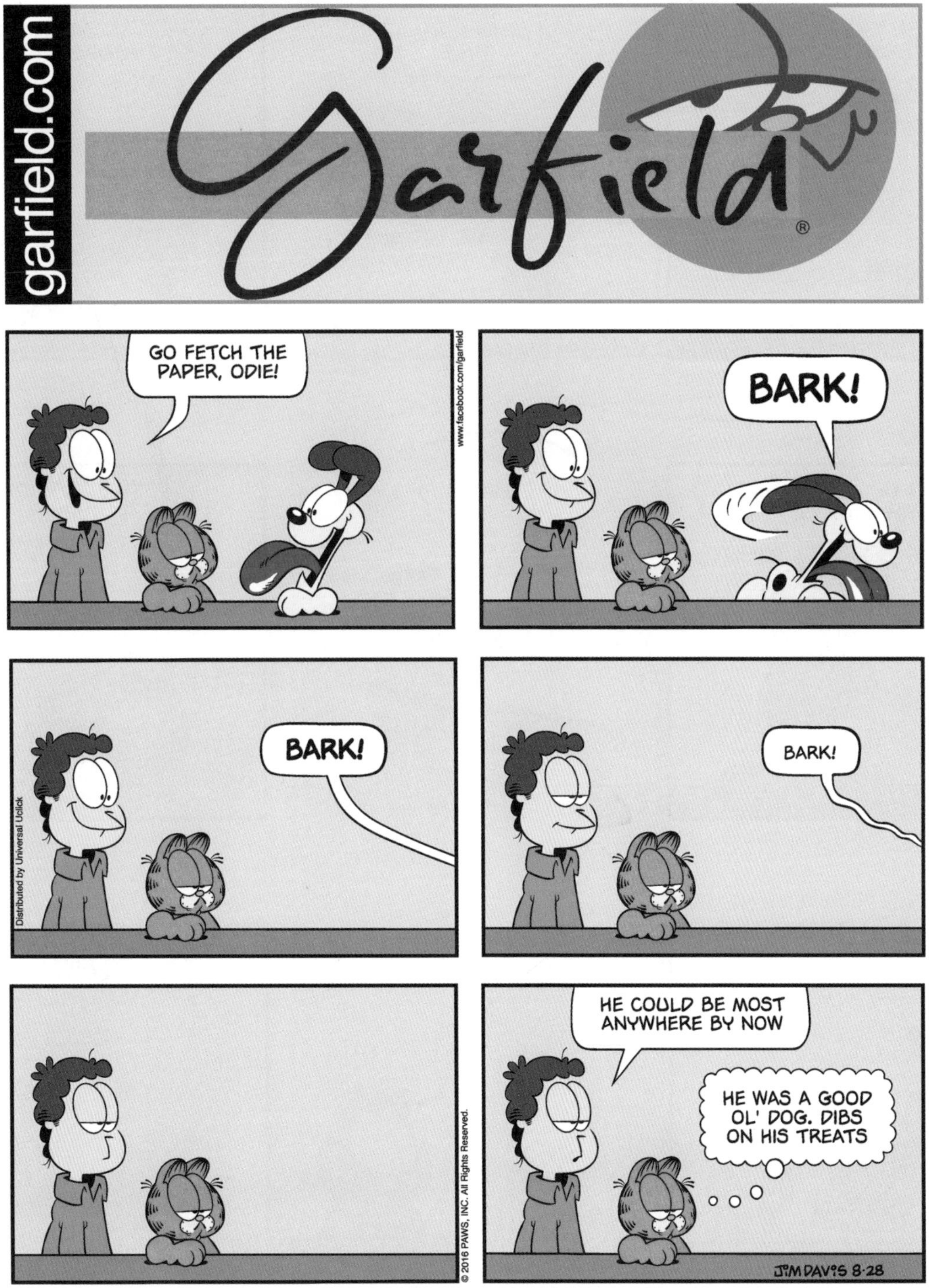
garfield.com
Garfield®
GO FETCH THE PAPER, ODIE!
www.facebook.com/garfield
BARK!
Distributed by Universal Uclick
BARK!
BARK!
© 2016 PAWS, INC. All Rights Reserved.
HE COULD BE MOST ANYWHERE BY NOW
HE WAS A GOOD OL' DOG. DIBS ON HIS TREATS
JIM DAVIS 8-28

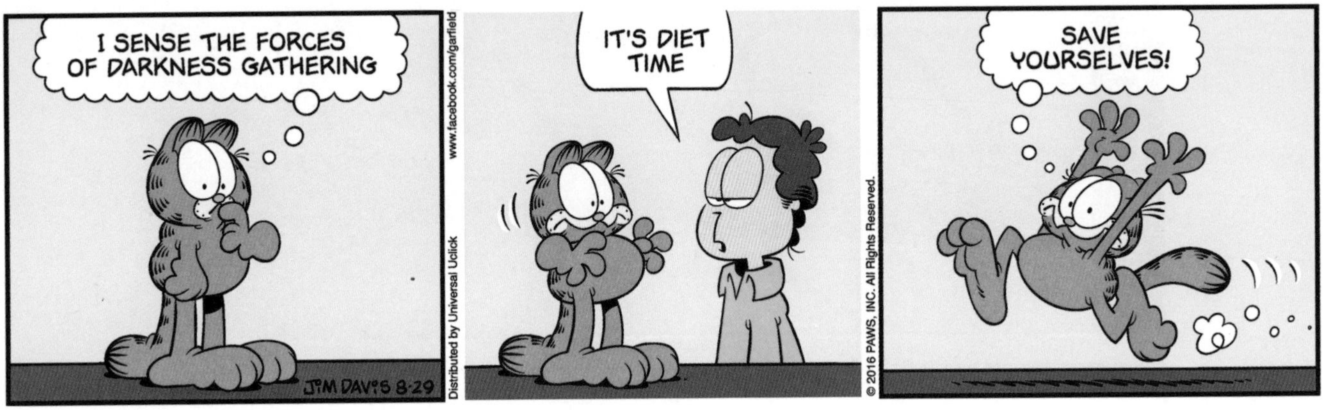
I SENSE THE FORCES OF DARKNESS GATHERING
JIM DAVIS 8-29
www.facebook.com/garfield
Distributed by Universal Uclick
IT'S DIET TIME
© 2016 PAWS, INC. All Rights Reserved.
SAVE YOURSELVES!

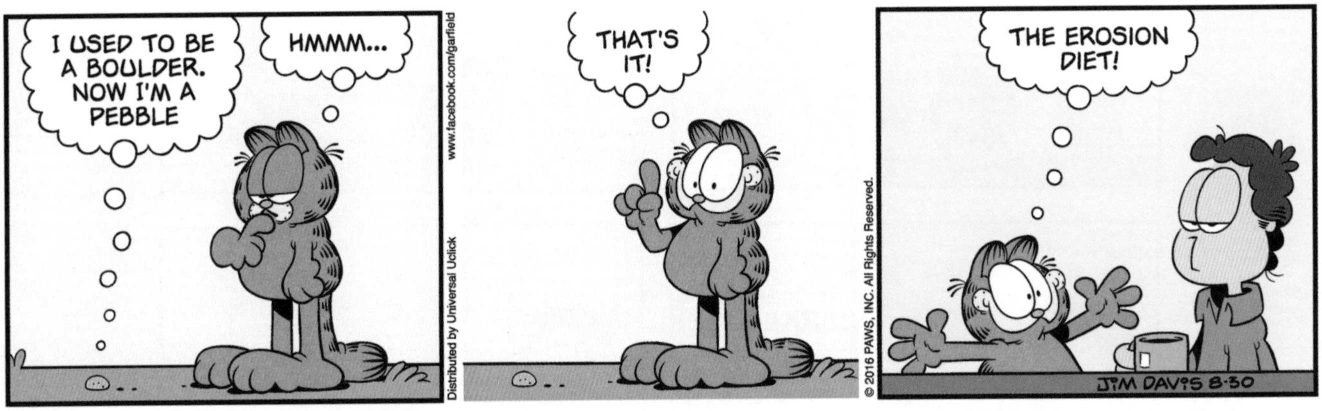
I USED TO BE A BOULDER. NOW I'M A PEBBLE
HMMM...
www.facebook.com/garfield
Distributed by Universal Uclick
THAT'S IT!
© 2016 PAWS, INC. All Rights Reserved.
THE EROSION DIET!
JIM DAVIS 8-30

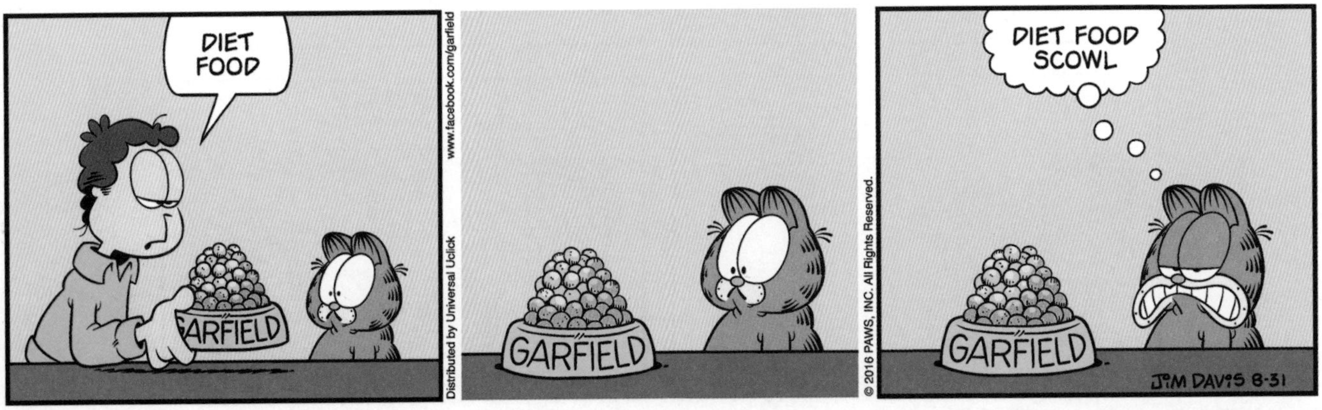
DIET FOOD
GARFIELD
www.facebook.com/garfield
Distributed by Universal Uclick
GARFIELD
© 2016 PAWS, INC. All Rights Reserved.
DIET FOOD SCOWL
GARFIELD
JIM DAVIS 8-31

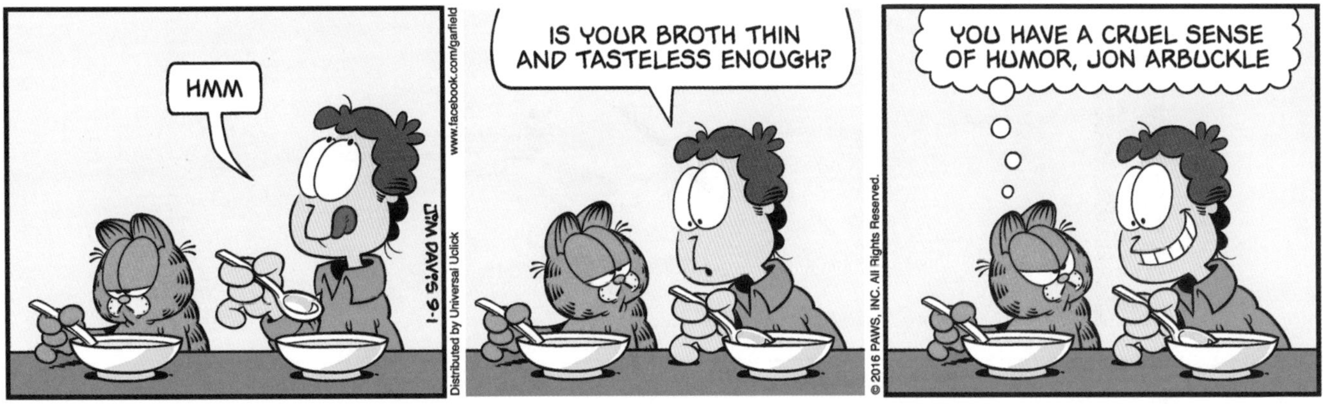
HMM
IS YOUR BROTH THIN AND TASTELESS ENOUGH?
YOU HAVE A CRUEL SENSE OF HUMOR, JON ARBUCKLE
JIM DAVIS 9-1
Distributed by Universal Uclick www.facebook.com/garfield
© 2016 PAWS, INC. All Rights Reserved.

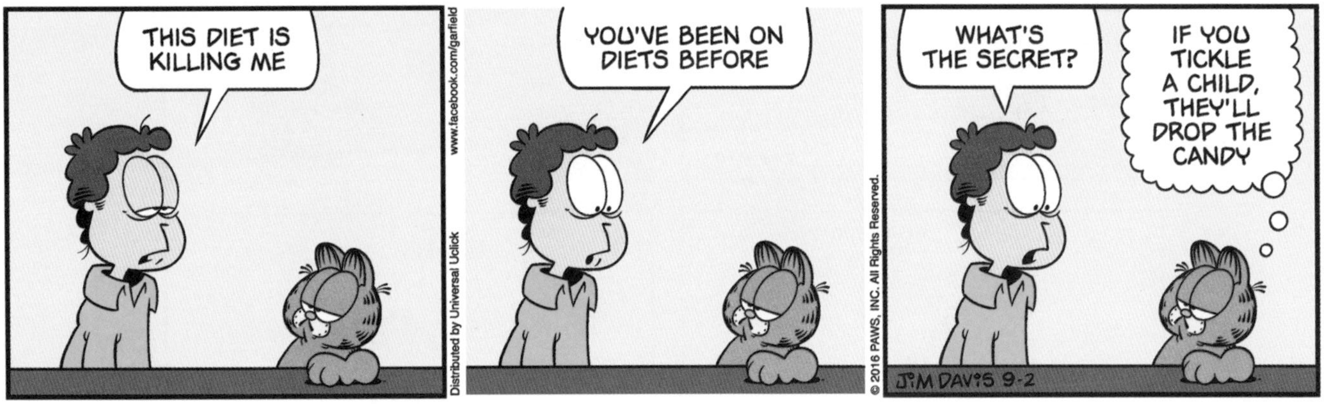
THIS DIET IS KILLING ME
YOU'VE BEEN ON DIETS BEFORE
WHAT'S THE SECRET?
IF YOU TICKLE A CHILD, THEY'LL DROP THE CANDY
JIM DAVIS 9-2
Distributed by Universal Uclick www.facebook.com/garfield
© 2016 PAWS, INC. All Rights Reserved.

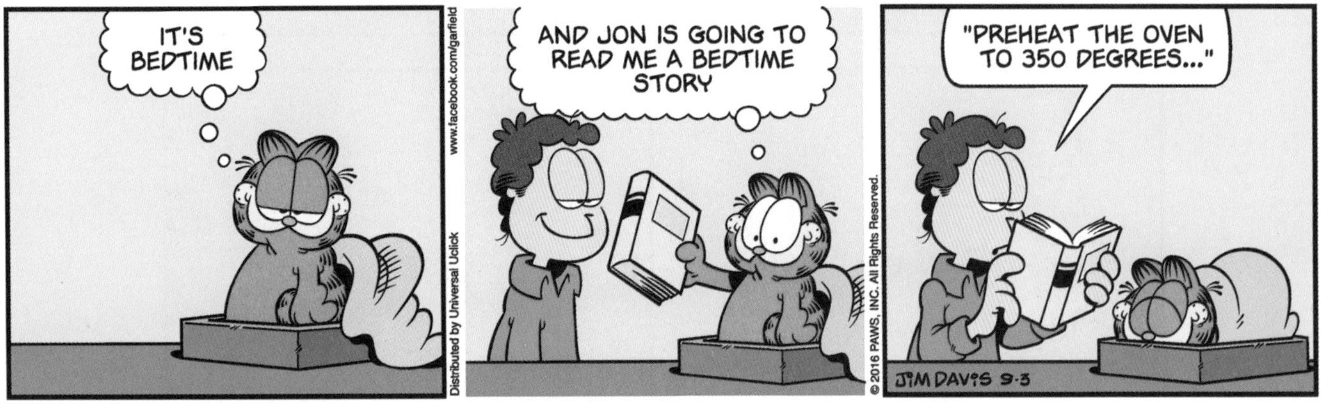
IT'S BEDTIME
AND JON IS GOING TO READ ME A BEDTIME STORY
"PREHEAT THE OVEN TO 350 DEGREES..."
JIM DAVIS 9-3
Distributed by Universal Uclick www.facebook.com/garfield
© 2016 PAWS, INC. All Rights Reserved.

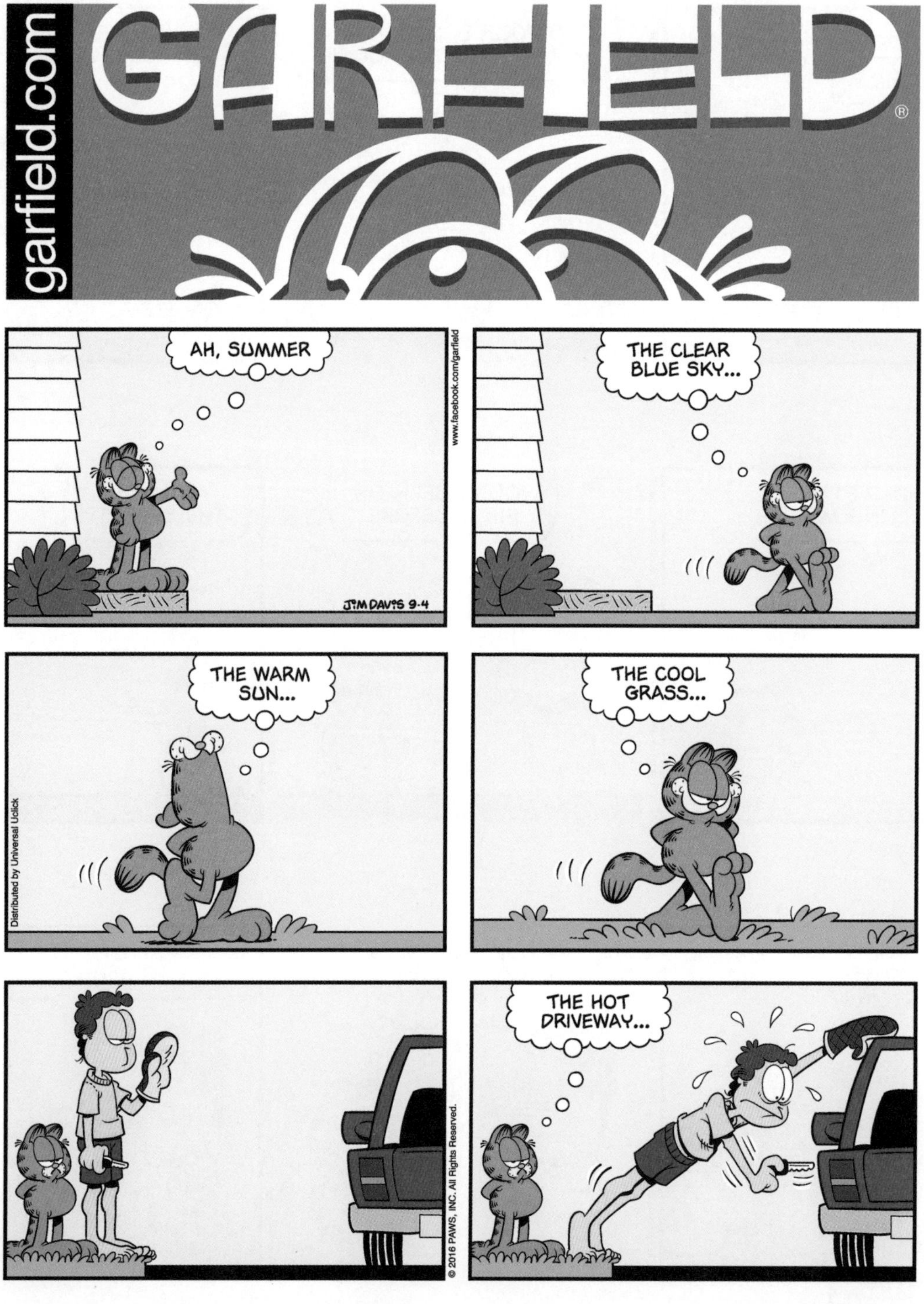
garfield.com
GARFIELD®
AH, SUMMER
JIM DAVIS 9-4
www.facebook.com/garfield
THE CLEAR BLUE SKY...
THE WARM SUN...
Distributed by Universal Uclick
THE COOL GRASS...
© 2016 PAWS, INC. All Rights Reserved.
THE HOT DRIVEWAY...

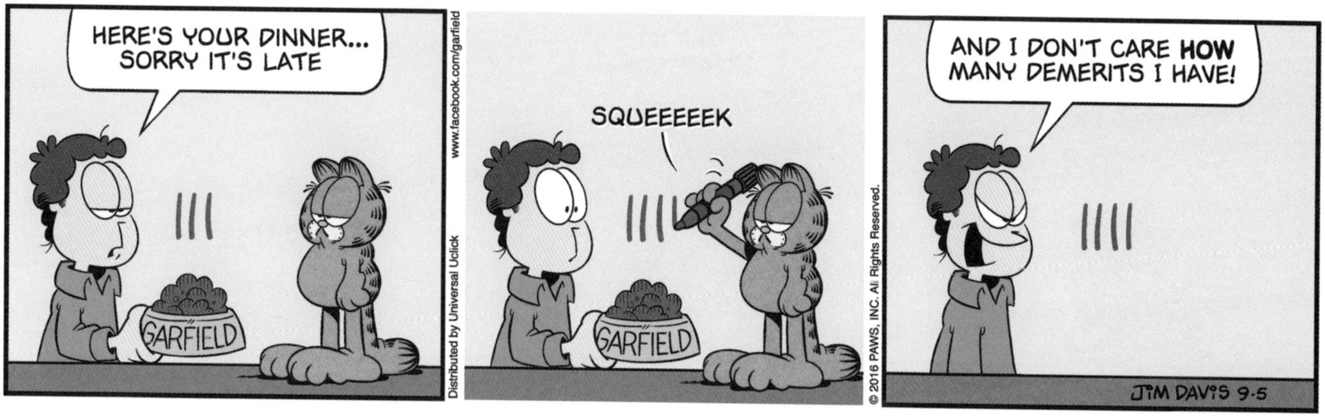
HERE'S YOUR DINNER... SORRY IT'S LATE
GARFIELD
www.facebook.com/garfield
Distributed by Universal Uclick
SQUEEEEEK
GARFIELD
© 2016 PAWS, INC. All Rights Reserved.
AND I DON'T CARE **HOW** MANY DEMERITS I HAVE!
JIM DAVIS 9-5

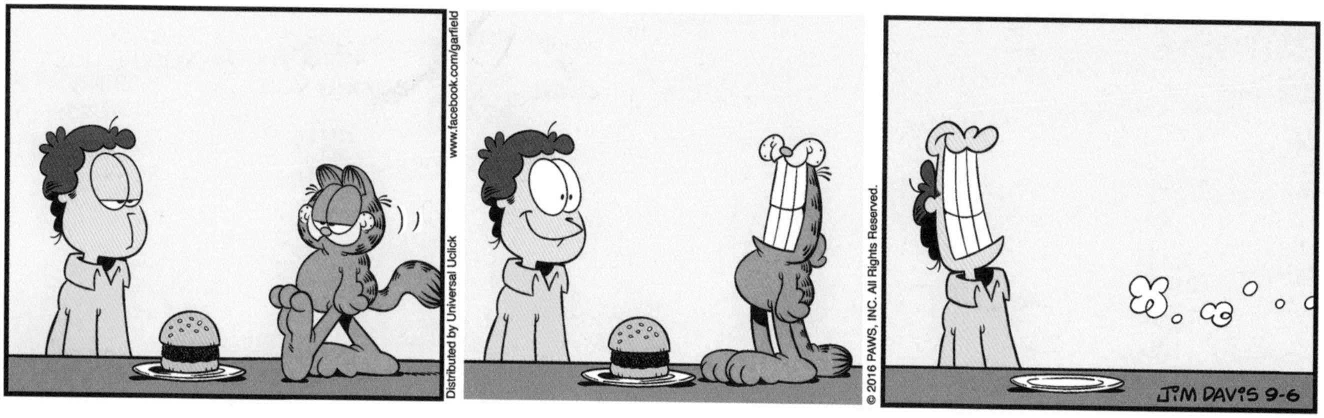
www.facebook.com/garfield
Distributed by Universal Uclick
© 2016 PAWS, INC. All Rights Reserved.
JIM DAVIS 9-6

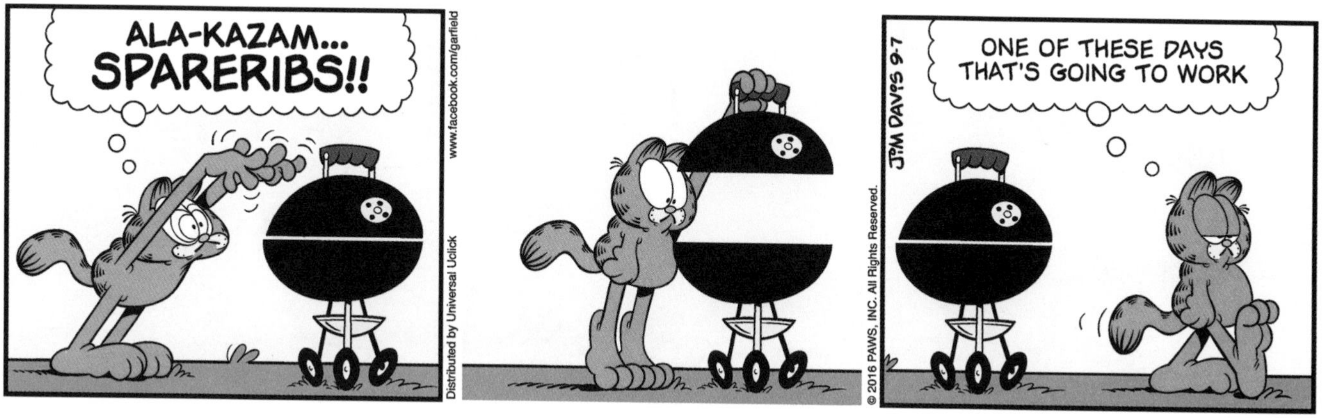
ALA-KAZAM... SPARERIBS!!
www.facebook.com/garfield
Distributed by Universal Uclick
JIM DAVIS 9-7
© 2016 PAWS, INC. All Rights Reserved.
ONE OF THESE DAYS THAT'S GOING TO WORK

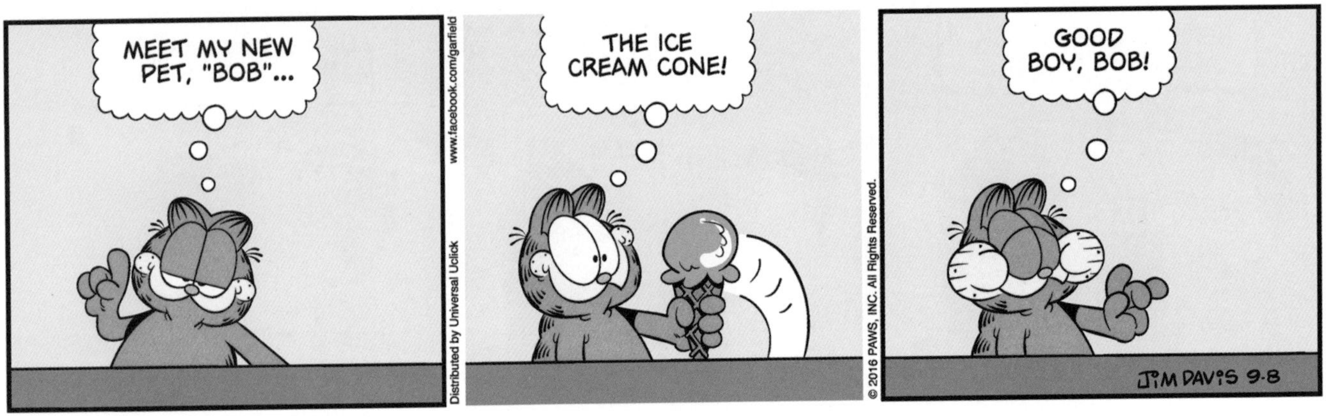
MEET MY NEW PET, "BOB"...
THE ICE CREAM CONE!
GOOD BOY, BOB!
JIM DAVIS 9-8
www.facebook.com/garfield
Distributed by Universal Uclick
© 2016 PAWS, INC. All Rights Reserved.

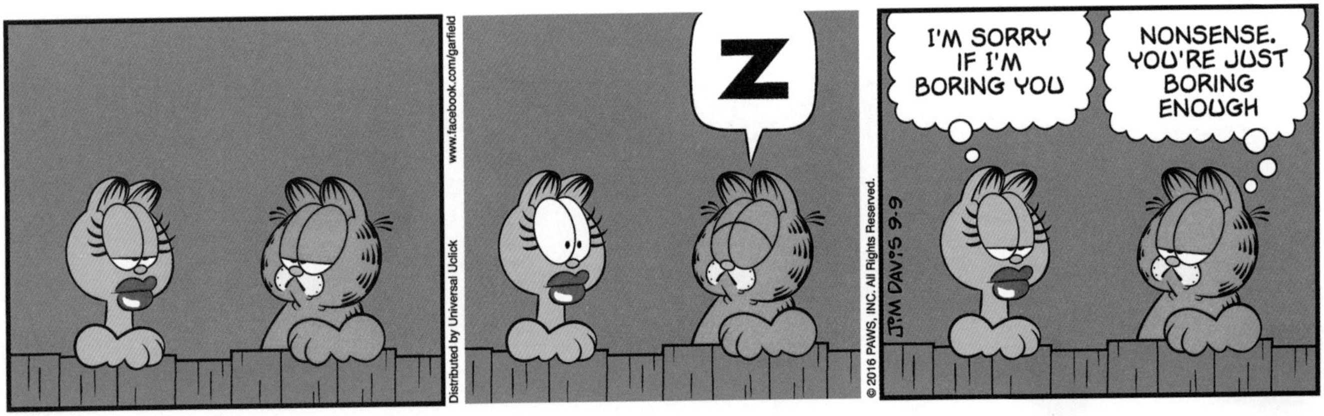
Z
I'M SORRY IF I'M BORING YOU
NONSENSE. YOU'RE JUST BORING ENOUGH
JIM DAVIS 9-9
www.facebook.com/garfield
Distributed by Universal Uclick
© 2016 PAWS, INC. All Rights Reserved.

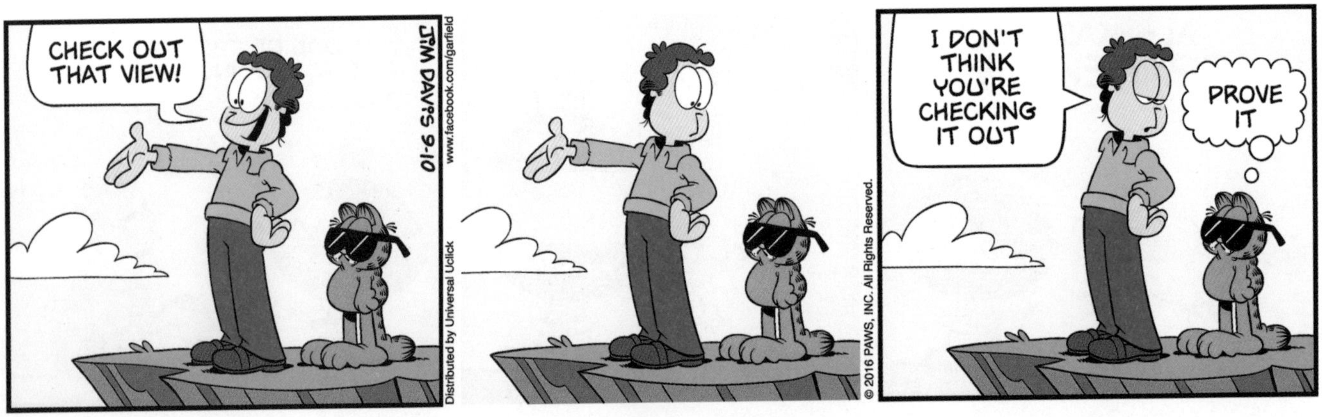
CHECK OUT THAT VIEW!
I DON'T THINK YOU'RE CHECKING IT OUT
PROVE IT
JIM DAVIS 9-10
www.facebook.com/garfield
Distributed by Universal Uclick
© 2016 PAWS, INC. All Rights Reserved.

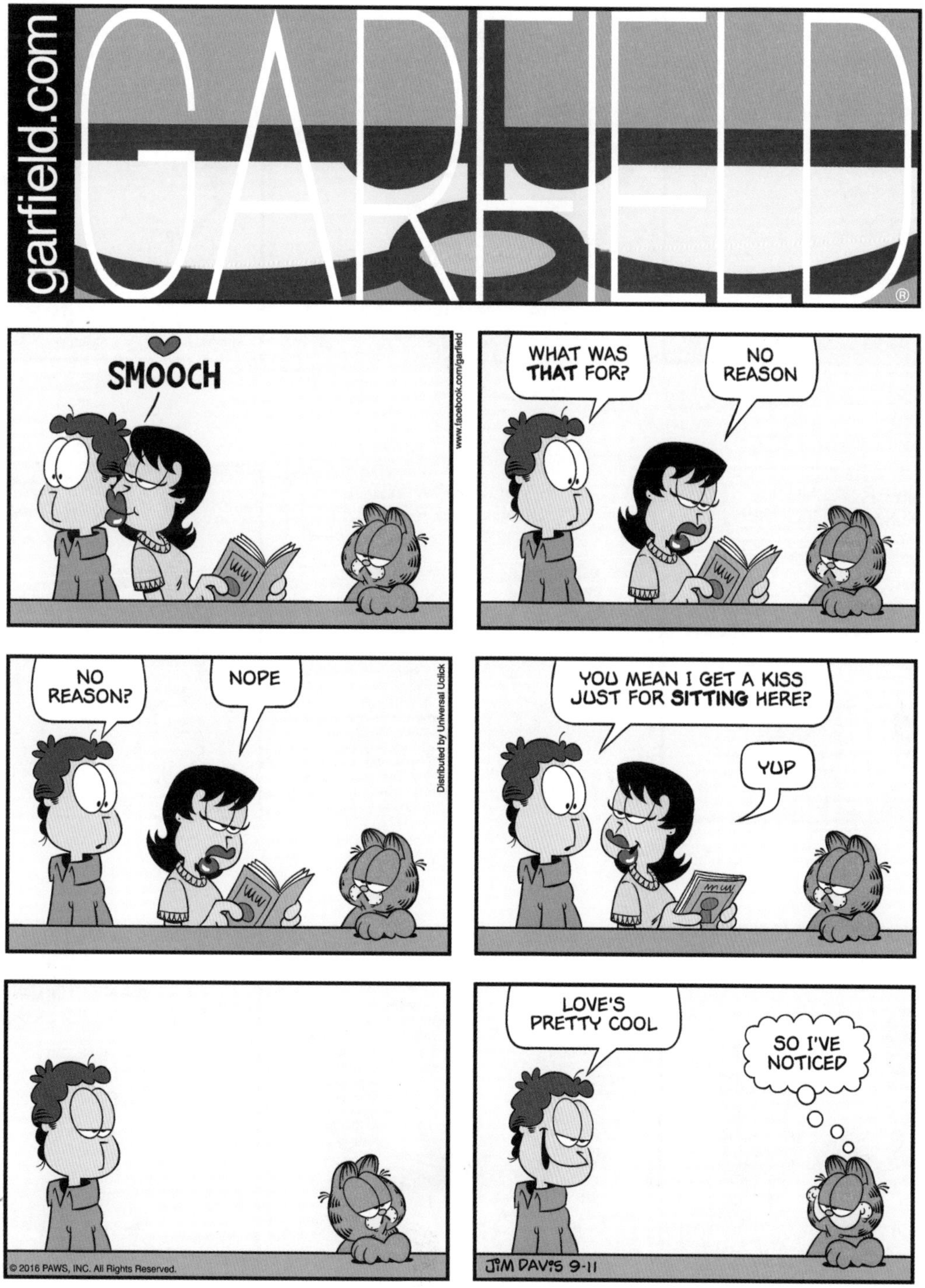
garfield.com
GARFIELD®
SMOOCH
www.facebook.com/garfield
WHAT WAS THAT FOR?
NO REASON
NO REASON?
NOPE
Distributed by Universal Uclick
YOU MEAN I GET A KISS JUST FOR SITTING HERE?
YUP
LOVE'S PRETTY COOL
SO I'VE NOTICED
© 2016 PAWS, INC. All Rights Reserved.
JIM DAVIS 9-11

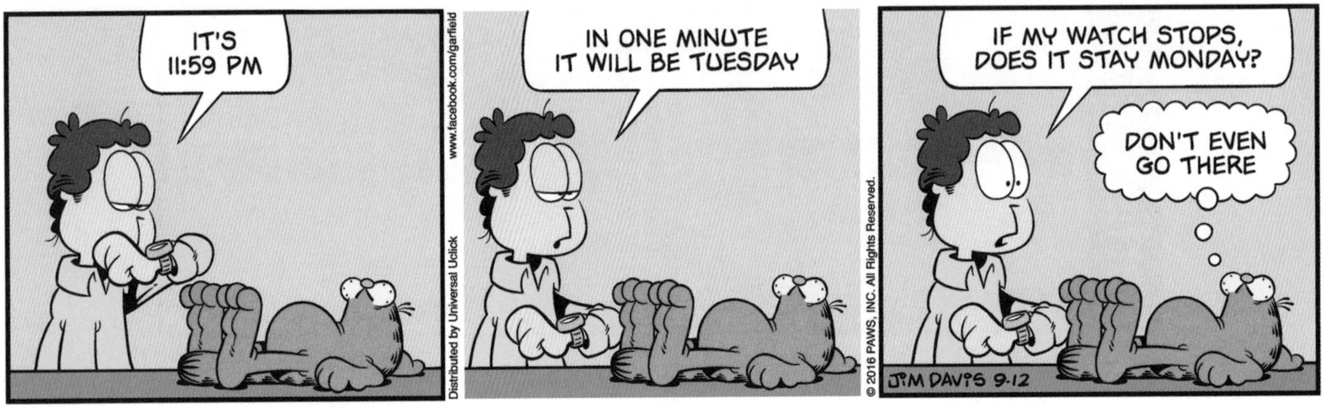
IT'S 11:59 PM
www.facebook.com/garfield
Distributed by Universal Uclick
IN ONE MINUTE IT WILL BE TUESDAY
© 2016 PAWS, INC. All Rights Reserved.
IF MY WATCH STOPS, DOES IT STAY MONDAY?
DON'T EVEN GO THERE
JIM DAVIS 9-12

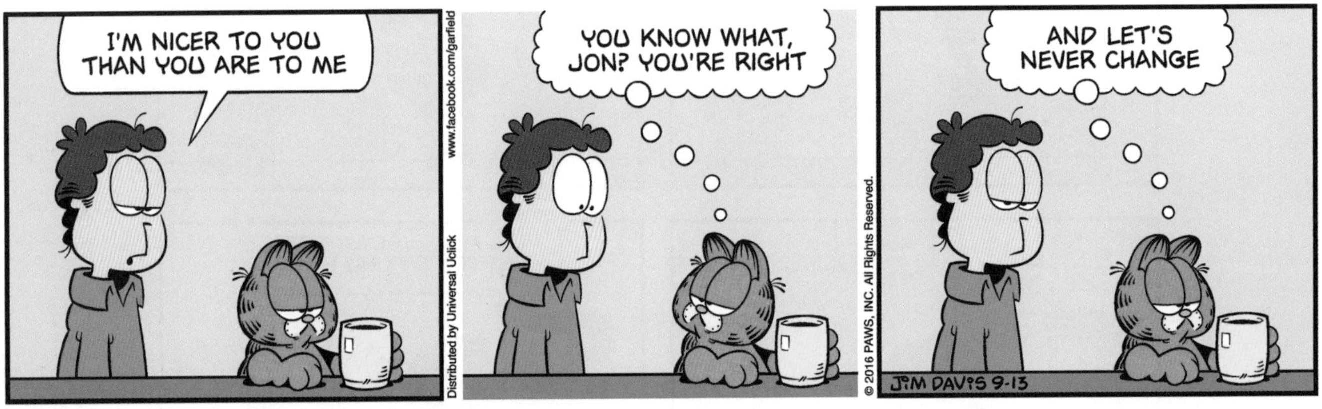
I'M NICER TO YOU THAN YOU ARE TO ME
www.facebook.com/garfield
Distributed by Universal Uclick
YOU KNOW WHAT, JON? YOU'RE RIGHT
© 2016 PAWS, INC. All Rights Reserved.
AND LET'S NEVER CHANGE
JIM DAVIS 9-13

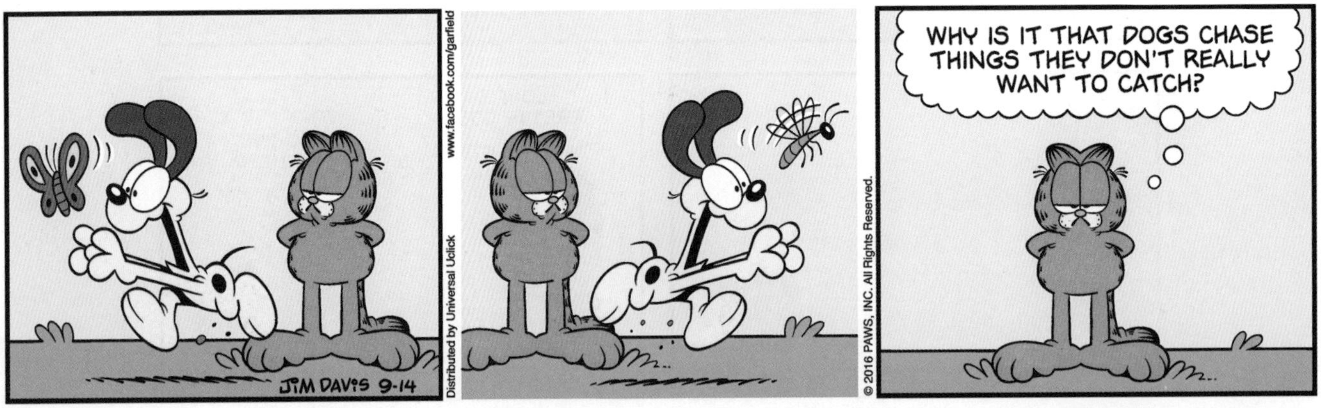
JIM DAVIS 9-14
www.facebook.com/garfield
Distributed by Universal Uclick
© 2016 PAWS, INC. All Rights Reserved.
WHY IS IT THAT DOGS CHASE THINGS THEY DON'T REALLY WANT TO CATCH?

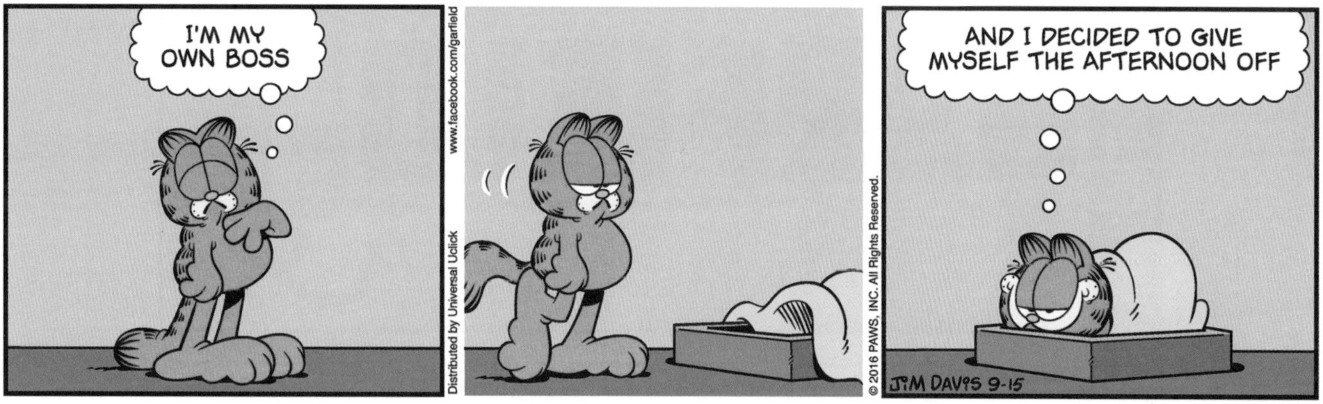
I'M MY OWN BOSS
AND I DECIDED TO GIVE MYSELF THE AFTERNOON OFF
JIM DAVIS 9-15
Distributed by Universal Uclick www.facebook.com/garfield
© 2016 PAWS, INC. All Rights Reserved.

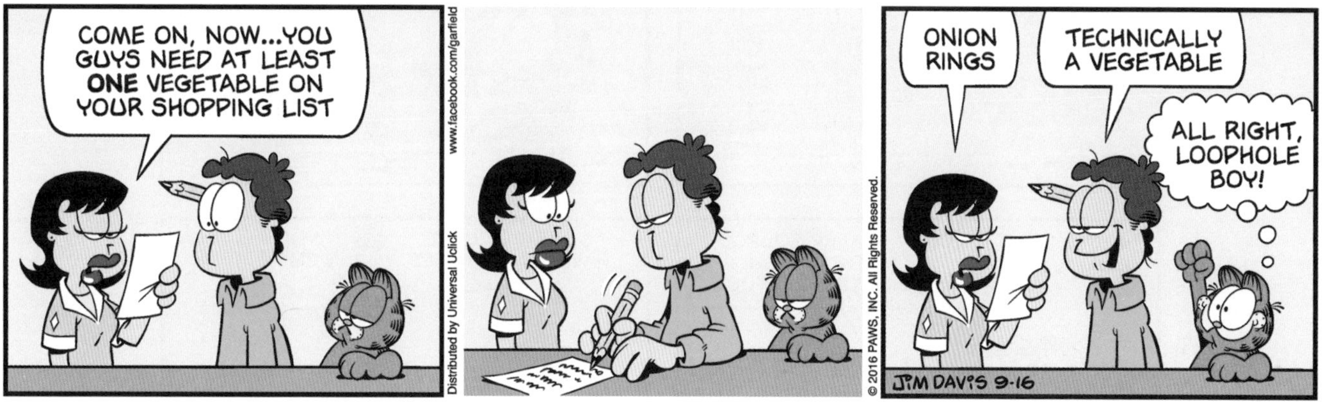
COME ON, NOW...YOU GUYS NEED AT LEAST **ONE** VEGETABLE ON YOUR SHOPPING LIST
ONION RINGS
TECHNICALLY A VEGETABLE
ALL RIGHT, LOOPHOLE BOY!
JIM DAVIS 9-16
Distributed by Universal Uclick www.facebook.com/garfield
© 2016 PAWS, INC. All Rights Reserved.

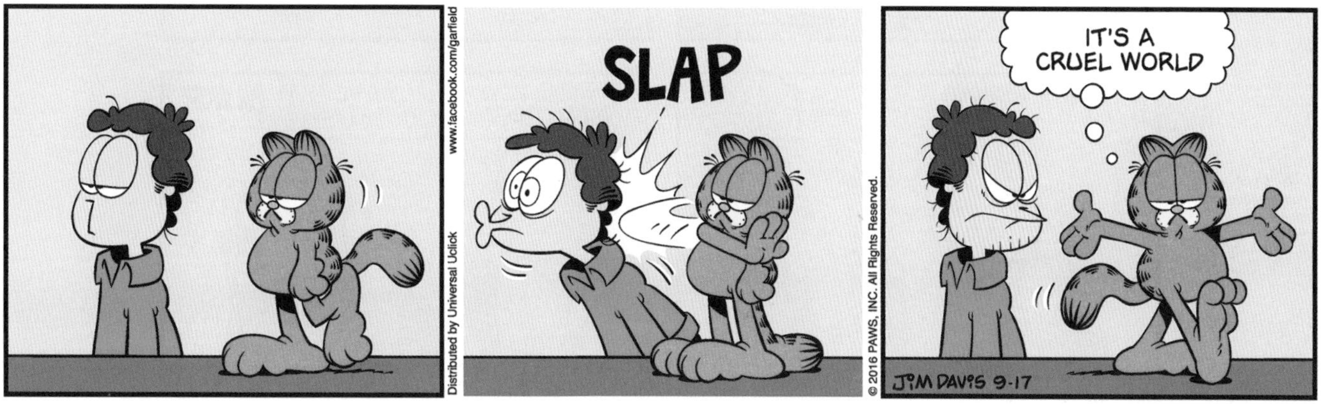
SLAP
IT'S A CRUEL WORLD
JIM DAVIS 9-17
Distributed by Universal Uclick www.facebook.com/garfield
© 2016 PAWS, INC. All Rights Reserved.

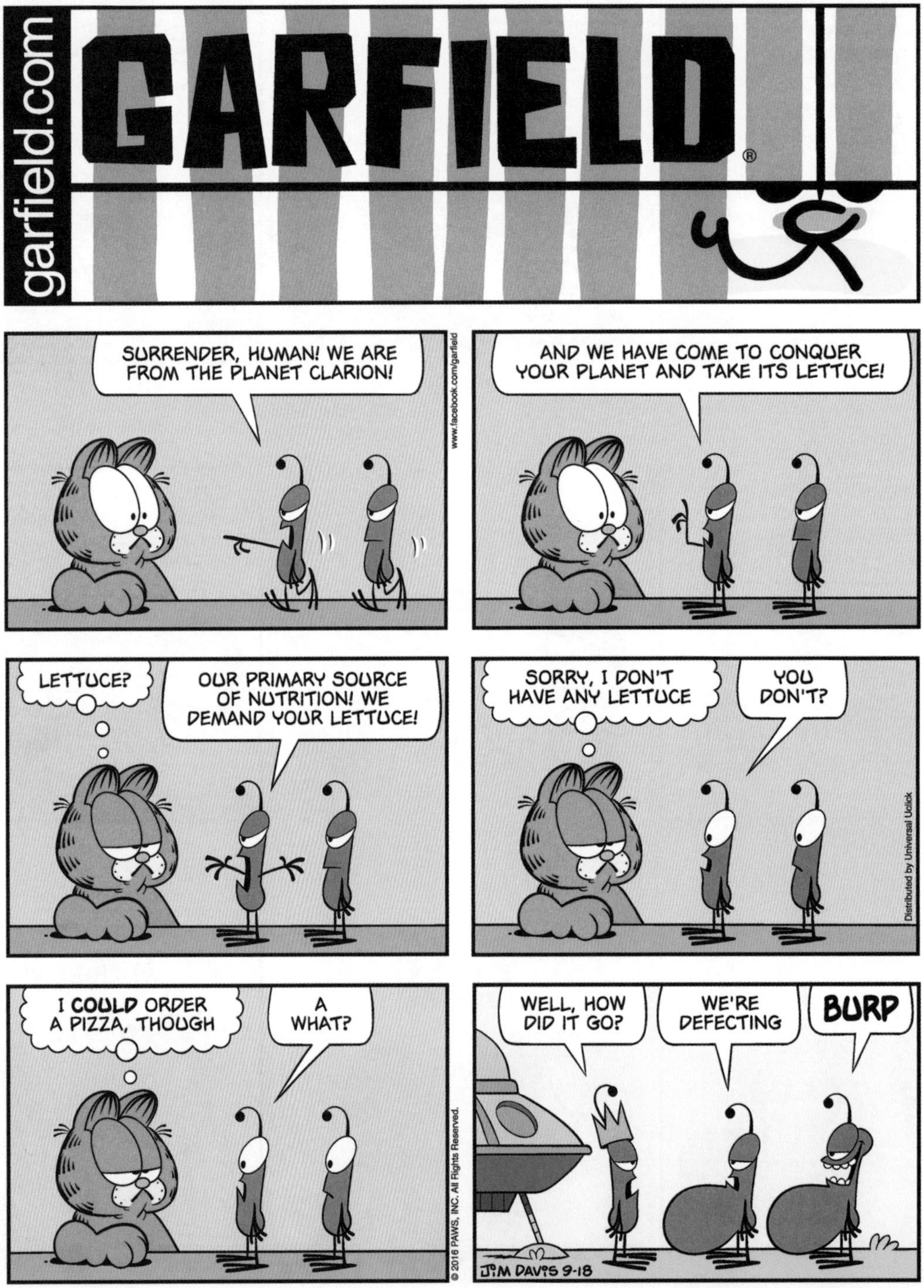
garfield.com
GARFIELD
SURRENDER, HUMAN! WE ARE FROM THE PLANET CLARION!
www.facebook.com/garfield
AND WE HAVE COME TO CONQUER YOUR PLANET AND TAKE ITS LETTUCE!
LETTUCE?
OUR PRIMARY SOURCE OF NUTRITION! WE DEMAND YOUR LETTUCE!
SORRY, I DON'T HAVE ANY LETTUCE
YOU DON'T?
Distributed by Universal Uclick
I COULD ORDER A PIZZA, THOUGH
A WHAT?
© 2016 PAWS, INC. All Rights Reserved.
WELL, HOW DID IT GO?
WE'RE DEFECTING
BURP
JIM DAVIS 9-18

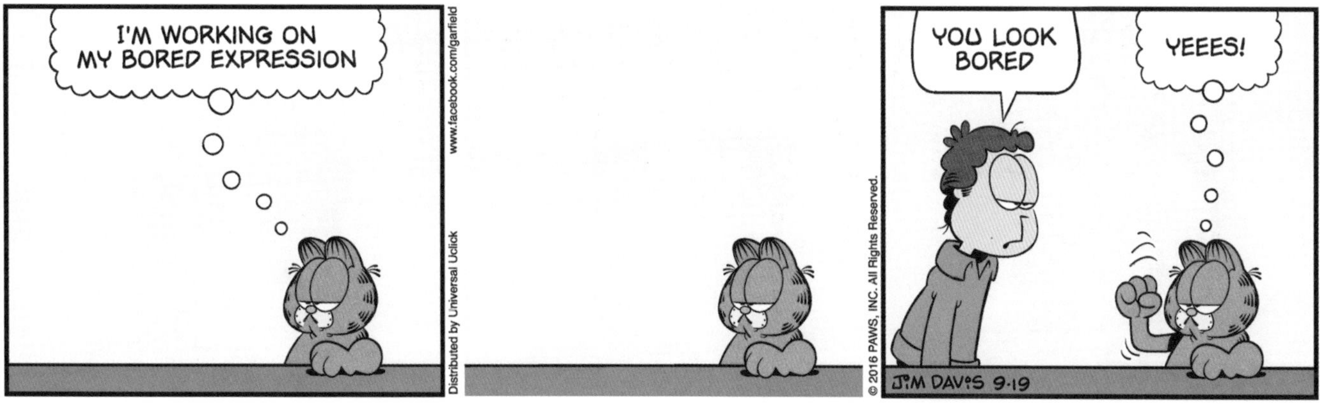
I'M WORKING ON MY BORED EXPRESSION
YOU LOOK BORED
YEEES!
JIM DAVIS 9·19
Distributed by Universal Uclick www.facebook.com/garfield
© 2016 PAWS, INC. All Rights Reserved.

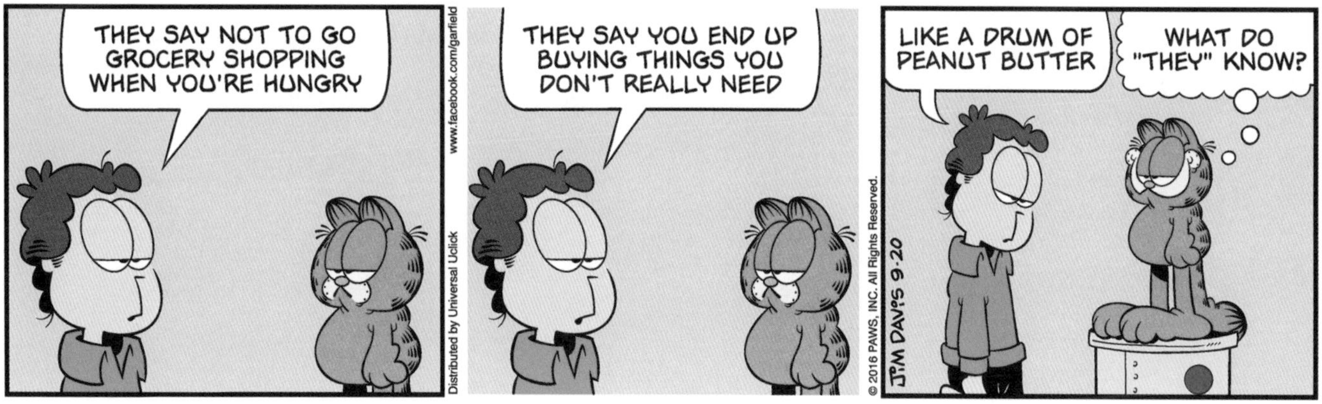
THEY SAY NOT TO GO GROCERY SHOPPING WHEN YOU'RE HUNGRY
THEY SAY YOU END UP BUYING THINGS YOU DON'T REALLY NEED
LIKE A DRUM OF PEANUT BUTTER
WHAT DO "THEY" KNOW?
JIM DAVIS 9·20
Distributed by Universal Uclick www.facebook.com/garfield
© 2016 PAWS, INC. All Rights Reserved.

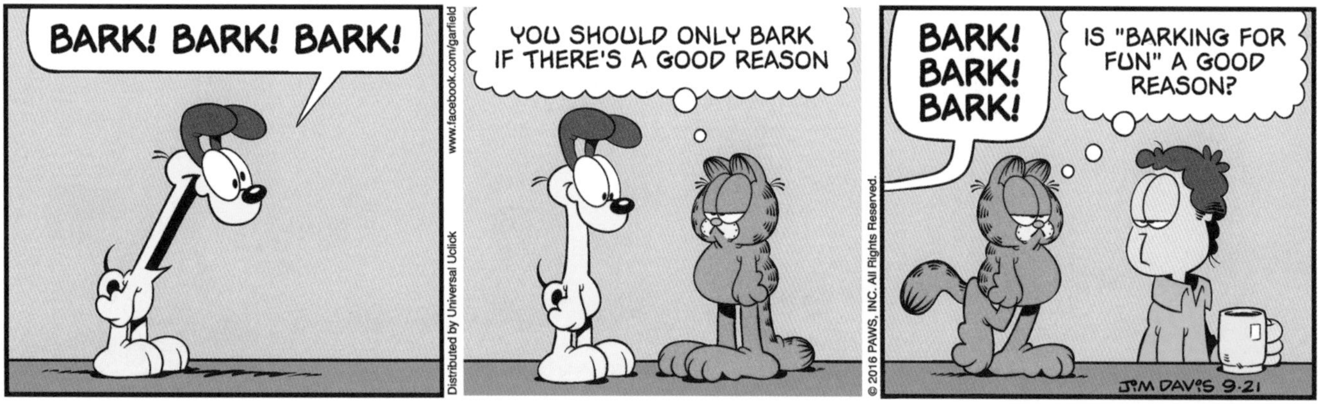
BARK! BARK! BARK!
YOU SHOULD ONLY BARK IF THERE'S A GOOD REASON
BARK! BARK! BARK!
IS "BARKING FOR FUN" A GOOD REASON?
JIM DAVIS 9·21
Distributed by Universal Uclick www.facebook.com/garfield
© 2016 PAWS, INC. All Rights Reserved.

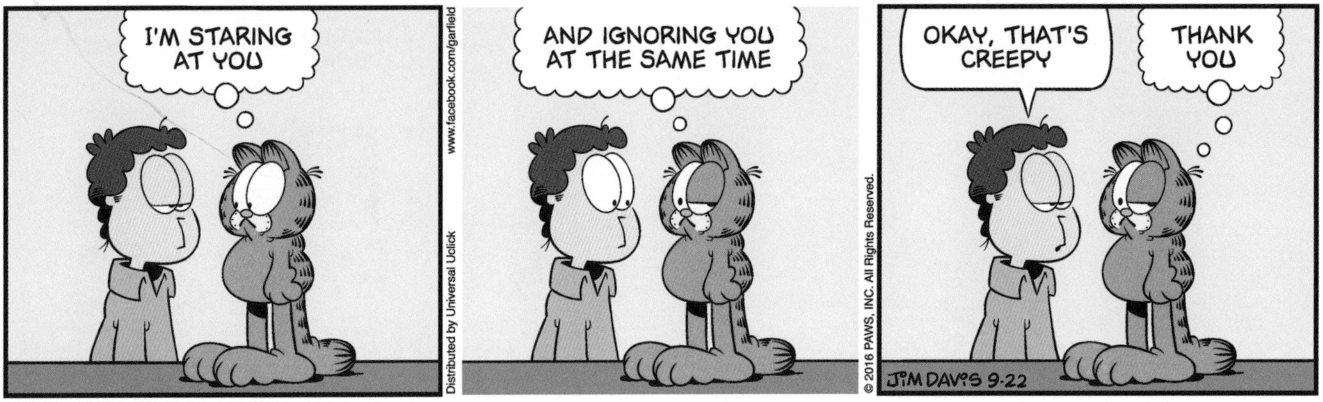
I'M STARING AT YOU
AND IGNORING YOU AT THE SAME TIME
OKAY, THAT'S CREEPY
THANK YOU
JIM DAVIS 9-22

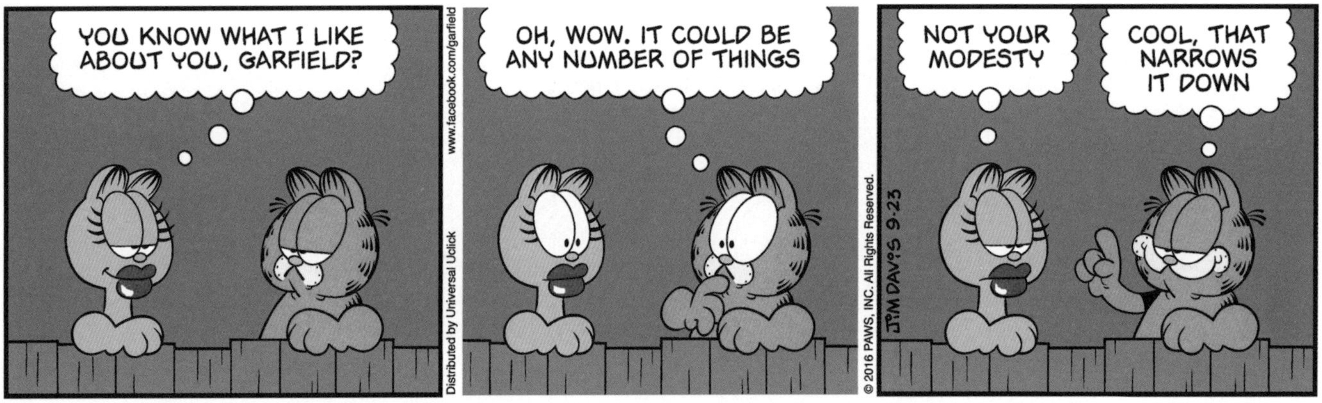
YOU KNOW WHAT I LIKE ABOUT YOU, GARFIELD?
OH, WOW. IT COULD BE ANY NUMBER OF THINGS
NOT YOUR MODESTY
COOL, THAT NARROWS IT DOWN
JIM DAVIS 9-23

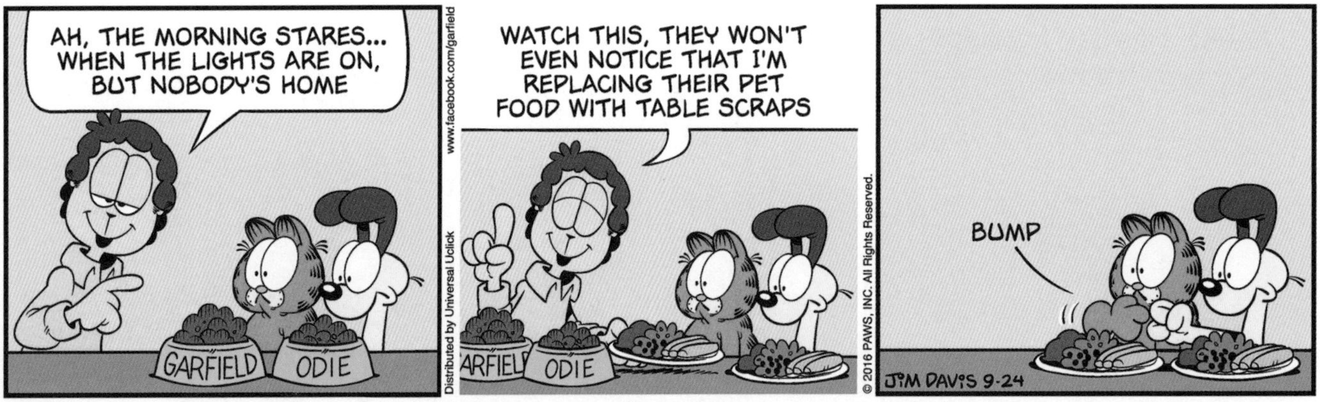
AH, THE MORNING STARES... WHEN THE LIGHTS ARE ON, BUT NOBODY'S HOME
GARFIELD
ODIE
WATCH THIS, THEY WON'T EVEN NOTICE THAT I'M REPLACING THEIR PET FOOD WITH TABLE SCRAPS
BUMP
JIM DAVIS 9-24

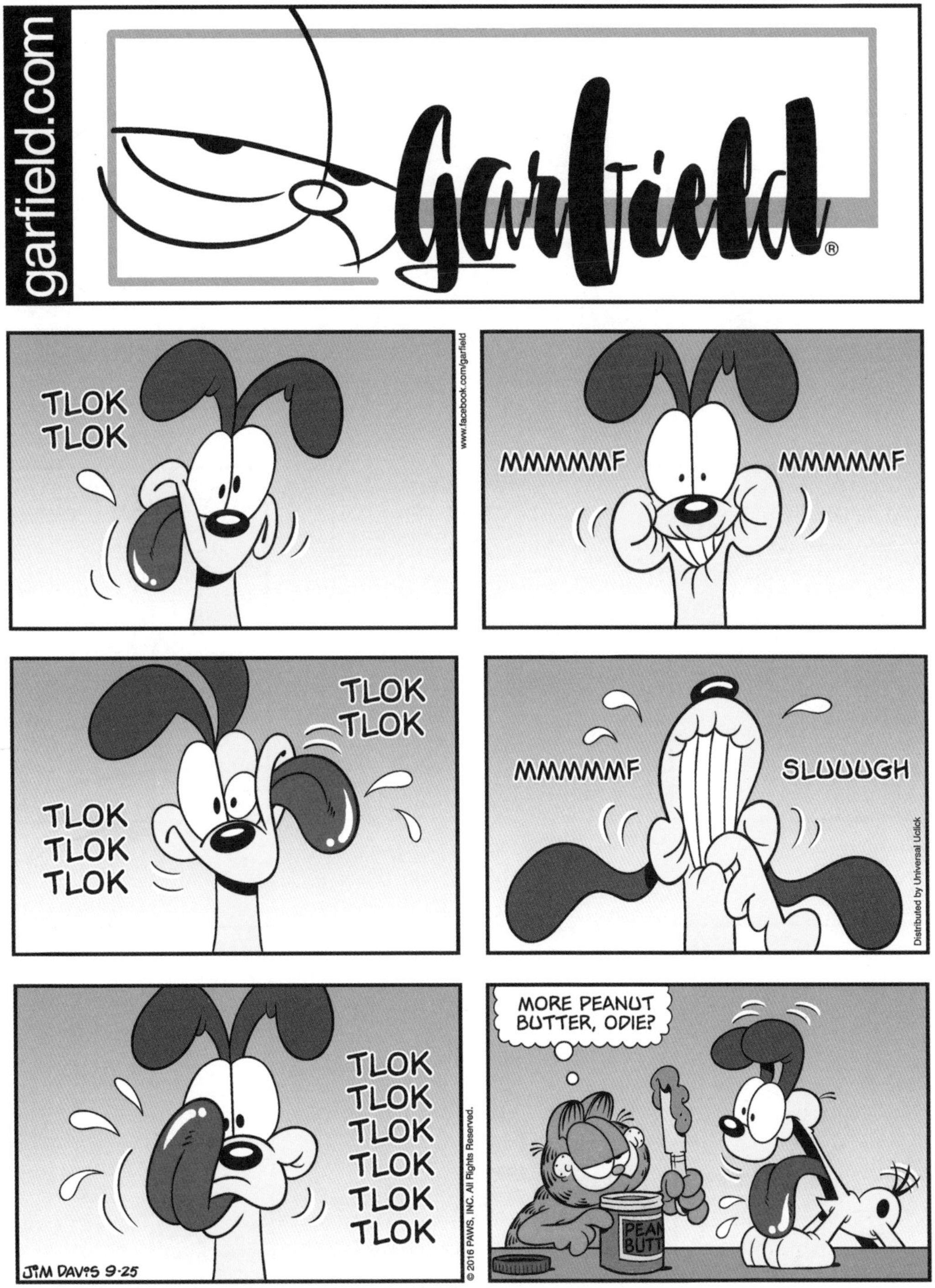
garfield.com
Garfield®
www.facebook.com/garfield
TLOK
TLOK
MMMMMF
MMMMMF
TLOK
TLOK
TLOK
TLOK
TLOK
MMMMMF
SLUUUGH
Distributed by Universal Uclick
TLOK
TLOK
TLOK
TLOK
TLOK
TLOK
JIM DAVIS 9-25
© 2016 PAWS, INC. All Rights Reserved.
MORE PEANUT BUTTER, ODIE?
PEAN
BUTT

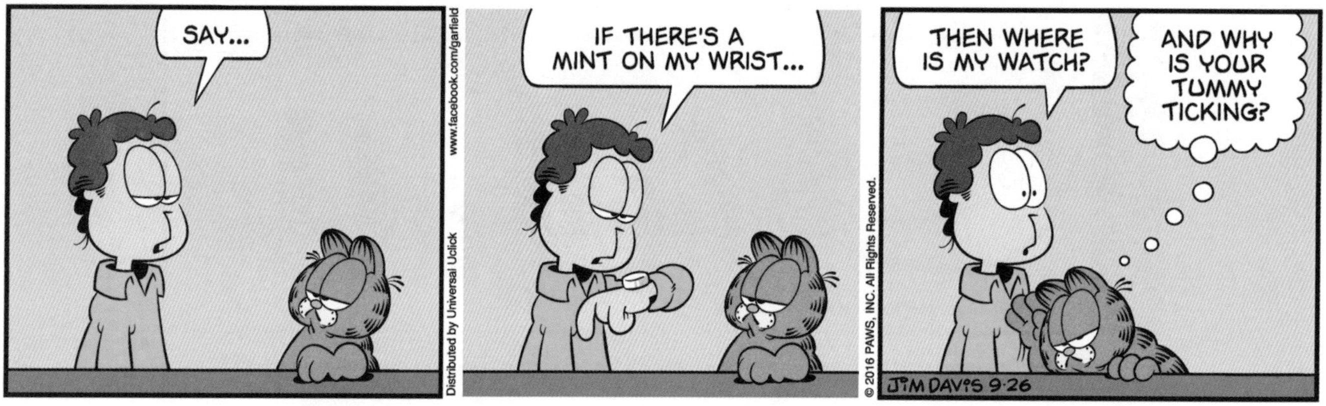
SAY...
IF THERE'S A MINT ON MY WRIST...
THEN WHERE IS MY WATCH?
AND WHY IS YOUR TUMMY TICKING?
JIM DAVIS 9·26
Distributed by Universal Uclick www.facebook.com/garfield
© 2016 PAWS, INC. All Rights Reserved.

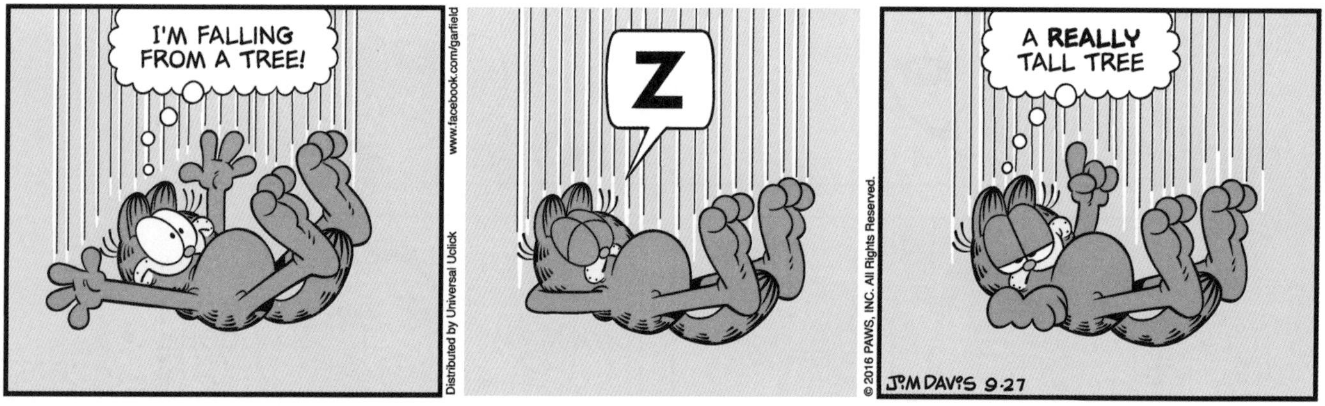
I'M FALLING FROM A TREE!
Z
A **REALLY** TALL TREE
JIM DAVIS 9·27
Distributed by Universal Uclick www.facebook.com/garfield
© 2016 PAWS, INC. All Rights Reserved.

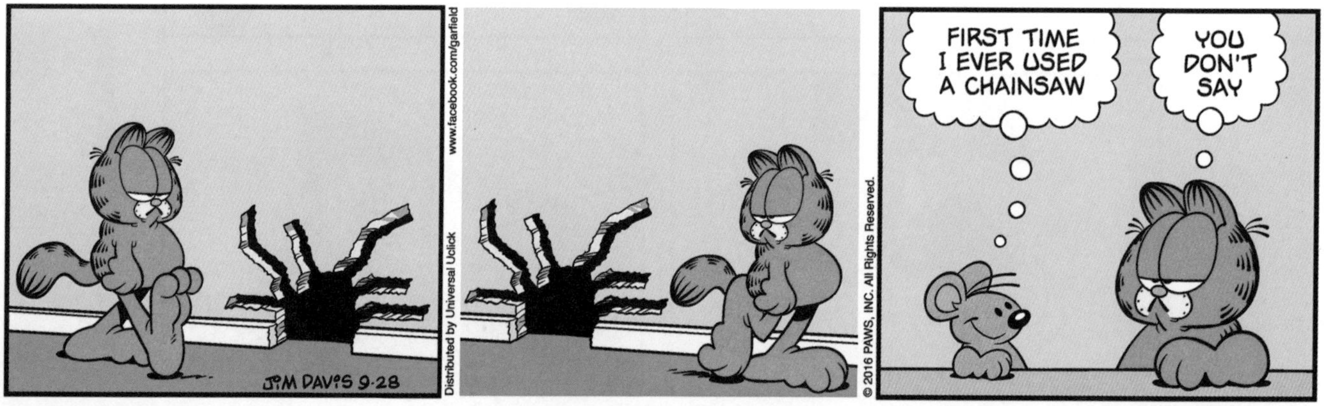
JIM DAVIS 9·28
Distributed by Universal Uclick www.facebook.com/garfield
© 2016 PAWS, INC. All Rights Reserved.
FIRST TIME I EVER USED A CHAINSAW
YOU DON'T SAY

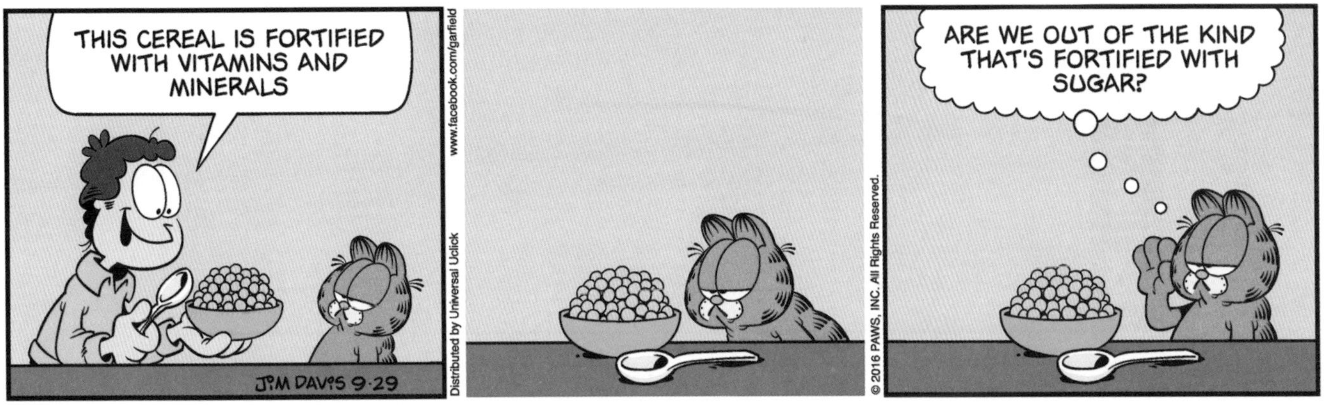
THIS CEREAL IS FORTIFIED WITH VITAMINS AND MINERALS
JIM DAVIS 9-29
Distributed by Universal Uclick www.facebook.com/garfield
© 2016 PAWS, INC. All Rights Reserved.
ARE WE OUT OF THE KIND THAT'S FORTIFIED WITH SUGAR?

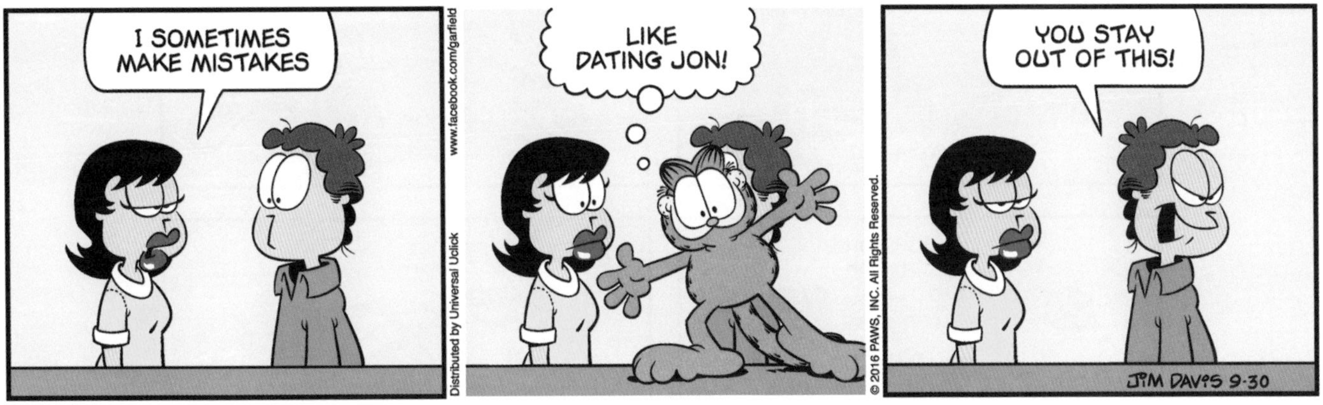
I SOMETIMES MAKE MISTAKES
Distributed by Universal Uclick www.facebook.com/garfield
LIKE DATING JON!
© 2016 PAWS, INC. All Rights Reserved.
YOU STAY OUT OF THIS!
JIM DAVIS 9-30

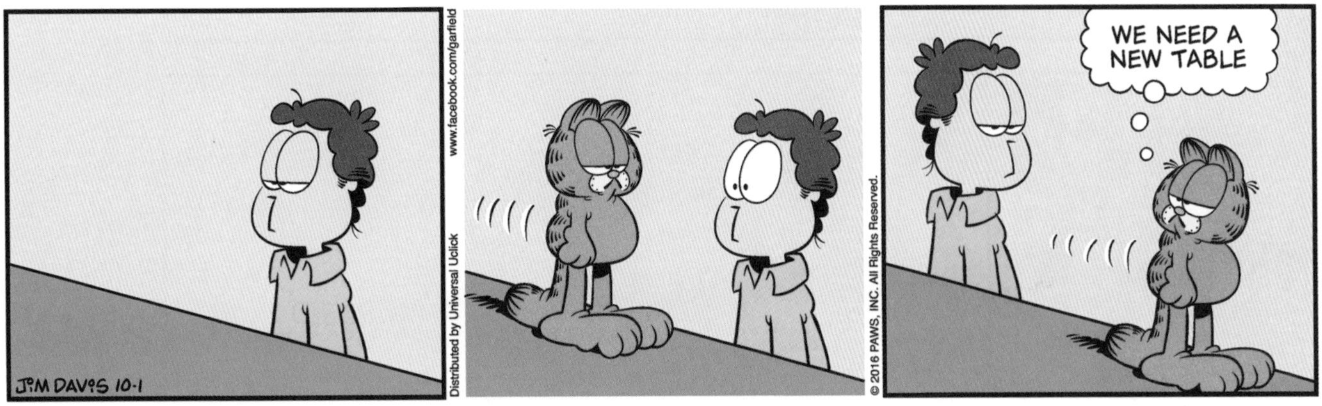
JIM DAVIS 10-1
Distributed by Universal Uclick www.facebook.com/garfield
© 2016 PAWS, INC. All Rights Reserved.
WE NEED A NEW TABLE

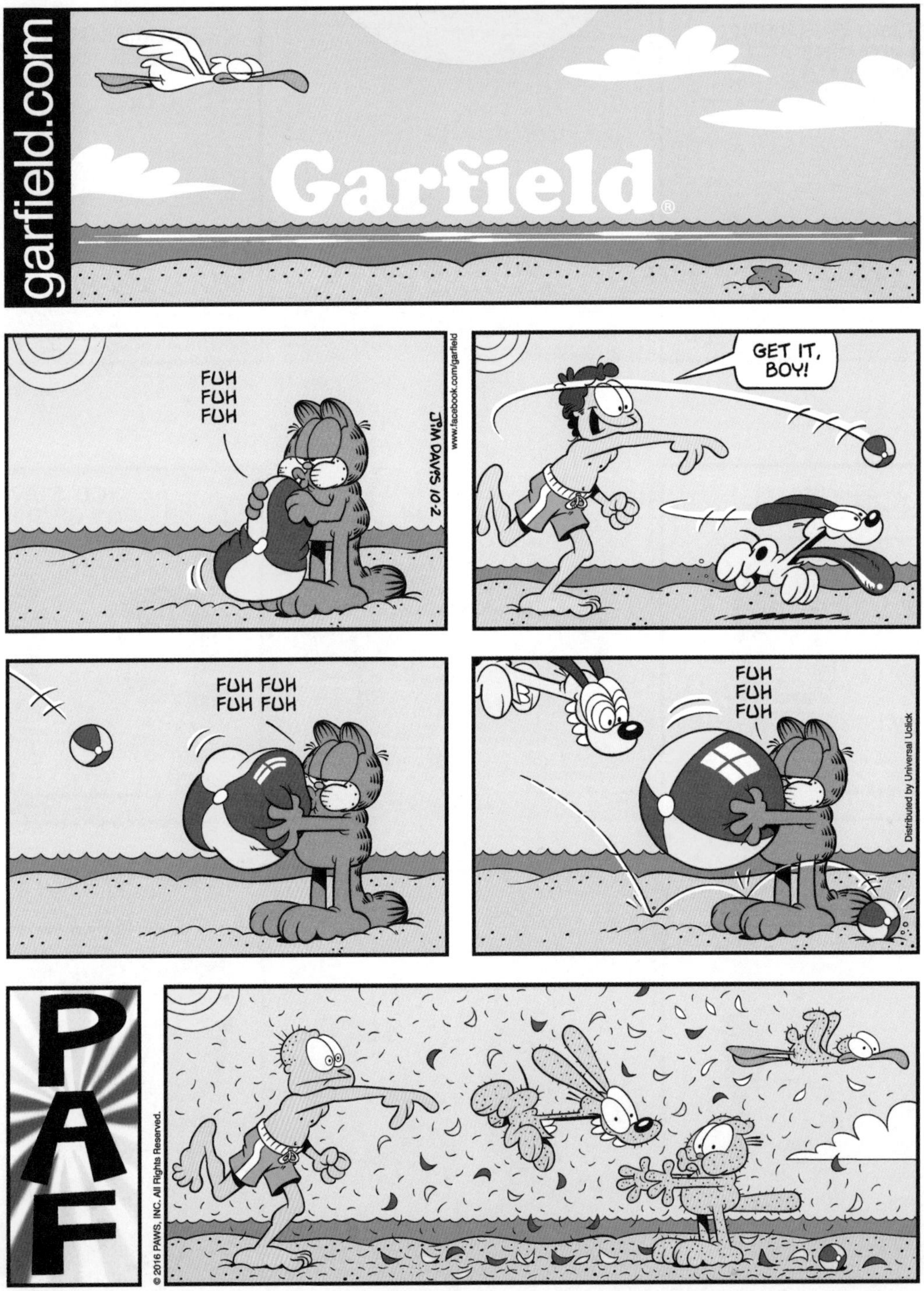
garfield.com
Garfield®
FUH
FUH
FUH
JIM DAVIS 10-2
www.facebook.com/garfield
GET IT, BOY!
FUH FUH
FUH FUH
FUH
FUH
FUH
Distributed by Universal Uclick
PAF
© 2016 PAWS, INC. All Rights Reserved.

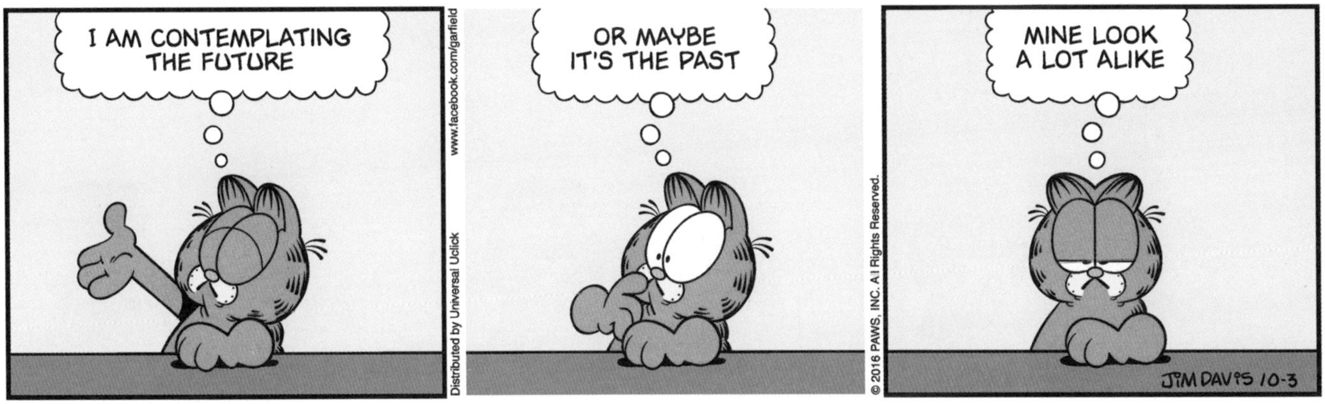
I AM CONTEMPLATING THE FUTURE
OR MAYBE IT'S THE PAST
MINE LOOK A LOT ALIKE
JIM DAVIS 10-3
Distributed by Universal Uclick www.facebook.com/garfield
© 2016 PAWS, INC. All Rights Reserved.

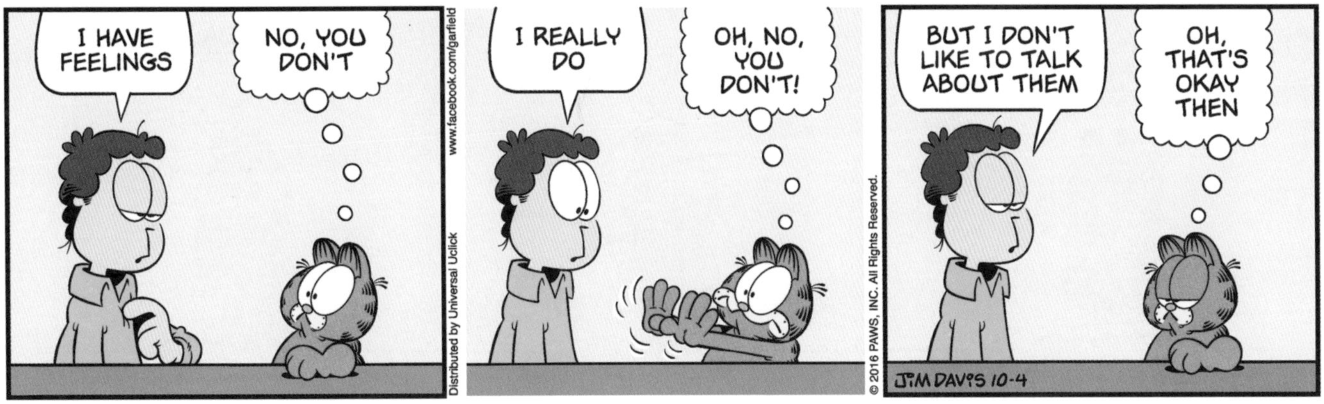
I HAVE FEELINGS
NO, YOU DON'T
I REALLY DO
OH, NO, YOU DON'T!
BUT I DON'T LIKE TO TALK ABOUT THEM
OH, THAT'S OKAY THEN
JIM DAVIS 10-4
Distributed by Universal Uclick www.facebook.com/garfield
© 2016 PAWS, INC. All Rights Reserved.

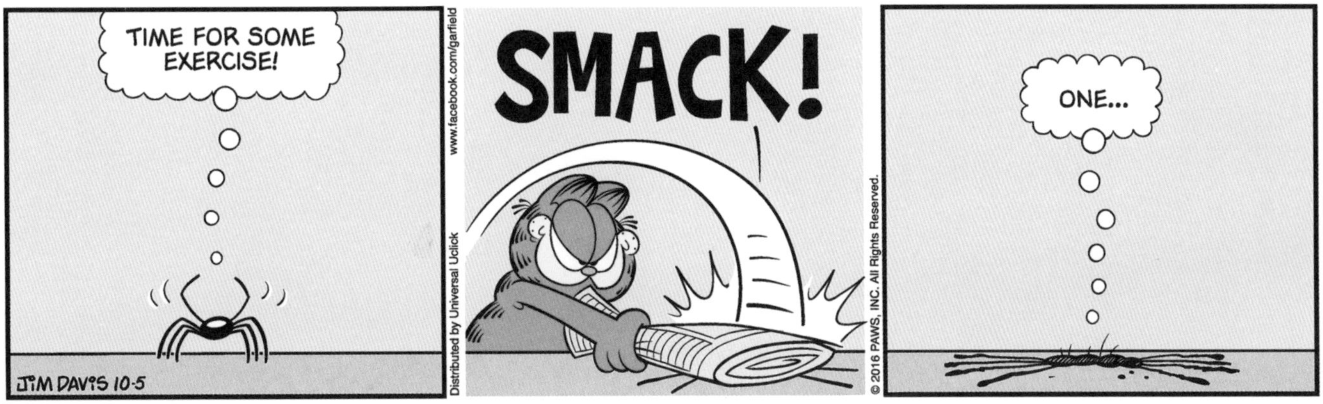
TIME FOR SOME EXERCISE!
JIM DAVIS 10-5
SMACK!
ONE...
Distributed by Universal Uclick www.facebook.com/garfield
© 2016 PAWS, INC. All Rights Reserved.

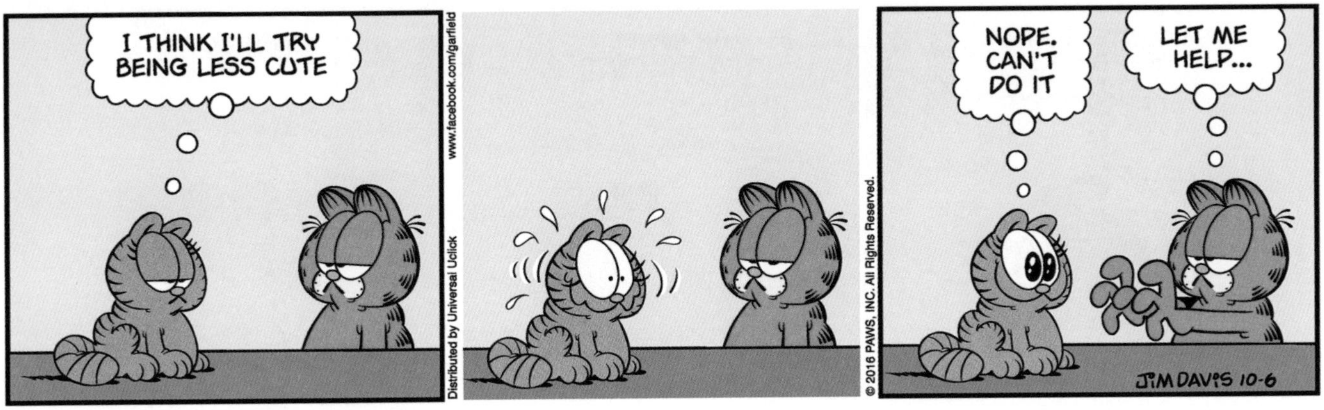
I THINK I'LL TRY BEING LESS CUTE
www.facebook.com/garfield
Distributed by Universal Uclick
© 2016 PAWS, INC. All Rights Reserved.
NOPE. CAN'T DO IT
LET ME HELP...
JIM DAVIS 10-6

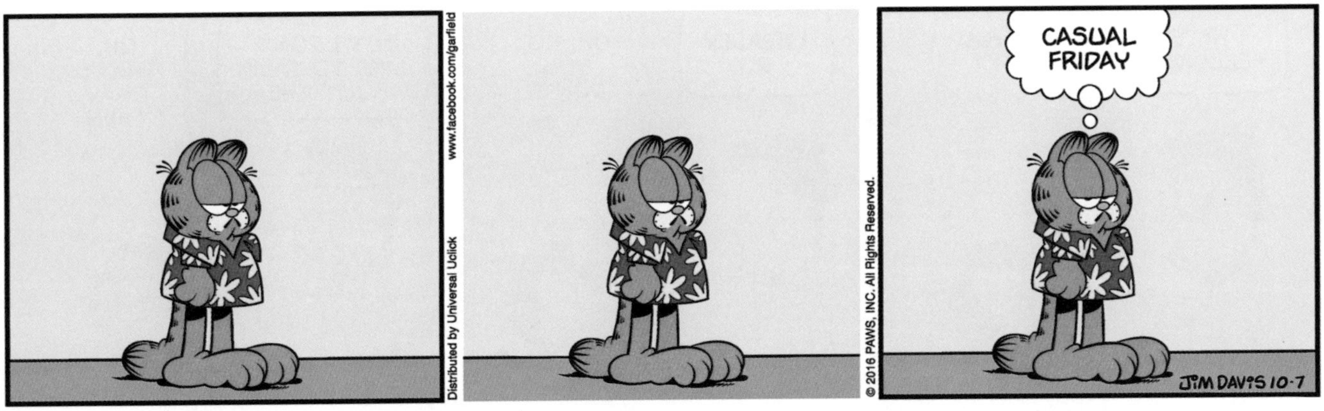
www.facebook.com/garfield
Distributed by Universal Uclick
© 2016 PAWS, INC. All Rights Reserved.
CASUAL FRIDAY
JIM DAVIS 10-7

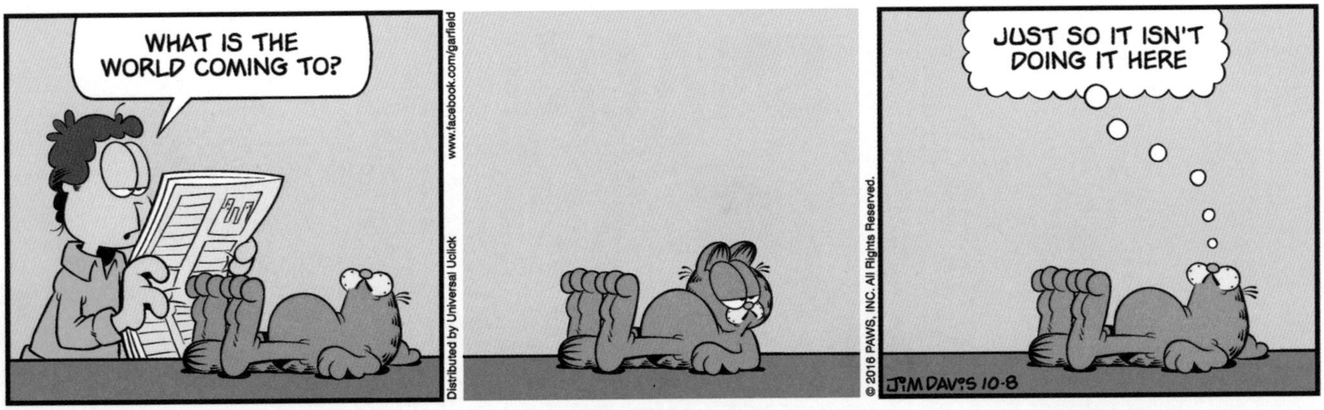
WHAT IS THE WORLD COMING TO?
www.facebook.com/garfield
Distributed by Universal Uclick
© 2016 PAWS, INC. All Rights Reserved.
JUST SO IT ISN'T DOING IT HERE
JIM DAVIS 10-8

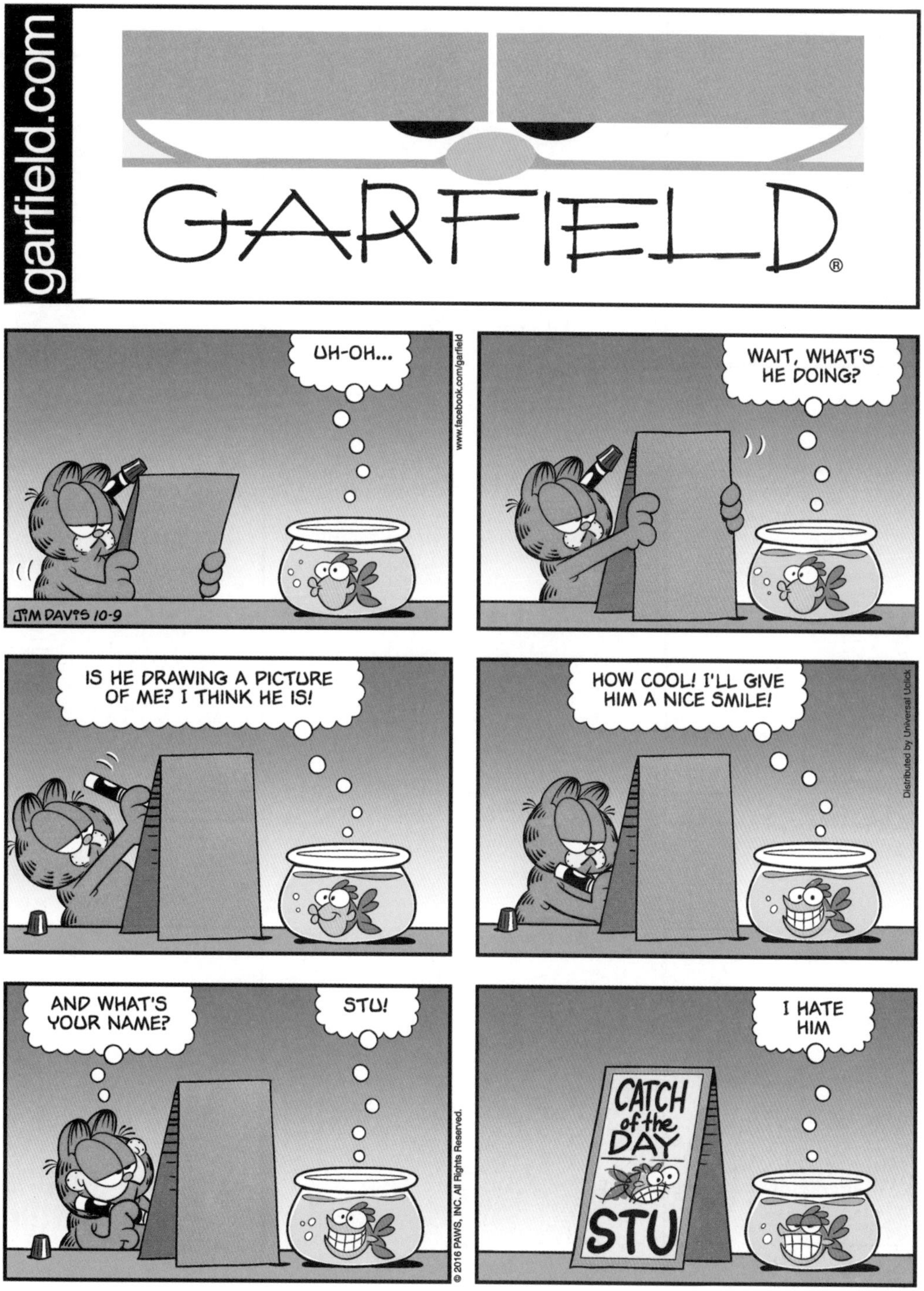
garfield.com
GARFIELD®
UH-OH...
JIM DAVIS 10-9
www.facebook.com/garfield
WAIT, WHAT'S HE DOING?
IS HE DRAWING A PICTURE OF ME? I THINK HE IS!
HOW COOL! I'LL GIVE HIM A NICE SMILE!
Distributed by Universal Uclick
AND WHAT'S YOUR NAME?
STU!
© 2016 PAWS, INC. All Rights Reserved.
I HATE HIM
CATCH of the DAY
STU

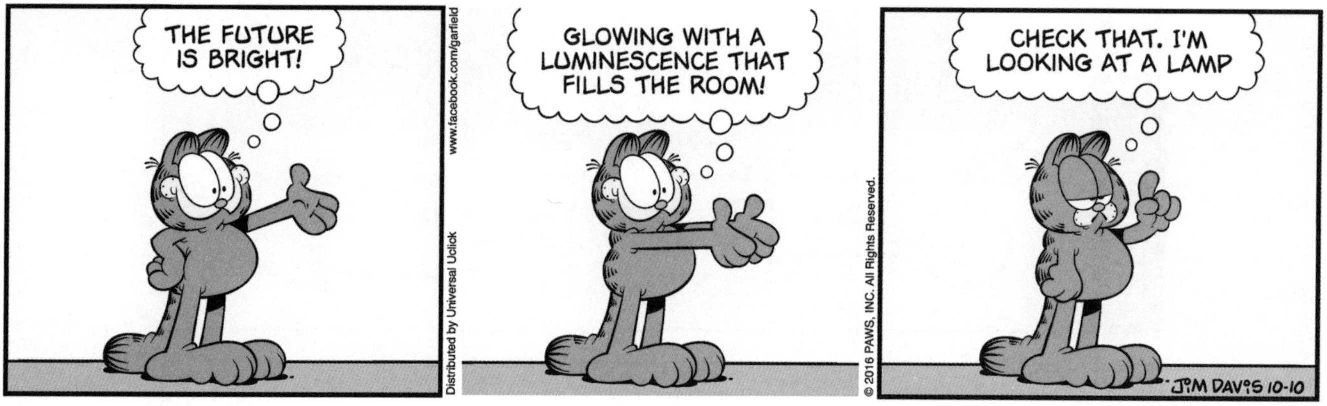
THE FUTURE IS BRIGHT!
GLOWING WITH A LUMINESCENCE THAT FILLS THE ROOM!
CHECK THAT. I'M LOOKING AT A LAMP
JIM DAVIS 10-10
Distributed by Universal Uclick www.facebook.com/garfield
© 2016 PAWS, INC. All Rights Reserved.

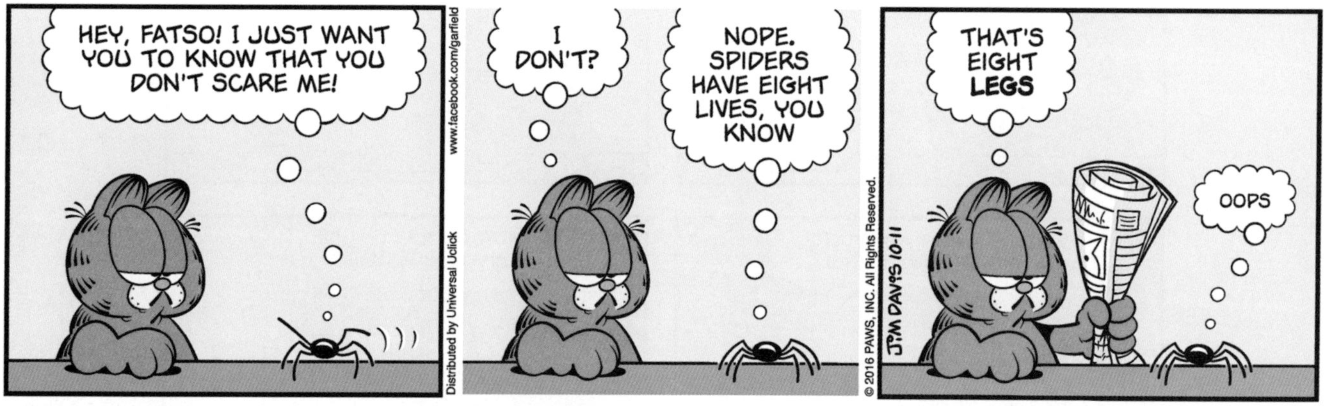
HEY, FATSO! I JUST WANT YOU TO KNOW THAT YOU DON'T SCARE ME!
I DON'T?
NOPE. SPIDERS HAVE EIGHT LIVES, YOU KNOW
THAT'S EIGHT **LEGS**
OOPS
JIM DAVIS 10-11
Distributed by Universal Uclick www.facebook.com/garfield
© 2016 PAWS, INC. All Rights Reserved.

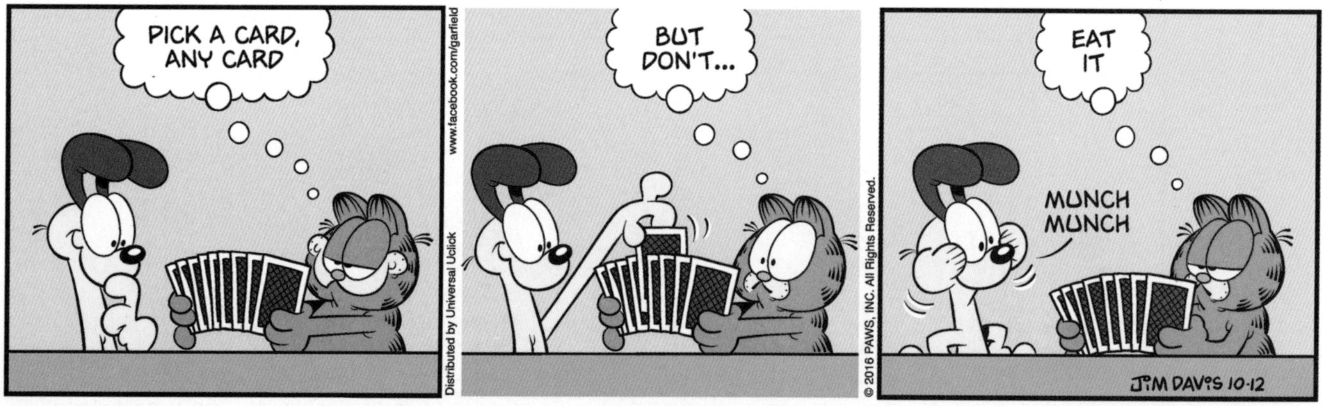
PICK A CARD, ANY CARD
BUT DON'T...
EAT IT
MUNCH MUNCH
JIM DAVIS 10-12
Distributed by Universal Uclick www.facebook.com/garfield
© 2016 PAWS, INC. All Rights Reserved.

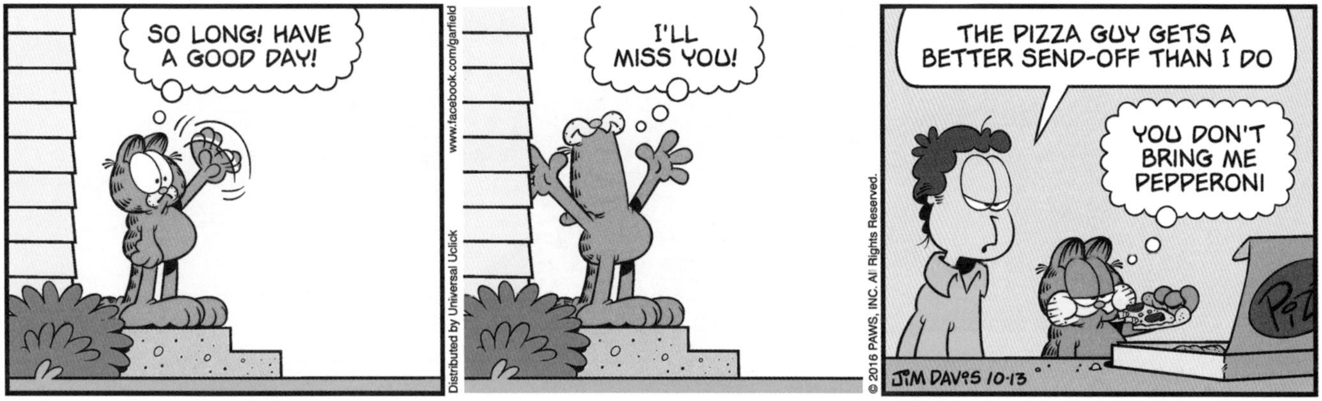
SO LONG! HAVE A GOOD DAY!
www.facebook.com/garfield
Distributed by Universal Uclick
I'LL MISS YOU!
THE PIZZA GUY GETS A BETTER SEND-OFF THAN I DO
YOU DON'T BRING ME PEPPERONI
© 2016 PAWS, INC. All Rights Reserved.
JIM DAVIS 10-13

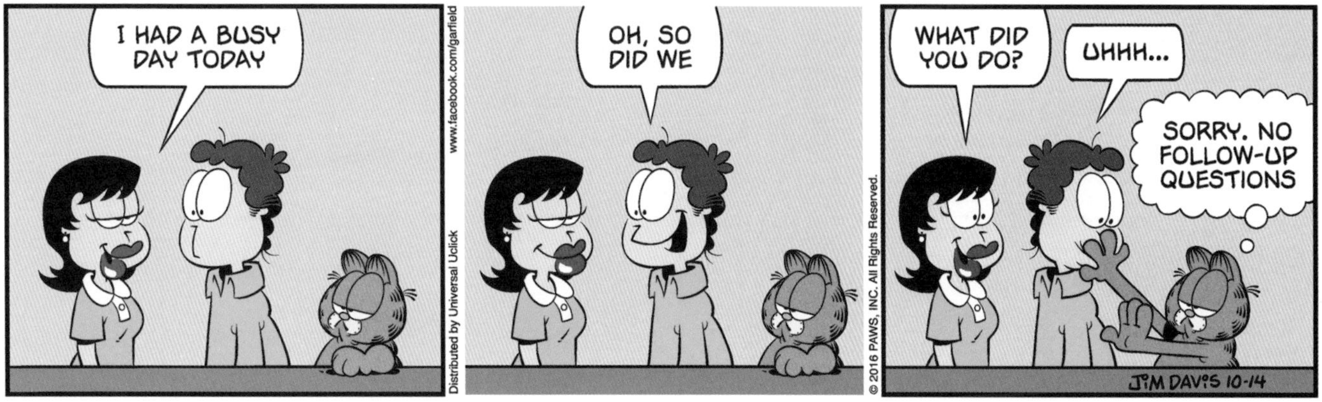
I HAD A BUSY DAY TODAY
www.facebook.com/garfield
Distributed by Universal Uclick
OH, SO DID WE
WHAT DID YOU DO?
UHHH...
SORRY. NO FOLLOW-UP QUESTIONS
© 2016 PAWS, INC. All Rights Reserved.
JIM DAVIS 10-14

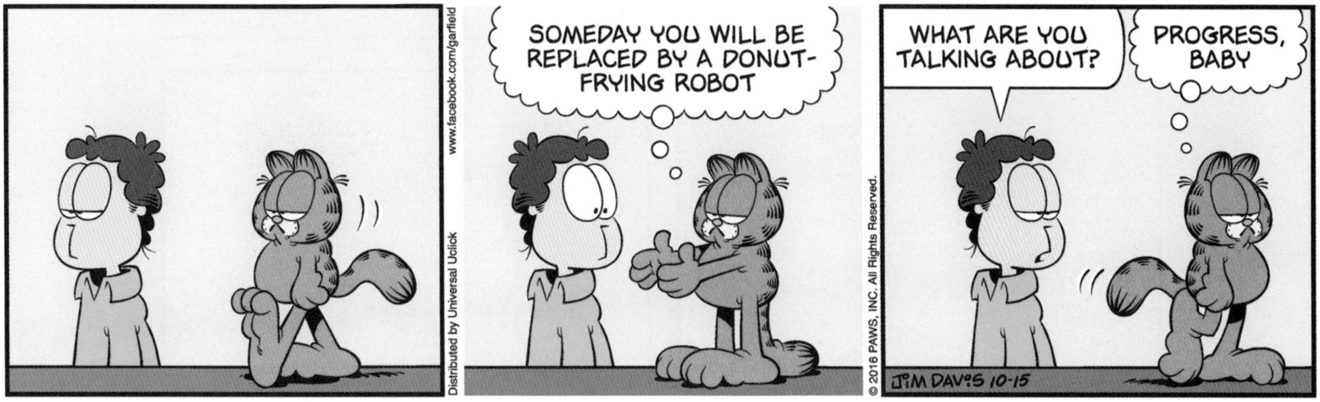
www.facebook.com/garfield
Distributed by Universal Uclick
SOMEDAY YOU WILL BE REPLACED BY A DONUT-FRYING ROBOT
WHAT ARE YOU TALKING ABOUT?
PROGRESS, BABY
© 2016 PAWS, INC. All Rights Reserved.
JIM DAVIS 10-15

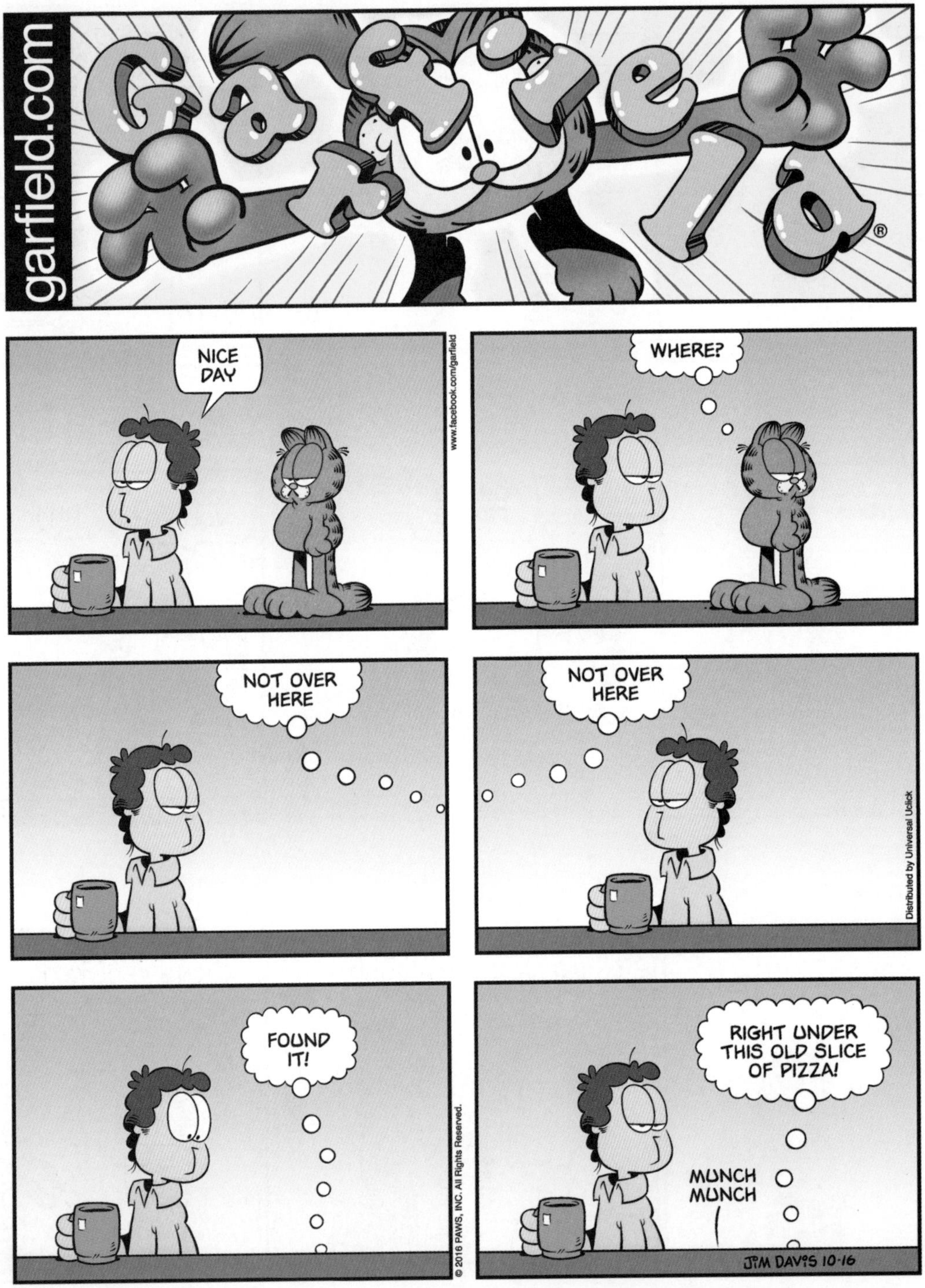
garfield.com
Garfield®
NICE DAY
www.facebook.com/garfield
WHERE?
NOT OVER HERE
NOT OVER HERE
Distributed by Universal Uclick
FOUND IT!
© 2016 PAWS, INC. All Rights Reserved.
RIGHT UNDER THIS OLD SLICE OF PIZZA!
MUNCH MUNCH
JIM DAVIS 10-16

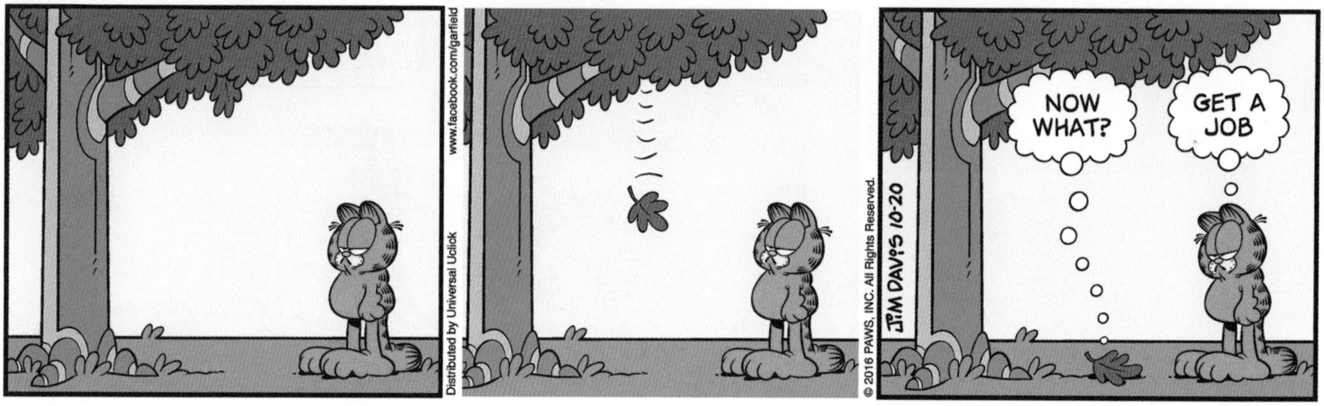
Distributed by Universal Uclick www.facebook.com/garfield
© 2016 PAWS, INC. All Rights Reserved.
JIM DAVIS 10-20
NOW WHAT?
GET A JOB

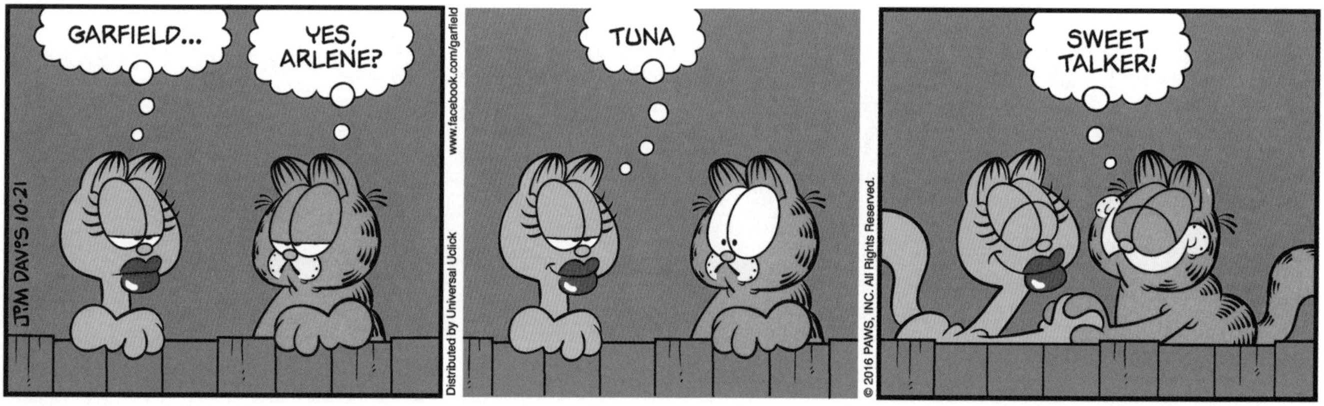
JIM DAVIS 10-21
GARFIELD...
YES, ARLENE?
Distributed by Universal Uclick www.facebook.com/garfield
TUNA
© 2016 PAWS, INC. All Rights Reserved.
SWEET TALKER!

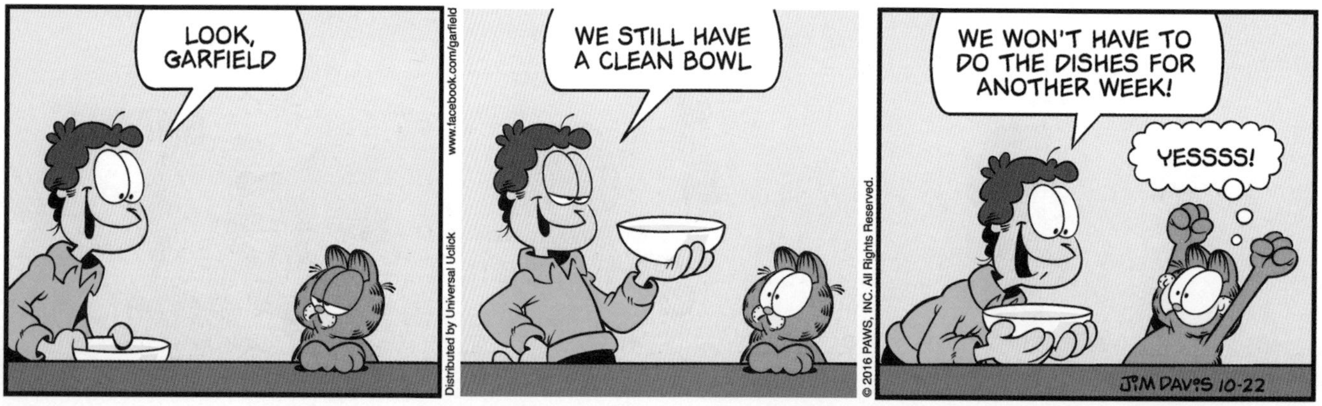
LOOK, GARFIELD
Distributed by Universal Uclick www.facebook.com/garfield
WE STILL HAVE A CLEAN BOWL
© 2016 PAWS, INC. All Rights Reserved.
WE WON'T HAVE TO DO THE DISHES FOR ANOTHER WEEK!
YESSSS!
JIM DAVIS 10-22

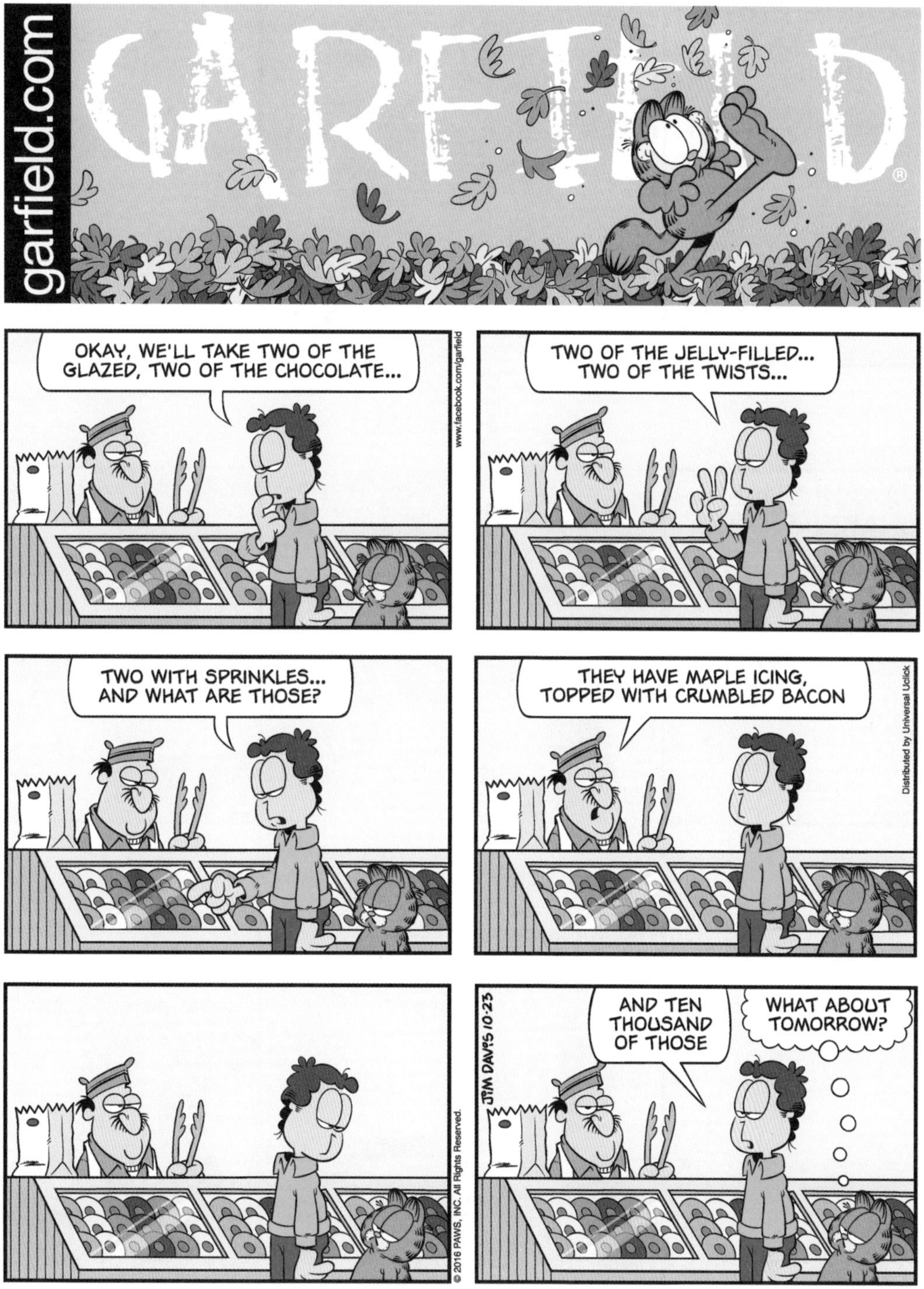

garfield.com
GARFIELD®
OKAY, WE'LL TAKE TWO OF THE GLAZED, TWO OF THE CHOCOLATE...
www.facebook.com/garfield
TWO OF THE JELLY-FILLED... TWO OF THE TWISTS...
TWO WITH SPRINKLES... AND WHAT ARE THOSE?
THEY HAVE MAPLE ICING, TOPPED WITH CRUMBLED BACON
Distributed by Universal Uclick
© 2016 PAWS, INC. All Rights Reserved.
JIM DAVIS 10-23
AND TEN THOUSAND OF THOSE
WHAT ABOUT TOMORROW?

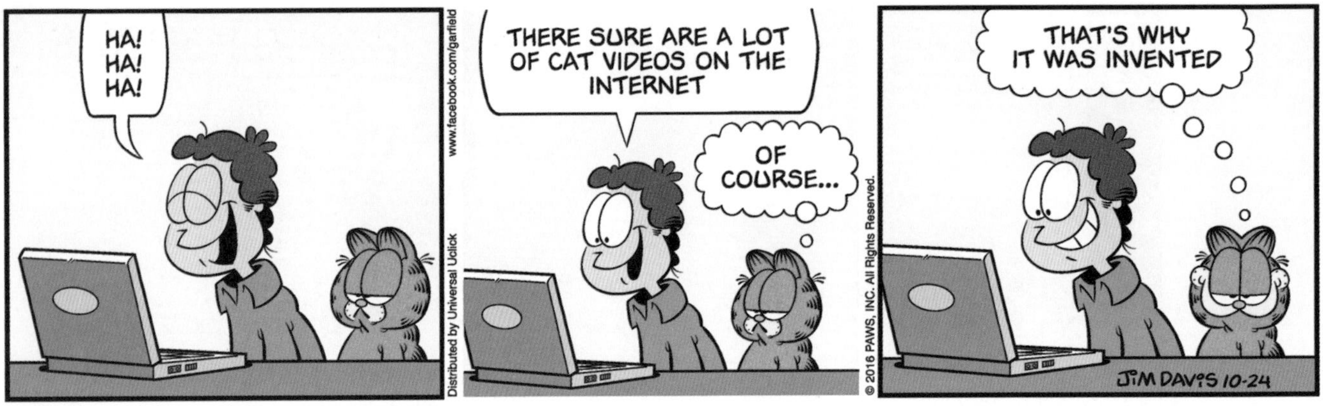
HA! HA! HA!
THERE SURE ARE A LOT OF CAT VIDEOS ON THE INTERNET
OF COURSE...
THAT'S WHY IT WAS INVENTED
JIM DAVIS 10-24
Distributed by Universal Uclick www.facebook.com/garfield
© 2016 PAWS, INC. All Rights Reserved.

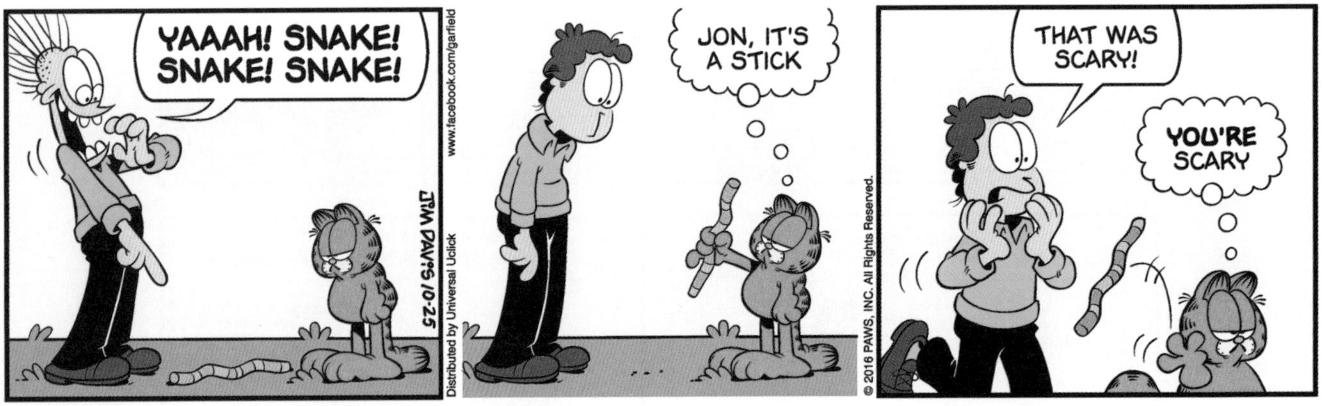
YAAAH! SNAKE! SNAKE! SNAKE!
JIM DAVIS 10-25
JON, IT'S A STICK
THAT WAS SCARY!
YOU'RE SCARY
Distributed by Universal Uclick www.facebook.com/garfield
© 2016 PAWS, INC. All Rights Reserved.

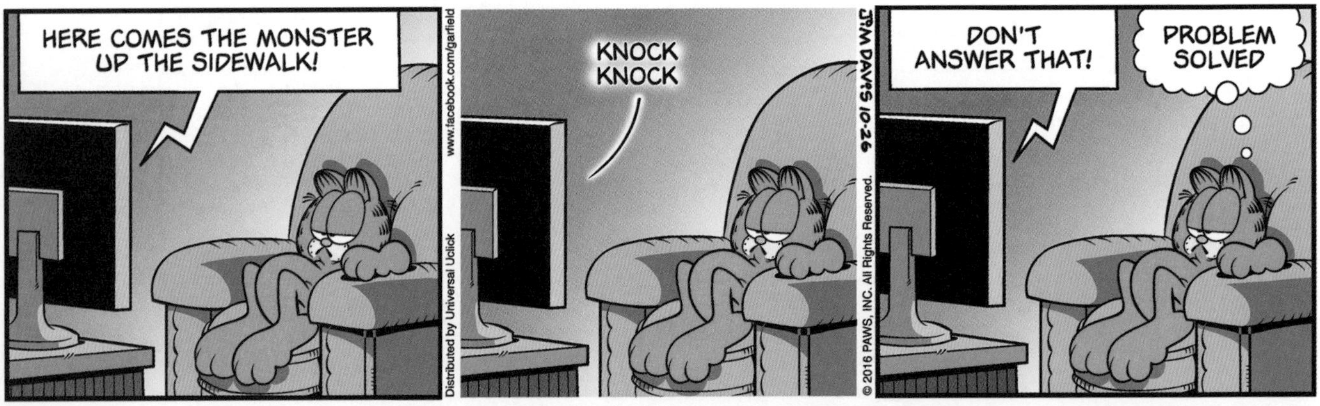
HERE COMES THE MONSTER UP THE SIDEWALK!
KNOCK KNOCK
DON'T ANSWER THAT!
PROBLEM SOLVED
JIM DAVIS 10-26
Distributed by Universal Uclick www.facebook.com/garfield
© 2016 PAWS, INC. All Rights Reserved.

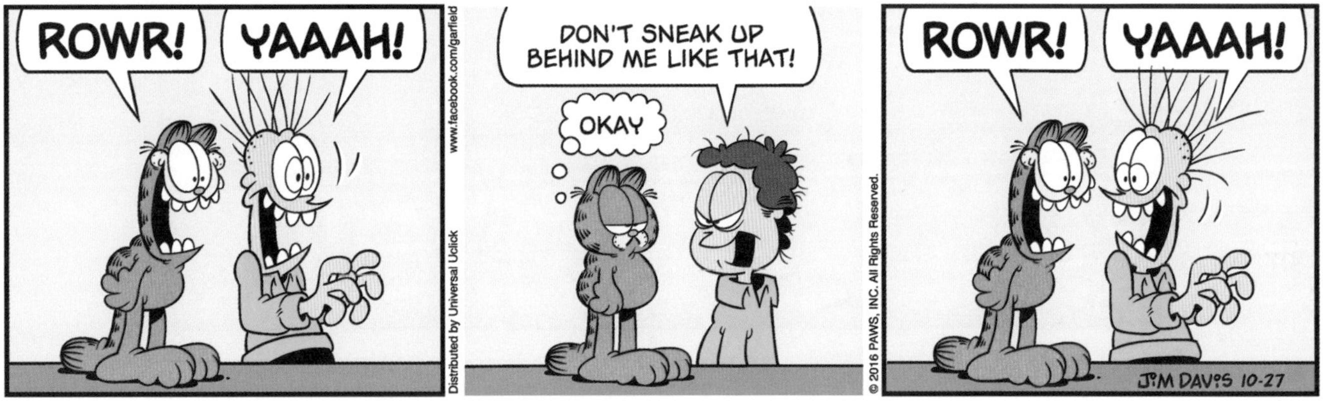
ROWR!
YAAAH!
Distributed by Universal Uclick www.facebook.com/garfield
DON'T SNEAK UP BEHIND ME LIKE THAT!
OKAY
© 2016 PAWS, INC. All Rights Reserved.
ROWR!
YAAAH!
JIM DAVIS 10-27

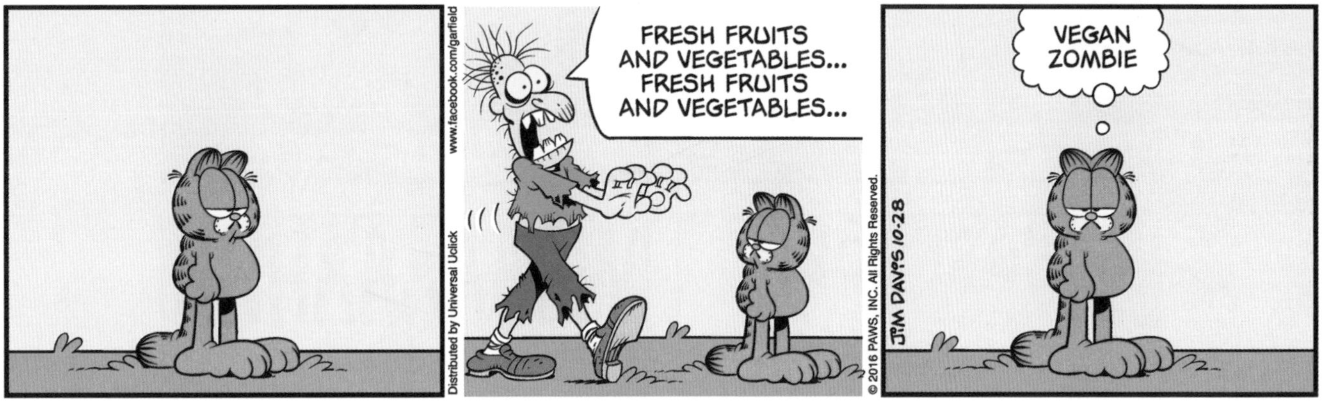
Distributed by Universal Uclick www.facebook.com/garfield
FRESH FRUITS AND VEGETABLES... FRESH FRUITS AND VEGETABLES...
© 2016 PAWS, INC. All Rights Reserved.
JIM DAVIS 10-28
VEGAN ZOMBIE

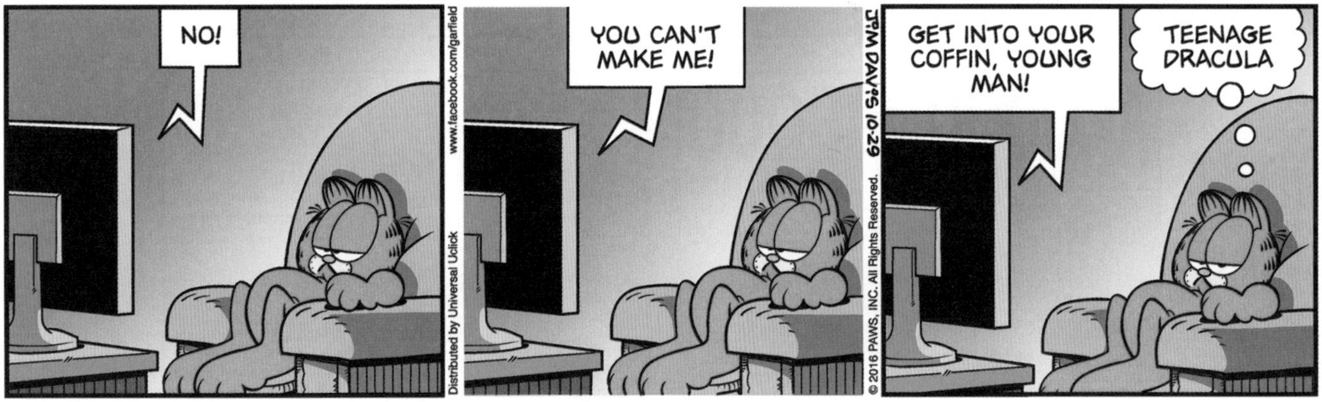
NO!
Distributed by Universal Uclick www.facebook.com/garfield
YOU CAN'T MAKE ME!
JIM DAVIS 10-29
© 2016 PAWS, INC. All Rights Reserved.
GET INTO YOUR COFFIN, YOUNG MAN!
TEENAGE DRACULA

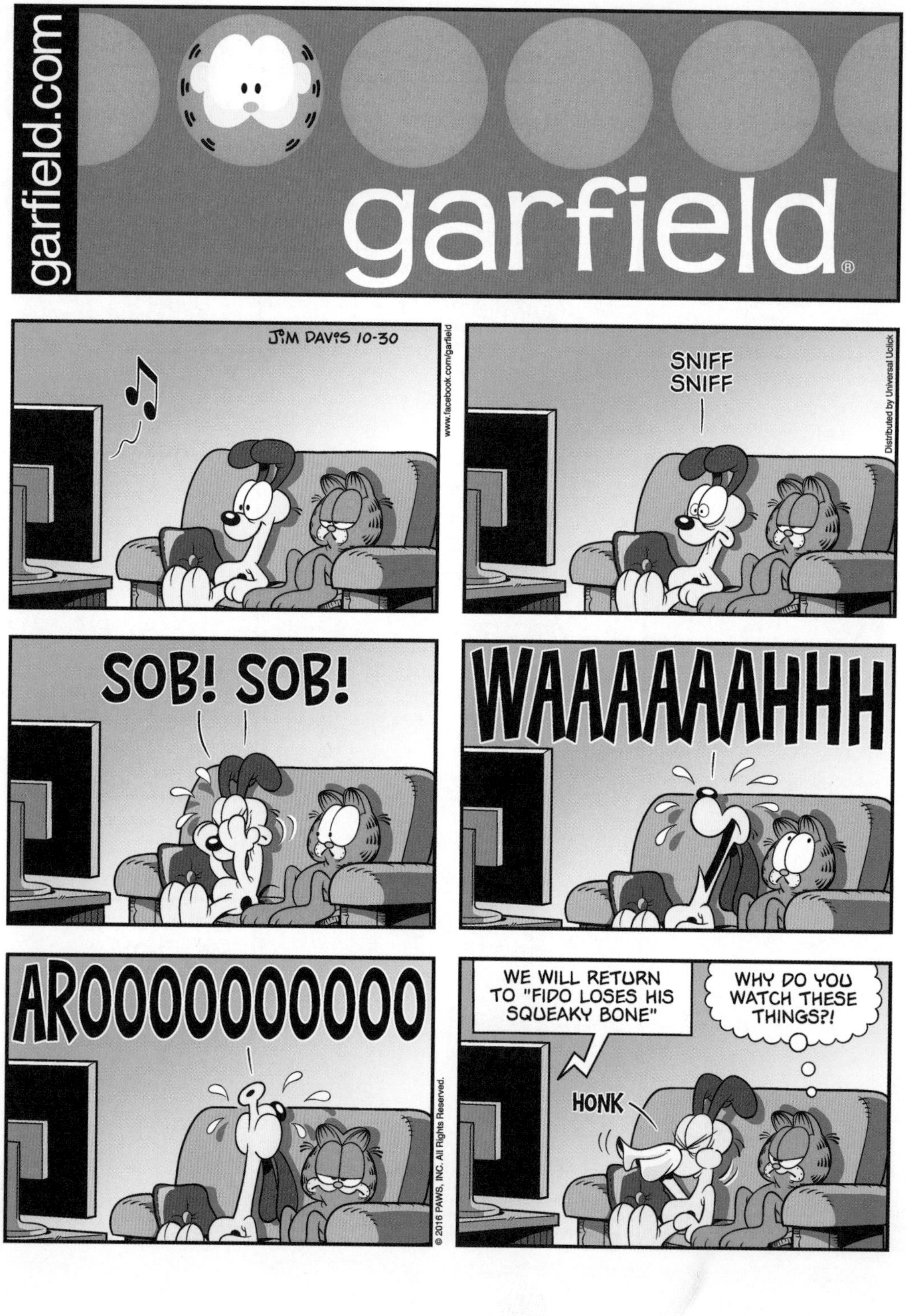
garfield.com
garfield®
JIM DAVIS 10-30
www.facebook.com/garfield
SNIFF SNIFF
Distributed by Universal Uclick
SOB! SOB!
WAAAAAAHHH
AROOOOOOOOOO
© 2016 PAWS, INC. All Rights Reserved.
WE WILL RETURN TO "FIDO LOSES HIS SQUEAKY BONE"
WHY DO YOU WATCH THESE THINGS?!
HONK

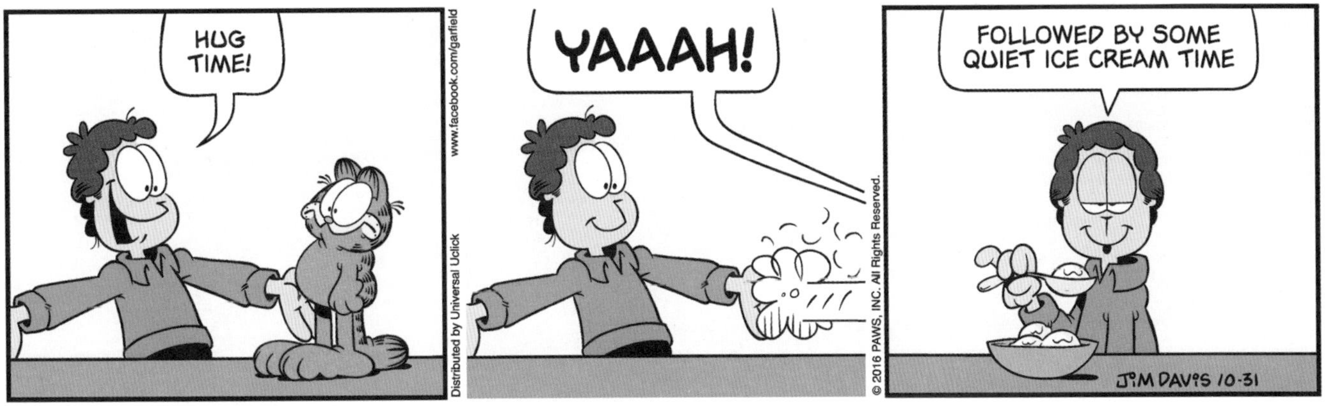
HUG TIME!
YAAAH!
FOLLOWED BY SOME QUIET ICE CREAM TIME
JIM DAVIS 10-31
Distributed by Universal Uclick www.facebook.com/garfield
© 2016 PAWS, INC. All Rights Reserved.

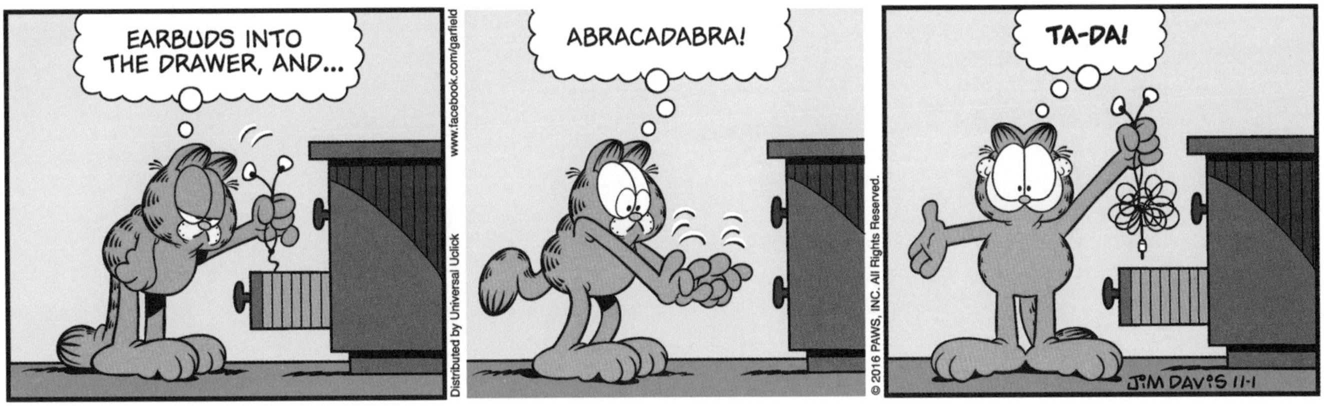
EARBUDS INTO THE DRAWER, AND...
ABRACADABRA!
TA-DA!
JIM DAVIS 11-1
Distributed by Universal Uclick www.facebook.com/garfield
© 2016 PAWS, INC. All Rights Reserved.

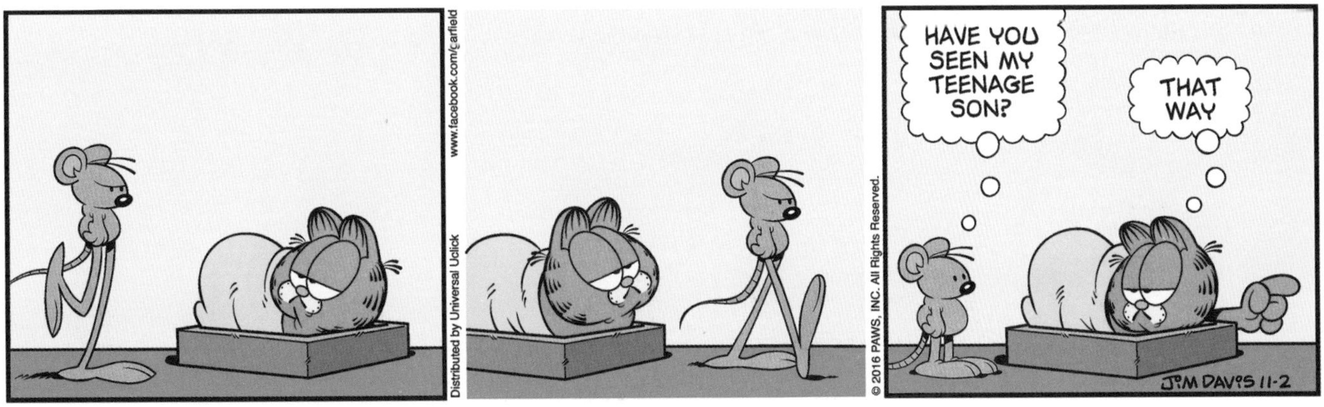
HAVE YOU SEEN MY TEENAGE SON?
THAT WAY
JIM DAVIS 11-2
Distributed by Universal Uclick www.facebook.com/garfield
© 2016 PAWS, INC. All Rights Reserved.

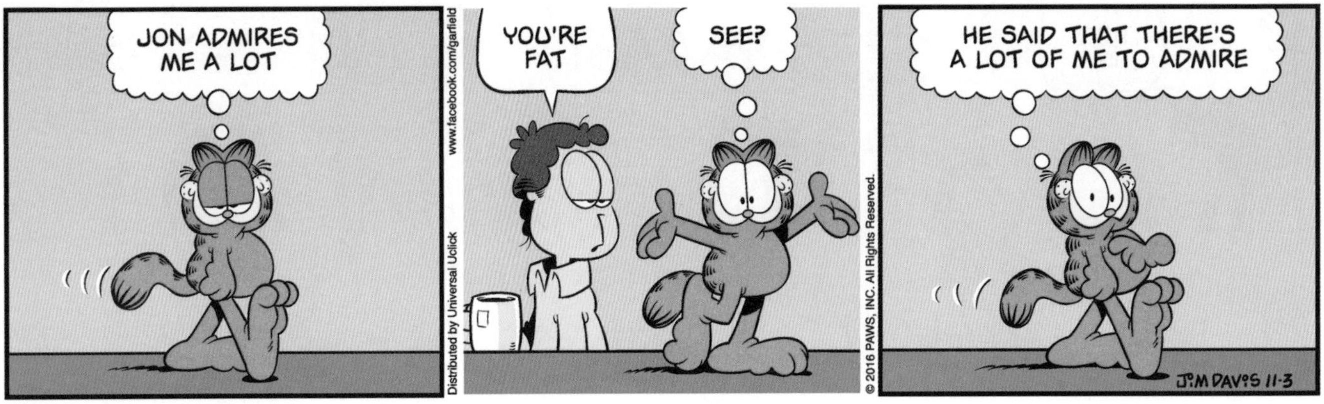
JON ADMIRES ME A LOT
Distributed by Universal Uclick www.facebook.com/garfield
YOU'RE FAT
SEE?
© 2016 PAWS, INC. All Rights Reserved.
HE SAID THAT THERE'S A LOT OF ME TO ADMIRE
JIM DAVIS 11-3

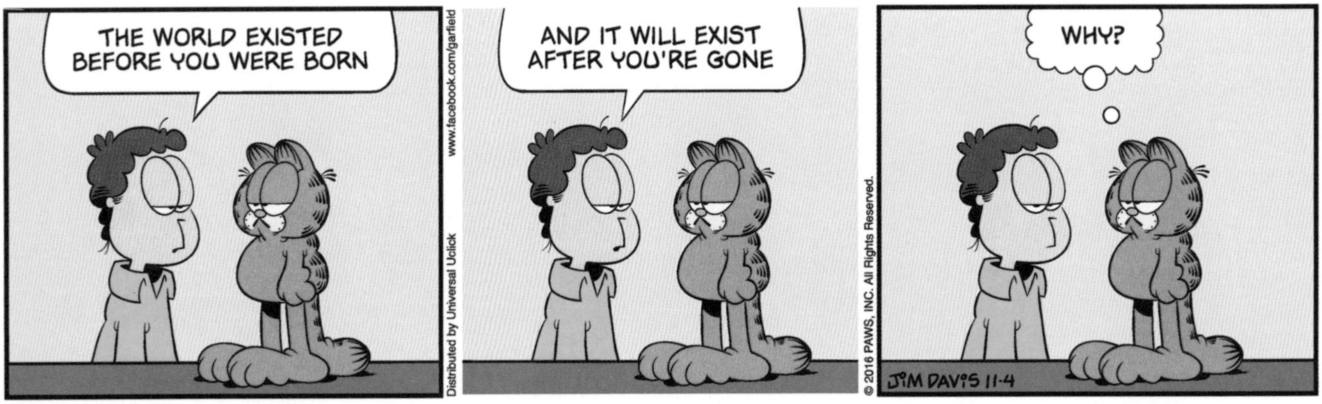
THE WORLD EXISTED BEFORE YOU WERE BORN
Distributed by Universal Uclick www.facebook.com/garfield
AND IT WILL EXIST AFTER YOU'RE GONE
© 2016 PAWS, INC. All Rights Reserved.
WHY?
JIM DAVIS 11-4

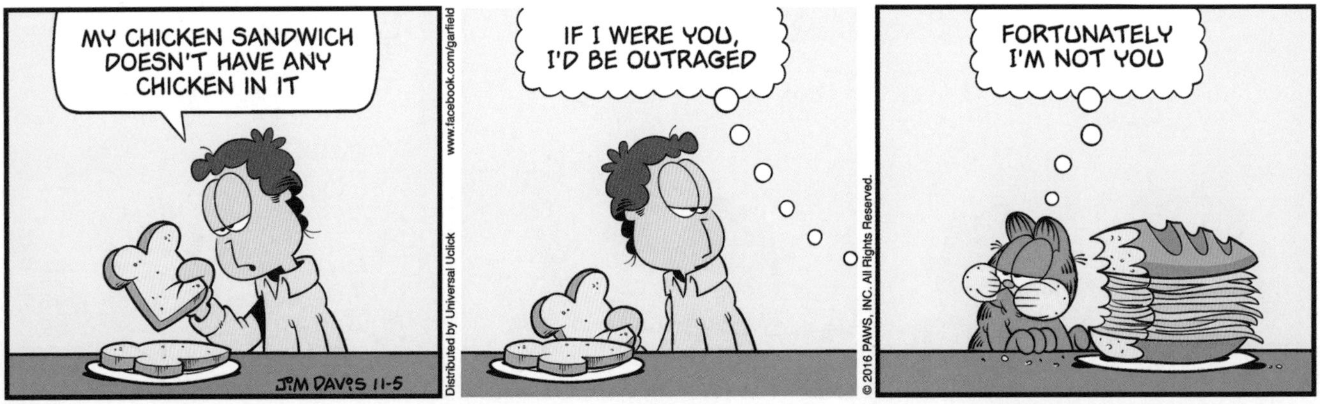
MY CHICKEN SANDWICH DOESN'T HAVE ANY CHICKEN IN IT
JIM DAVIS 11-5
Distributed by Universal Uclick www.facebook.com/garfield
IF I WERE YOU, I'D BE OUTRAGED
© 2016 PAWS, INC. All Rights Reserved.
FORTUNATELY I'M NOT YOU

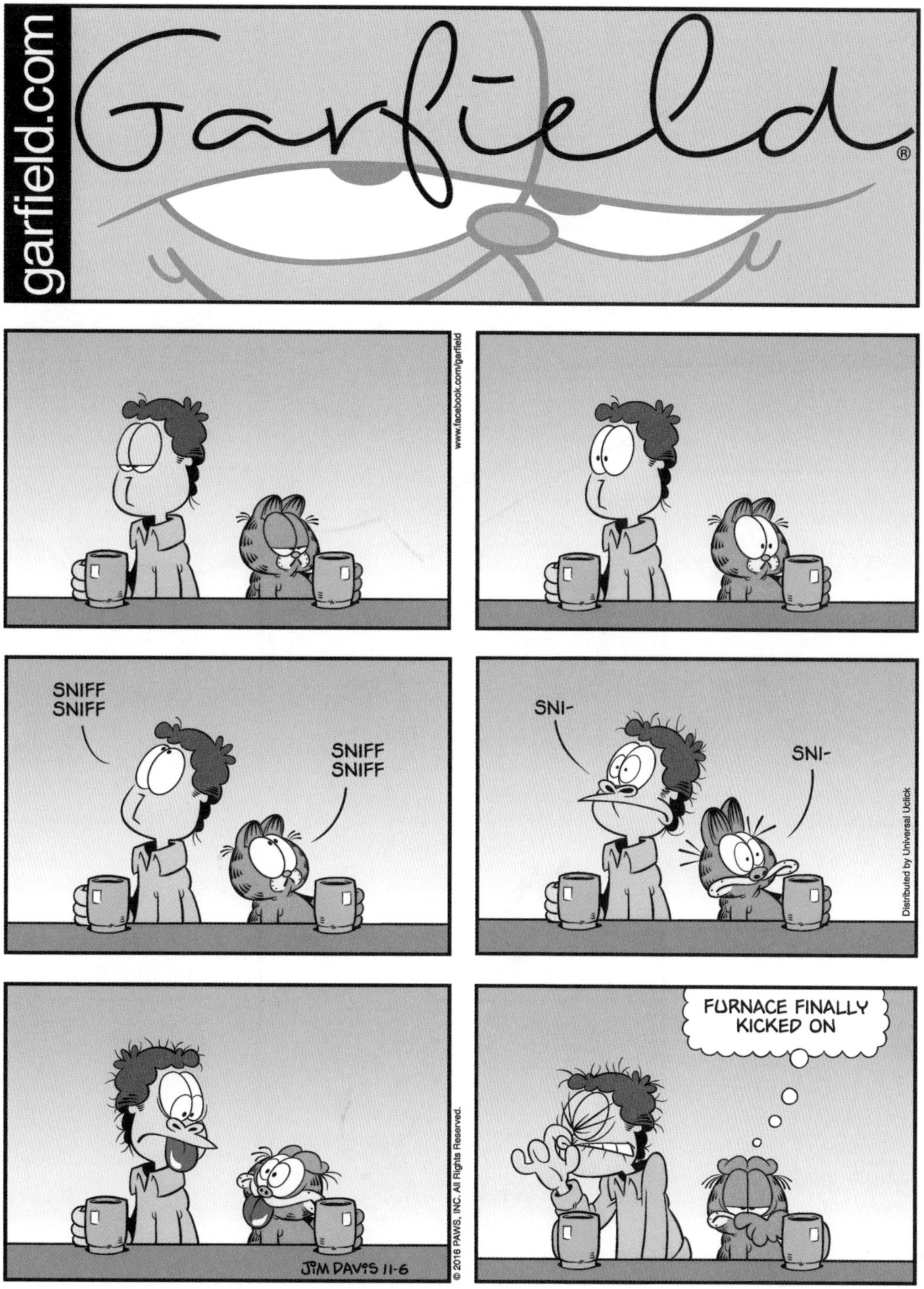
garfield.com
Garfield®
www.facebook.com/garfield
SNIFF SNIFF
SNIFF SNIFF
SNI-
SNI-
Distributed by Universal Uclick
JIM DAVIS 11-6
© 2016 PAWS, INC. All Rights Reserved.
FURNACE FINALLY KICKED ON

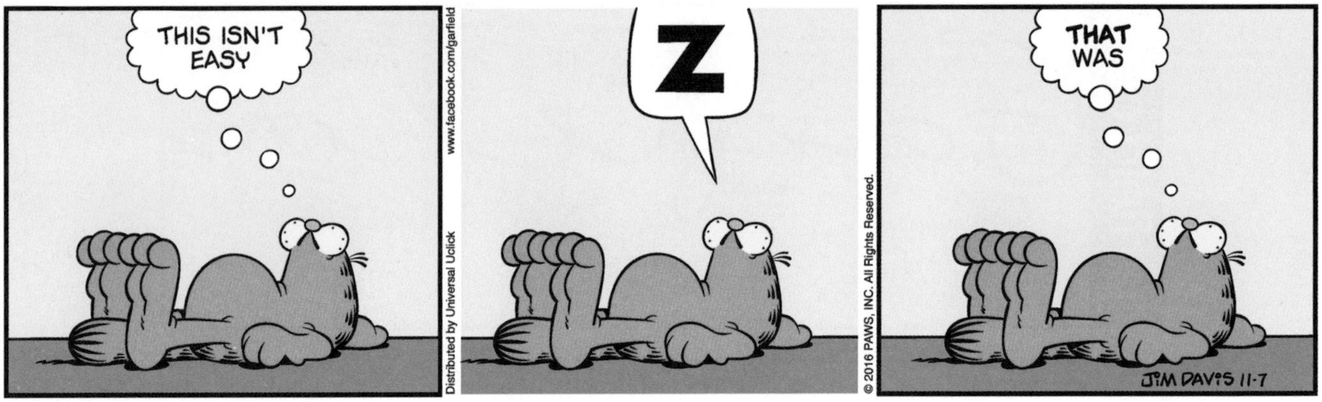
THIS ISN'T EASY
Distributed by Universal Uclick www.facebook.com/garfield
Z
© 2016 PAWS, INC. All Rights Reserved.
THAT WAS
JIM DAVIS 11-7

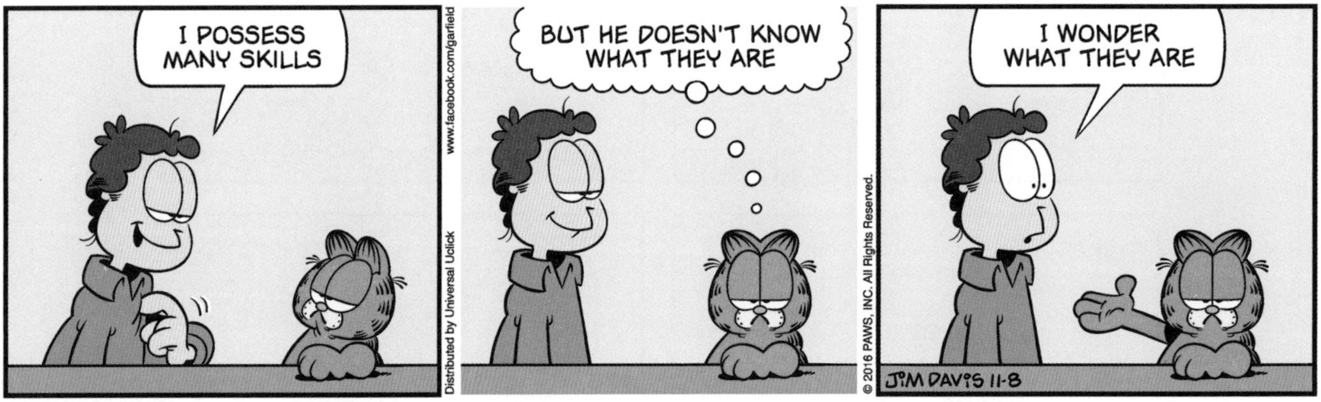
I POSSESS MANY SKILLS
Distributed by Universal Uclick www.facebook.com/garfield
BUT HE DOESN'T KNOW WHAT THEY ARE
© 2016 PAWS, INC. All Rights Reserved.
I WONDER WHAT THEY ARE
JIM DAVIS 11-8

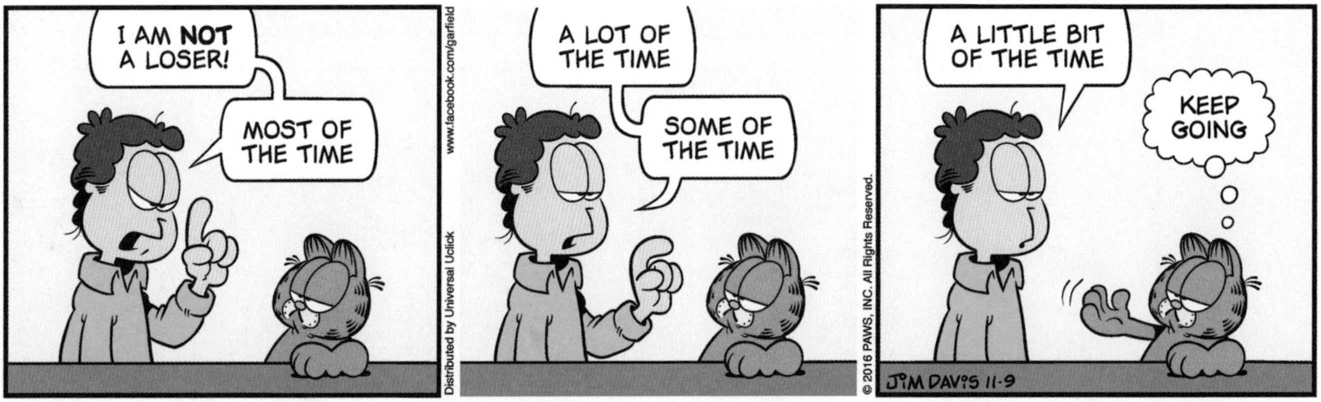
I AM NOT A LOSER!
MOST OF THE TIME
Distributed by Universal Uclick www.facebook.com/garfield
A LOT OF THE TIME
SOME OF THE TIME
© 2016 PAWS, INC. All Rights Reserved.
A LITTLE BIT OF THE TIME
KEEP GOING
JIM DAVIS 11-9

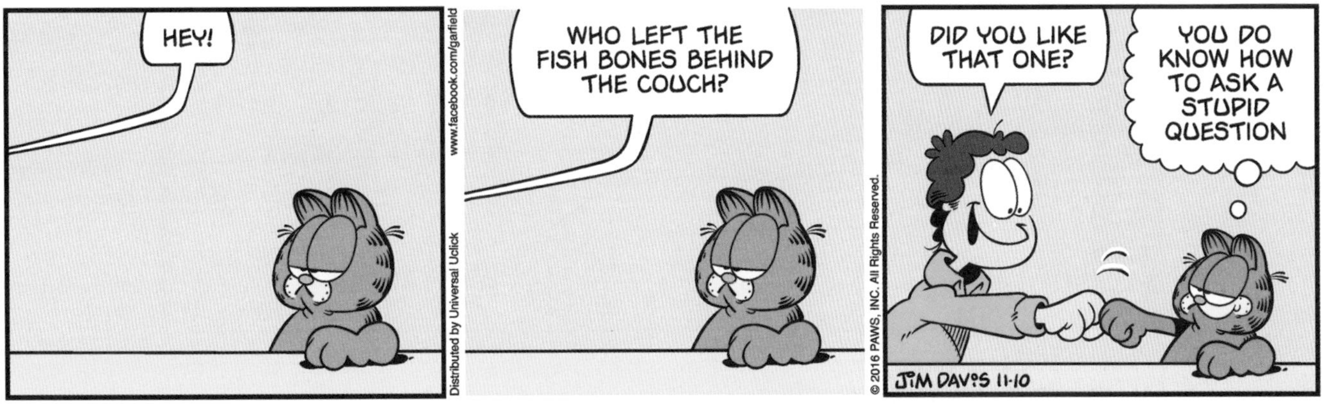
HEY!
WHO LEFT THE FISH BONES BEHIND THE COUCH?
DID YOU LIKE THAT ONE?
YOU DO KNOW HOW TO ASK A STUPID QUESTION
Distributed by Universal Uclick www.facebook.com/garfield
© 2016 PAWS, INC. All Rights Reserved.
JIM DAVIS 11-10

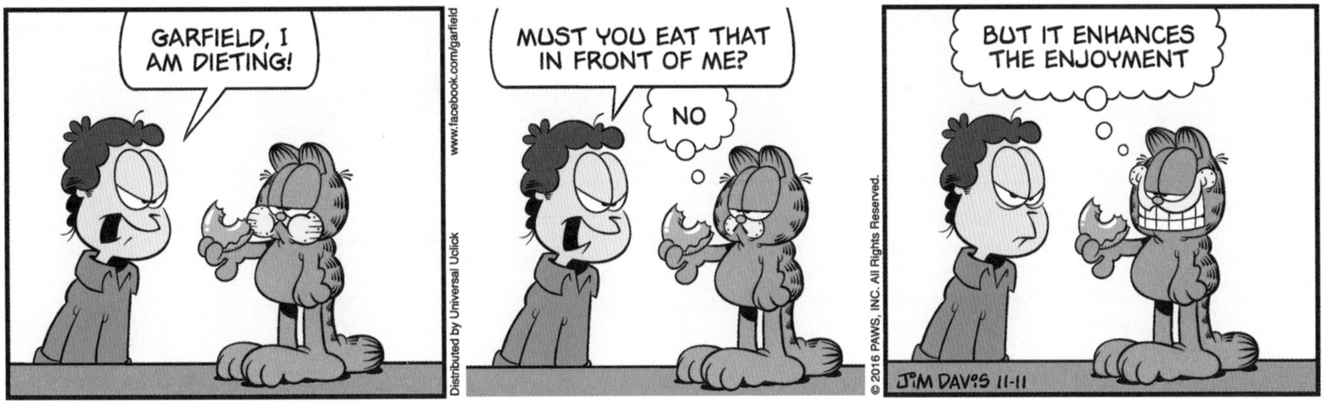
GARFIELD, I AM DIETING!
MUST YOU EAT THAT IN FRONT OF ME?
NO
BUT IT ENHANCES THE ENJOYMENT
Distributed by Universal Uclick www.facebook.com/garfield
© 2016 PAWS, INC. All Rights Reserved.
JIM DAVIS 11-11

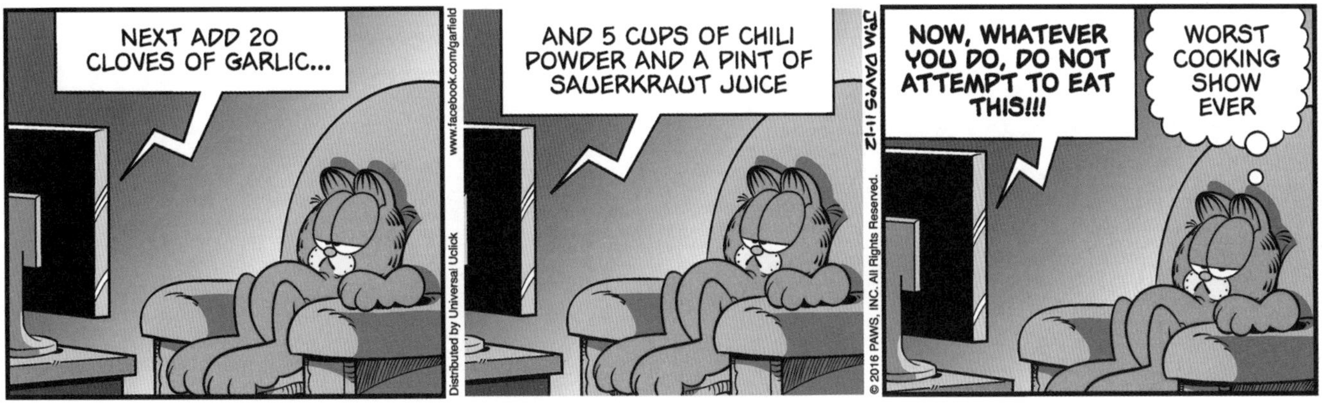
NEXT ADD 20 CLOVES OF GARLIC...
AND 5 CUPS OF CHILI POWDER AND A PINT OF SAUERKRAUT JUICE
NOW, WHATEVER YOU DO, DO NOT ATTEMPT TO EAT THIS!!!
WORST COOKING SHOW EVER
Distributed by Universal Uclick www.facebook.com/garfield
© 2016 PAWS, INC. All Rights Reserved.
JIM DAVIS 11-12

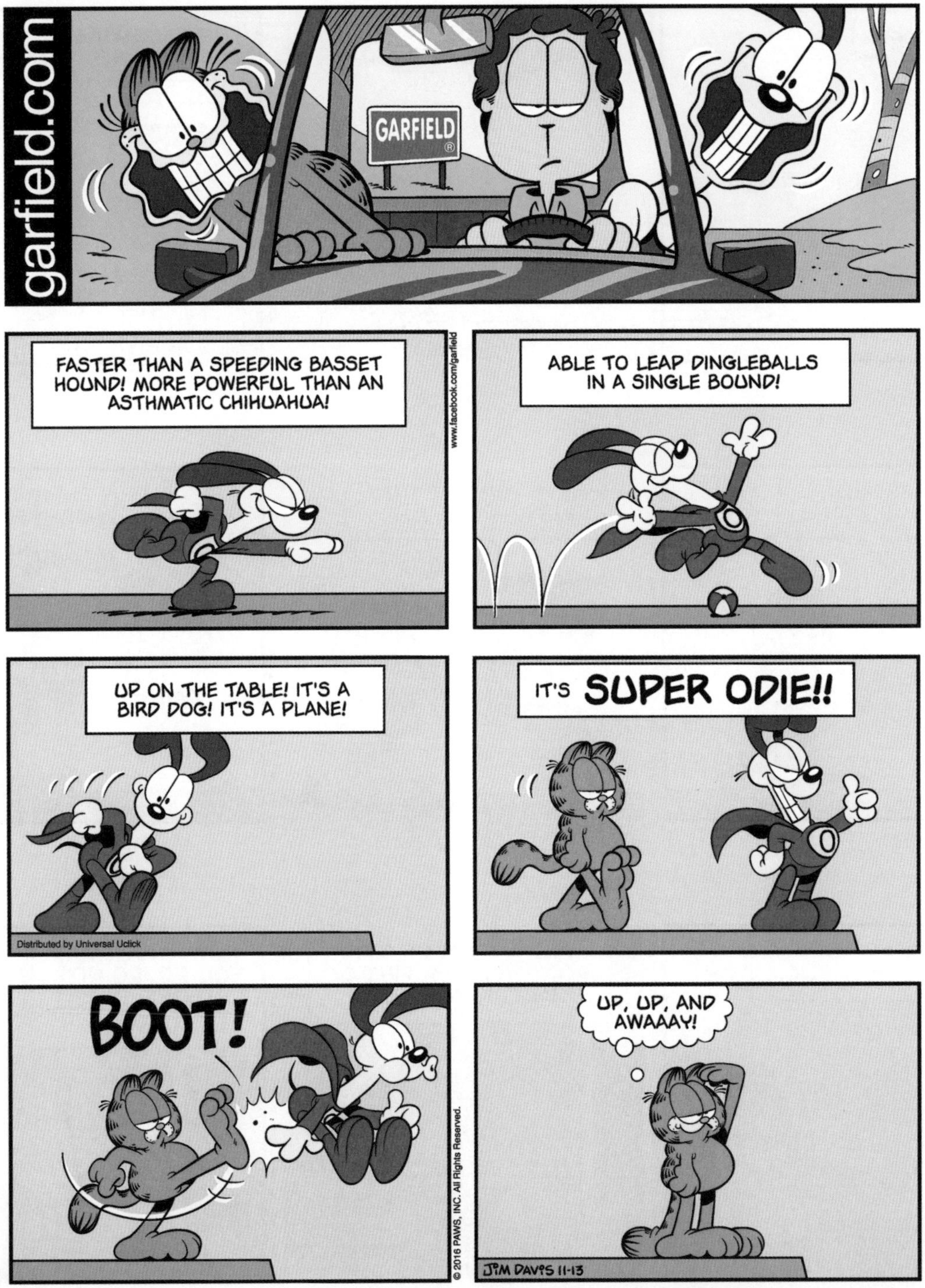
garfield.com
GARFIELD ®
FASTER THAN A SPEEDING BASSET HOUND! MORE POWERFUL THAN AN ASTHMATIC CHIHUAHUA!
www.facebook.com/garfield
ABLE TO LEAP DINGLEBALLS IN A SINGLE BOUND!
UP ON THE TABLE! IT'S A BIRD DOG! IT'S A PLANE!
Distributed by Universal Uclick
IT'S SUPER ODIE!!
BOOT!
© 2016 PAWS, INC. All Rights Reserved.
UP, UP, AND AWAAAY!
JIM DAVIS 11-13

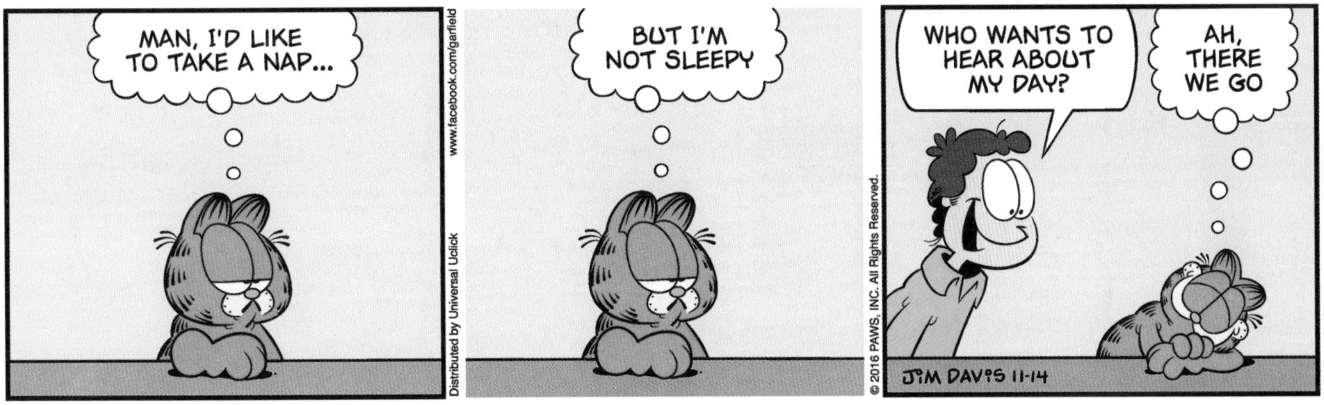
MAN, I'D LIKE TO TAKE A NAP...
Distributed by Universal Uclick www.facebook.com/garfield
BUT I'M NOT SLEEPY
WHO WANTS TO HEAR ABOUT MY DAY?
AH, THERE WE GO
© 2016 PAWS, INC. All Rights Reserved.
JIM DAVIS 11-14

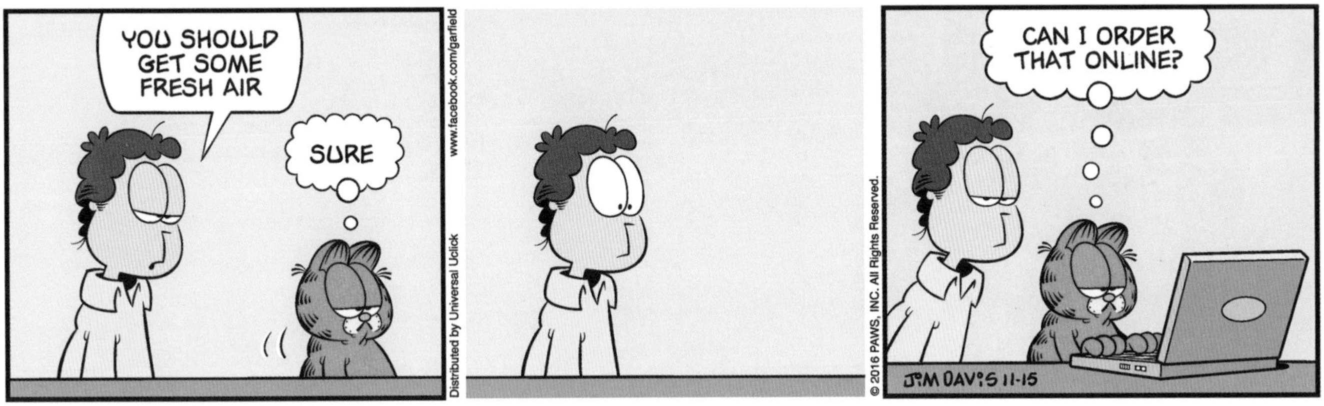
YOU SHOULD GET SOME FRESH AIR
SURE
Distributed by Universal Uclick www.facebook.com/garfield
CAN I ORDER THAT ONLINE?
© 2016 PAWS, INC. All Rights Reserved.
JIM DAVIS 11-15

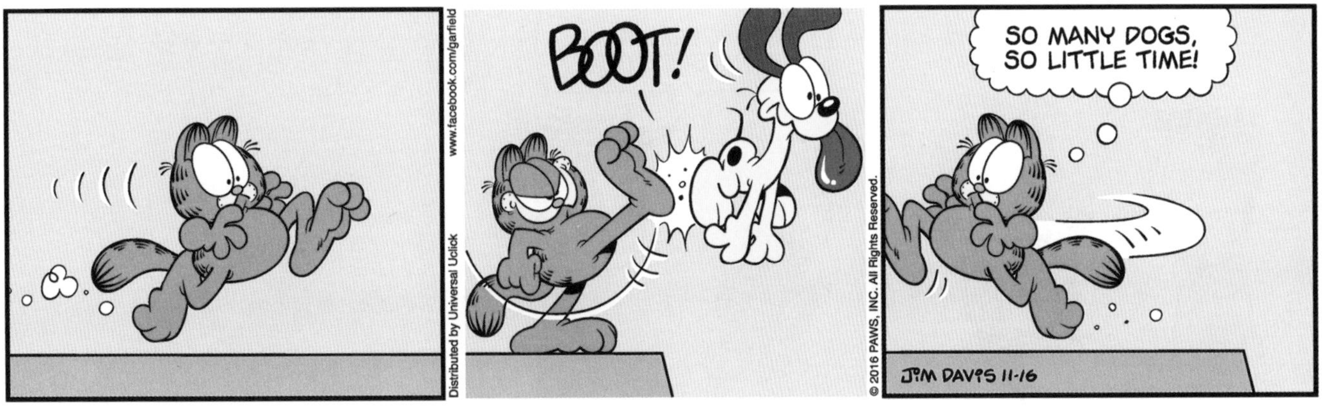
Distributed by Universal Uclick www.facebook.com/garfield
BOOT!
SO MANY DOGS, SO LITTLE TIME!
© 2016 PAWS, INC. All Rights Reserved.
JIM DAVIS 11-16

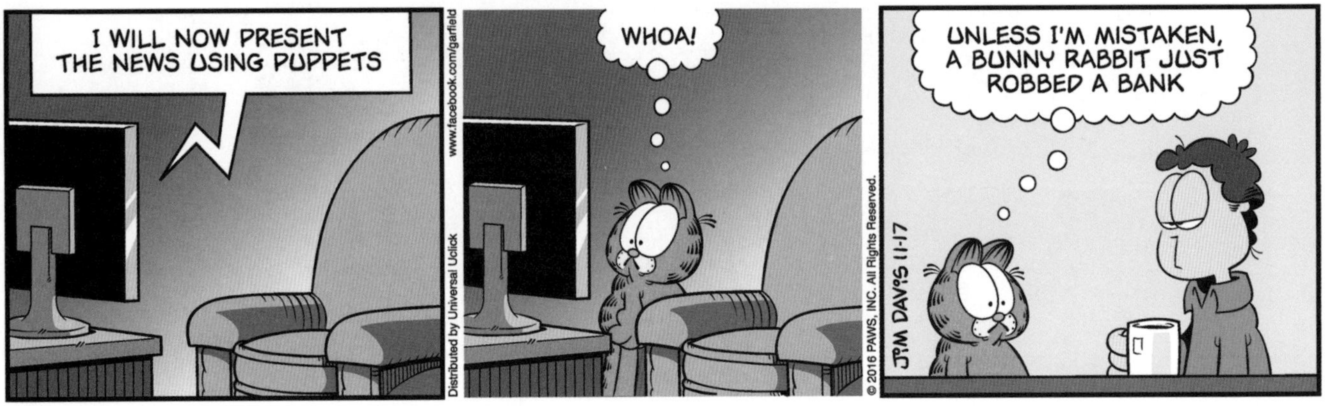
I WILL NOW PRESENT THE NEWS USING PUPPETS
WHOA!
UNLESS I'M MISTAKEN, A BUNNY RABBIT JUST ROBBED A BANK
Distributed by Universal Uclick www.facebook.com/garfield
© 2016 PAWS, INC. All Rights Reserved.
JIM DAVIS 11-17

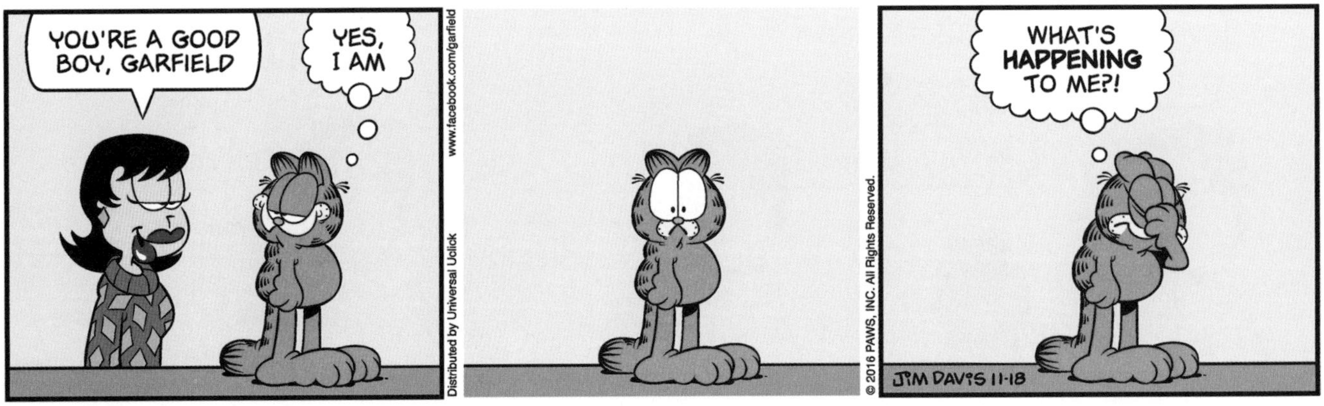
YOU'RE A GOOD BOY, GARFIELD
YES, I AM
WHAT'S **HAPPENING** TO ME?!
Distributed by Universal Uclick www.facebook.com/garfield
© 2016 PAWS, INC. All Rights Reserved.
JIM DAVIS 11-18

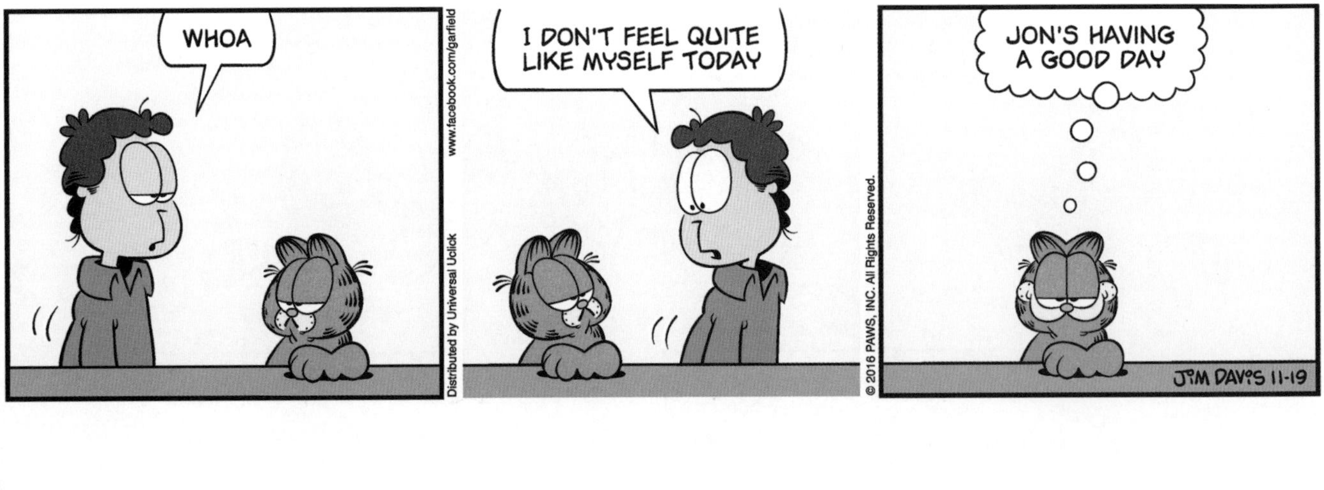
WHOA
I DON'T FEEL QUITE LIKE MYSELF TODAY
JON'S HAVING A GOOD DAY
Distributed by Universal Uclick www.facebook.com/garfield
© 2016 PAWS, INC. All Rights Reserved.
JIM DAVIS 11-19

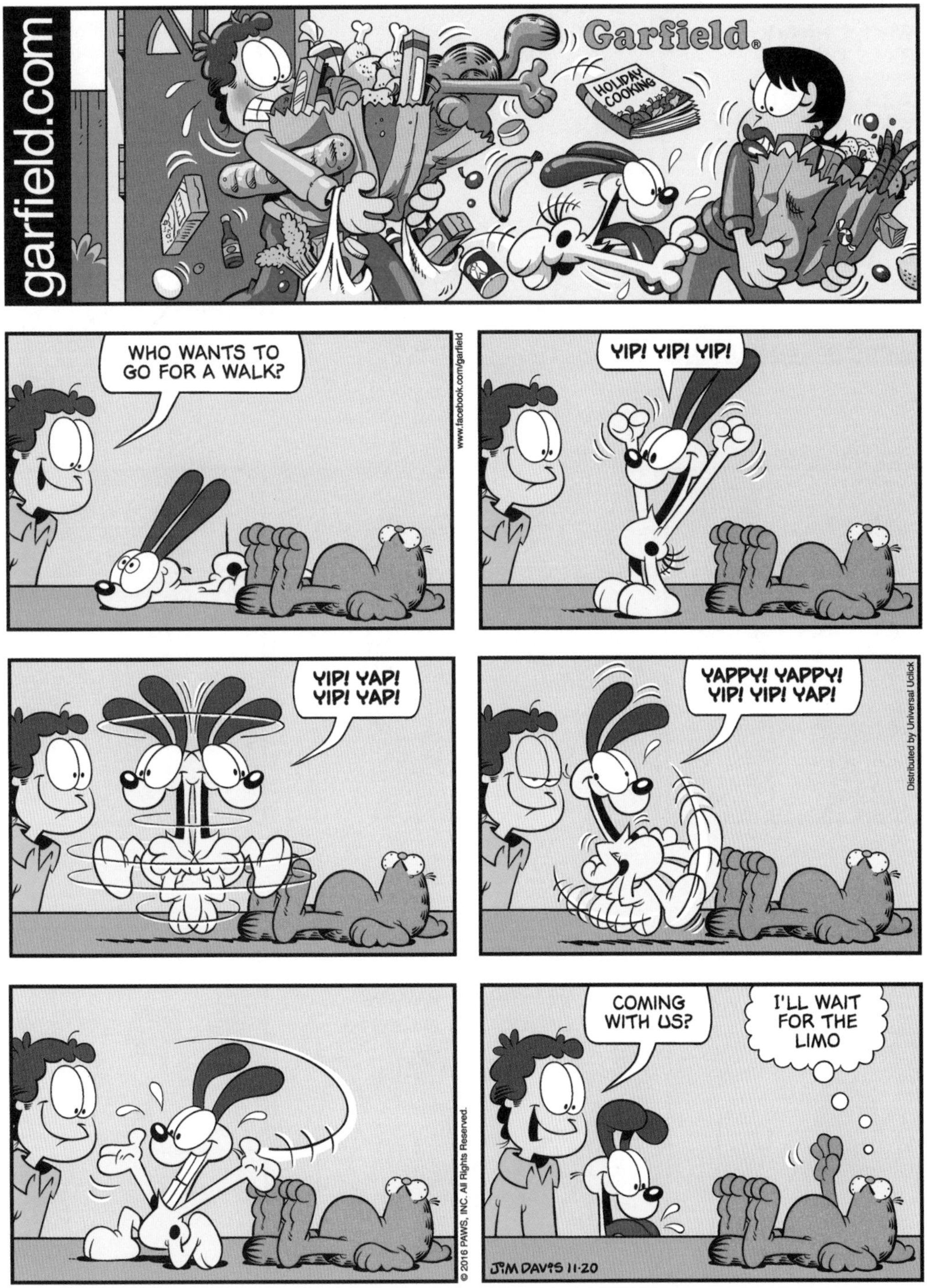
garfield.com
Garfield®
HOLIDAY COOKING
WHO WANTS TO GO FOR A WALK?
www.facebook.com/garfield
YIP! YIP! YIP!
YIP! YAP! YIP! YAP!
YAPPY! YAPPY! YIP! YIP! YAP!
Distributed by Universal Uclick
© 2016 PAWS, INC. All Rights Reserved.
COMING WITH US?
I'LL WAIT FOR THE LIMO
JIM DAVIS 11-20

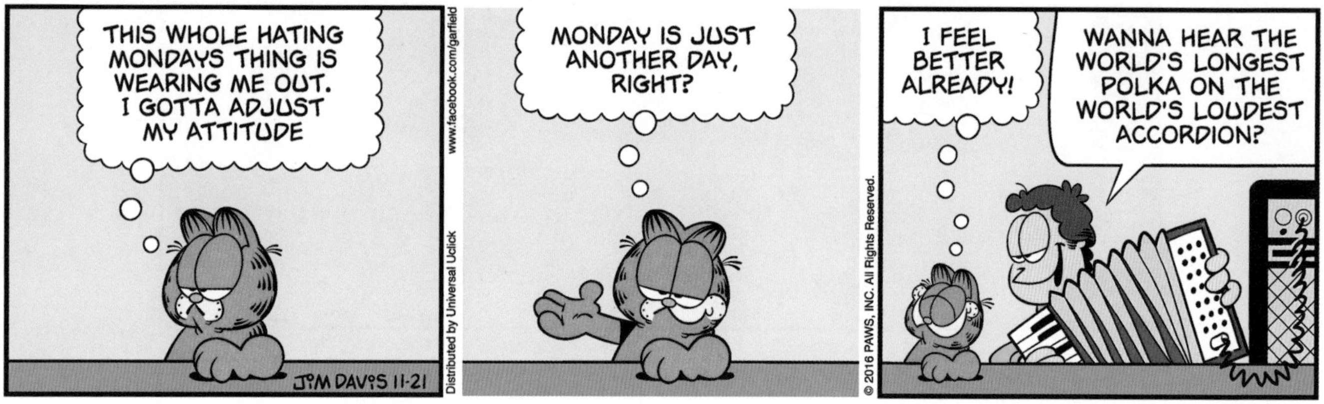
THIS WHOLE HATING MONDAYS THING IS WEARING ME OUT. I GOTTA ADJUST MY ATTITUDE
JIM DAVIS 11-21
Distributed by Universal Uclick www.facebook.com/garfield
MONDAY IS JUST ANOTHER DAY, RIGHT?
© 2016 PAWS, INC. All Rights Reserved.
I FEEL BETTER ALREADY!
WANNA HEAR THE WORLD'S LONGEST POLKA ON THE WORLD'S LOUDEST ACCORDION?

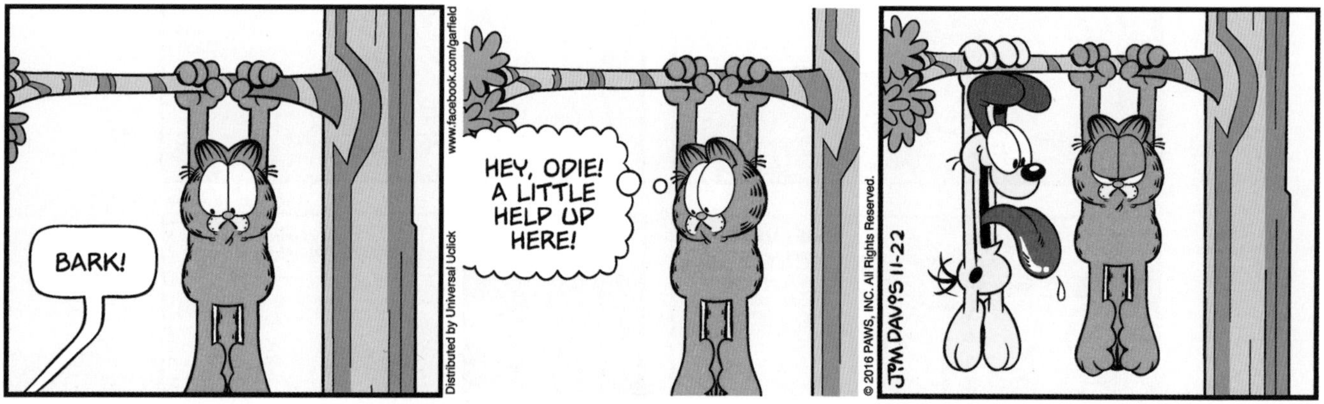
BARK!
Distributed by Universal Uclick www.facebook.com/garfield
HEY, ODIE! A LITTLE HELP UP HERE!
© 2016 PAWS, INC. All Rights Reserved.
JIM DAVIS 11-22

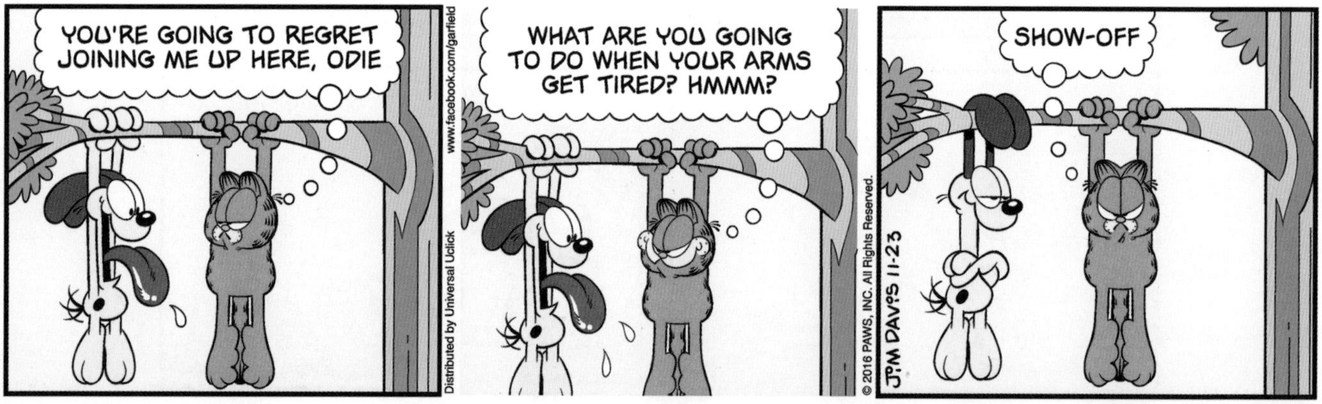
YOU'RE GOING TO REGRET JOINING ME UP HERE, ODIE
Distributed by Universal Uclick www.facebook.com/garfield
WHAT ARE YOU GOING TO DO WHEN YOUR ARMS GET TIRED? HMMM?
© 2016 PAWS, INC. All Rights Reserved.
JIM DAVIS 11-23
SHOW-OFF

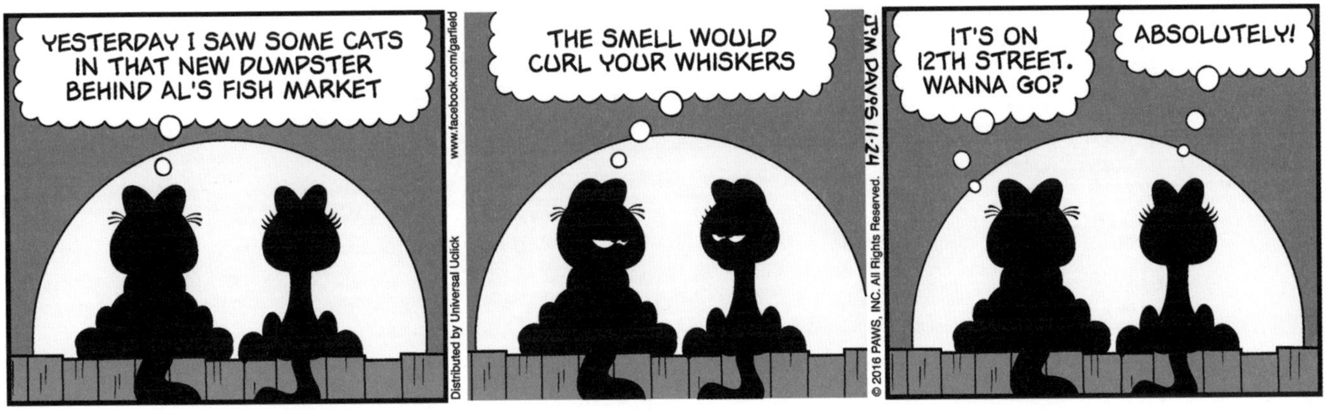
YESTERDAY I SAW SOME CATS IN THAT NEW DUMPSTER BEHIND AL'S FISH MARKET
THE SMELL WOULD CURL YOUR WHISKERS
IT'S ON 12TH STREET. WANNA GO?
ABSOLUTELY!
JIM DAVIS 11-24
Distributed by Universal Uclick www.facebook.com/garfield
© 2016 PAWS, INC. All Rights Reserved.

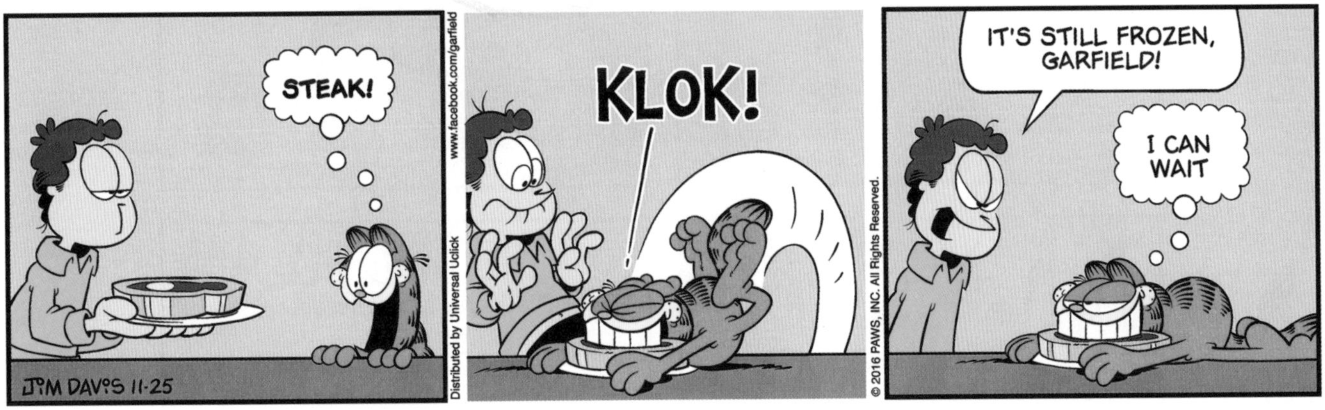
STEAK!
JIM DAVIS 11-25
KLOK!
IT'S STILL FROZEN, GARFIELD!
I CAN WAIT
Distributed by Universal Uclick www.facebook.com/garfield
© 2016 PAWS, INC. All Rights Reserved.

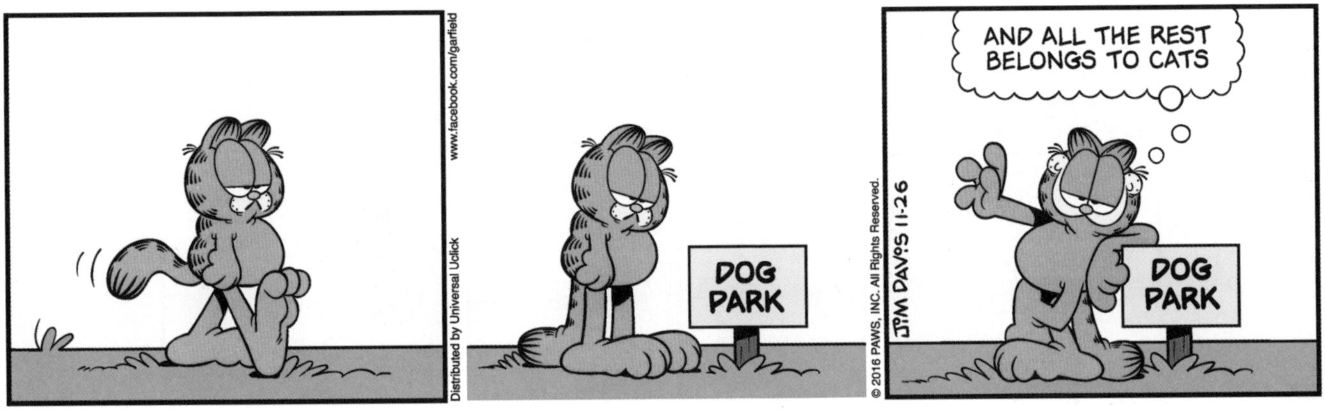
DOG PARK
AND ALL THE REST BELONGS TO CATS
DOG PARK
JIM DAVIS 11-26
Distributed by Universal Uclick www.facebook.com/garfield
© 2016 PAWS, INC. All Rights Reserved.

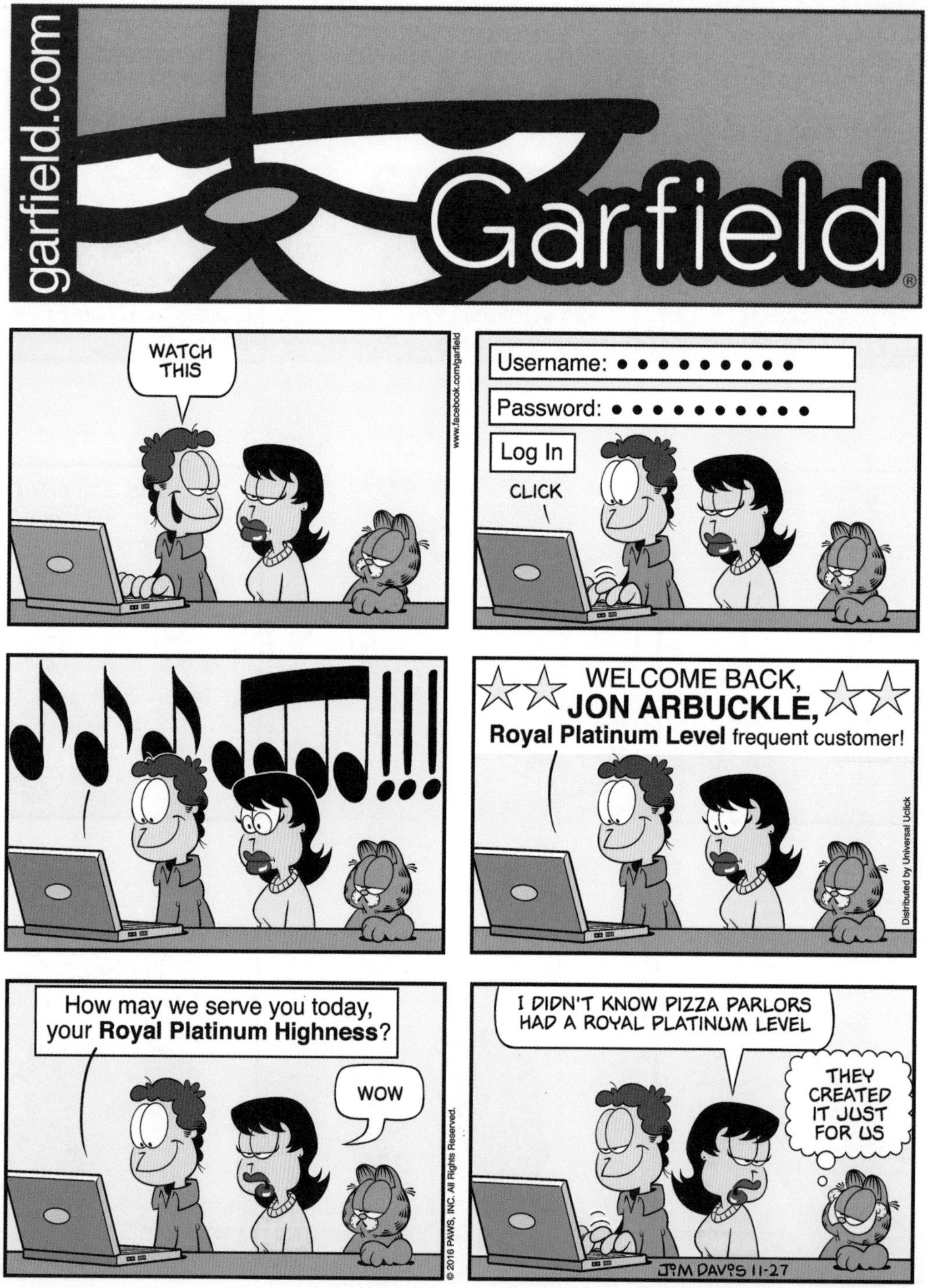
garfield.com
Garfield
WATCH THIS
www.facebook.com/garfield
Username: ●●●●●●●●●●
Password: ●●●●●●●●●●●
Log In
CLICK
!!!
WELCOME BACK, JON ARBUCKLE, Royal Platinum Level frequent customer!
Distributed by Universal Uclick
How may we serve you today, your Royal Platinum Highness?
WOW
© 2016 PAWS, INC. All Rights Reserved.
I DIDN'T KNOW PIZZA PARLORS HAD A ROYAL PLATINUM LEVEL
THEY CREATED IT JUST FOR US
JIM DAVIS 11-27

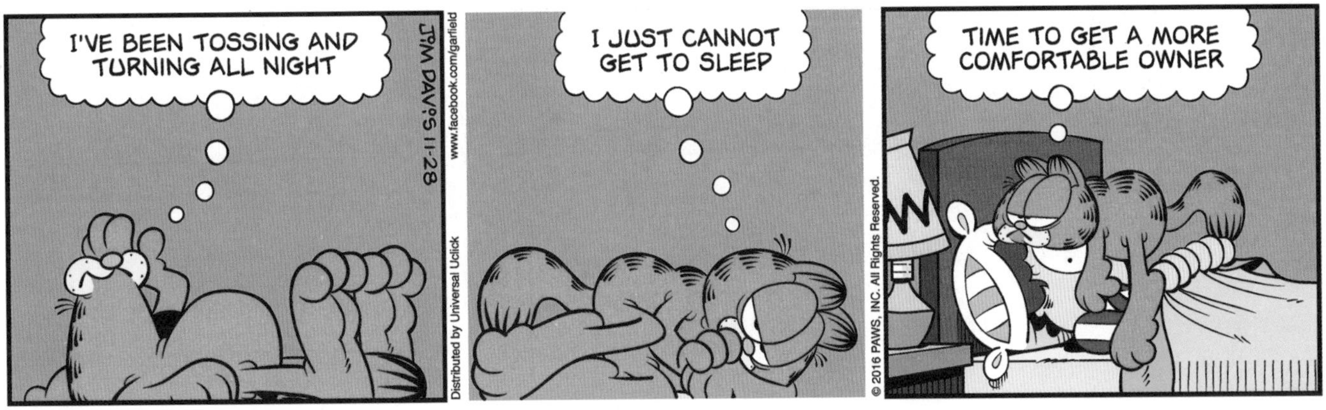
I'VE BEEN TOSSING AND TURNING ALL NIGHT
JIM DAVIS 11-28
www.facebook.com/garfield
Distributed by Universal Uclick
I JUST CANNOT GET TO SLEEP
© 2016 PAWS, INC. All Rights Reserved.
TIME TO GET A MORE COMFORTABLE OWNER

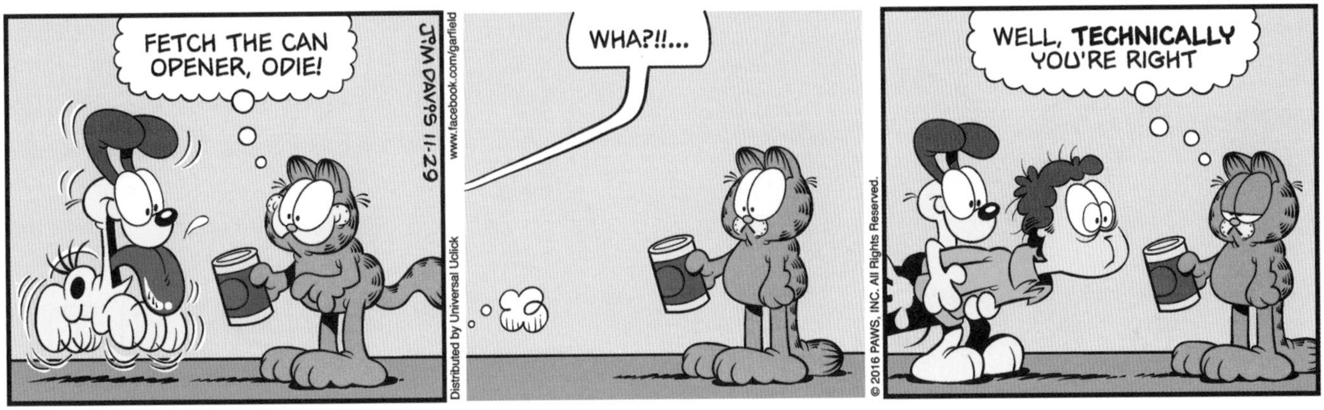
FETCH THE CAN OPENER, ODIE!
JIM DAVIS 11-29
www.facebook.com/garfield
Distributed by Universal Uclick
WHA?!!...
© 2016 PAWS, INC. All Rights Reserved.
WELL, **TECHNICALLY** YOU'RE RIGHT

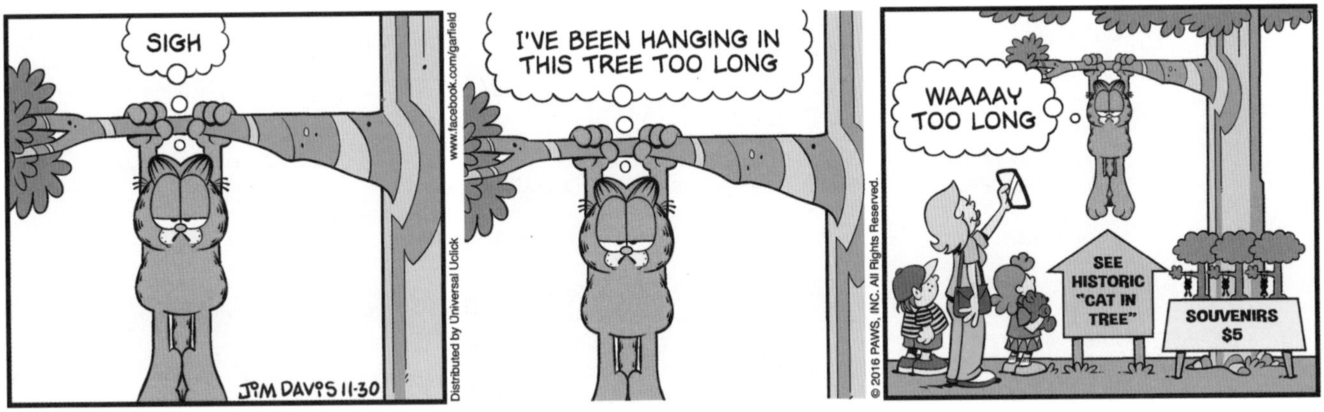
SIGH
JIM DAVIS 11-30
www.facebook.com/garfield
Distributed by Universal Uclick
I'VE BEEN HANGING IN THIS TREE TOO LONG
© 2016 PAWS, INC. All Rights Reserved.
WAAAAY TOO LONG
SEE HISTORIC "CAT IN TREE"
SOUVENIRS $5

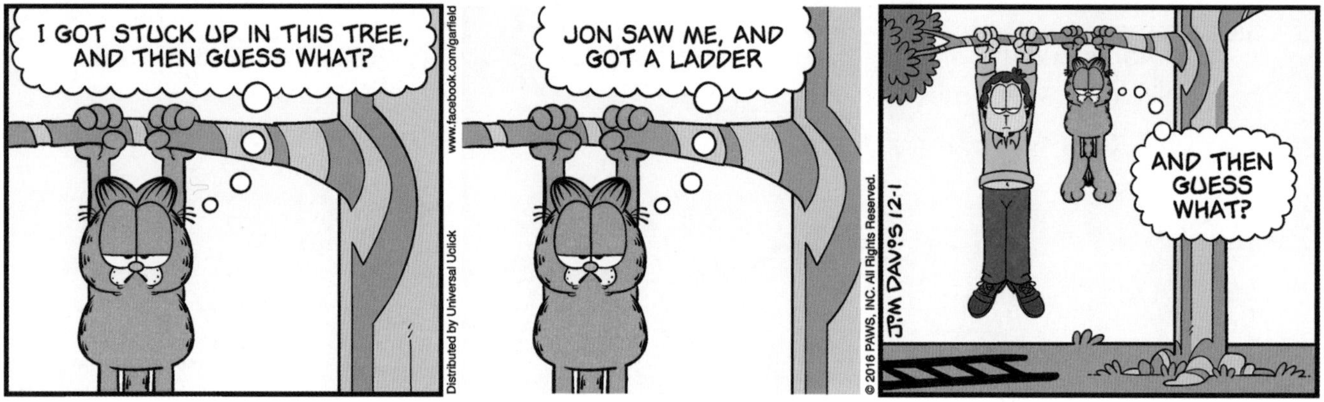
I GOT STUCK UP IN THIS TREE, AND THEN GUESS WHAT?
Distributed by Universal Uclick www.facebook.com/garfield
JON SAW ME, AND GOT A LADDER
© 2016 PAWS, INC. All Rights Reserved.
JIM DAVIS 12-1
AND THEN GUESS WHAT?

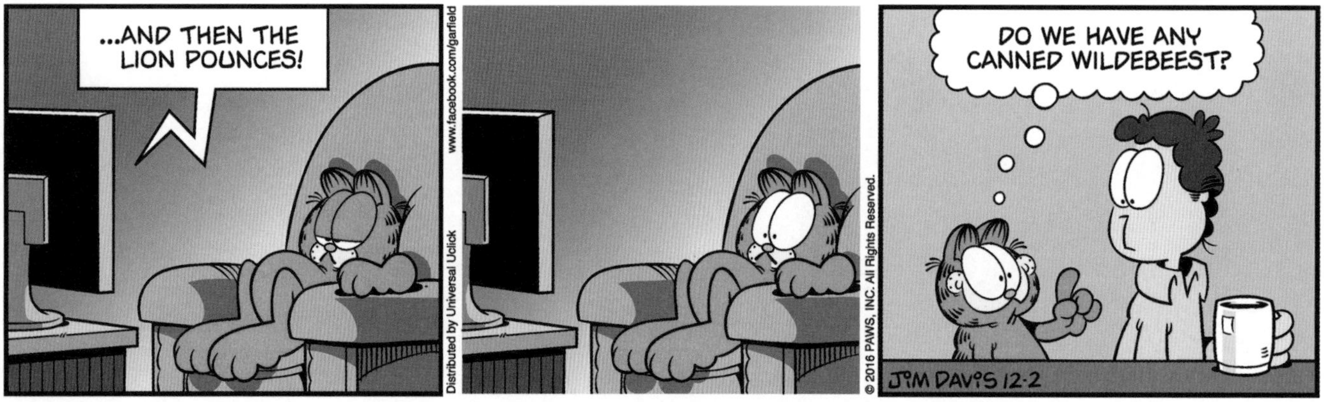
...AND THEN THE LION POUNCES!
Distributed by Universal Uclick www.facebook.com/garfield
© 2016 PAWS, INC. All Rights Reserved.
DO WE HAVE ANY CANNED WILDEBEEST?
JIM DAVIS 12-2

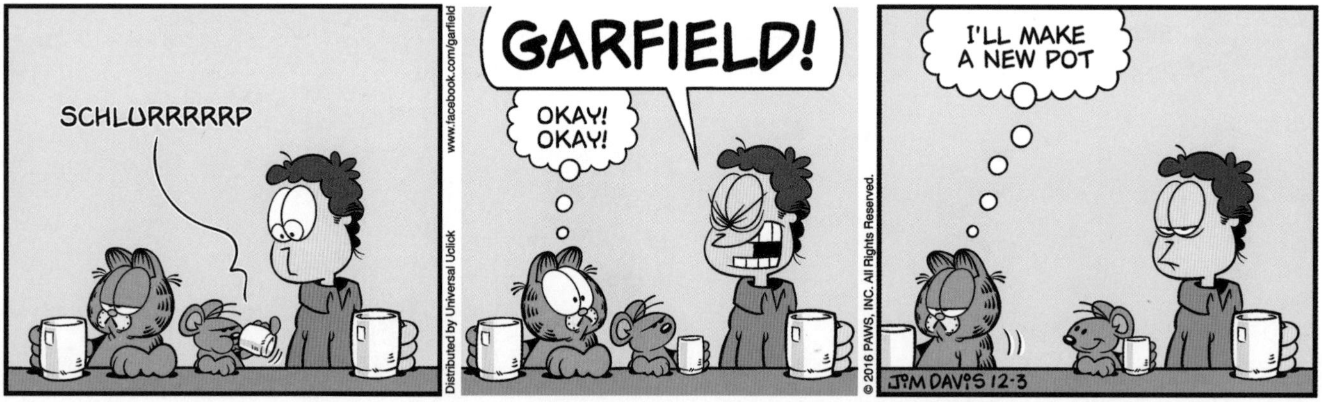
SCHLURRRRRP
Distributed by Universal Uclick www.facebook.com/garfield
GARFIELD!
OKAY! OKAY!
© 2016 PAWS, INC. All Rights Reserved.
I'LL MAKE A NEW POT
JIM DAVIS 12-3

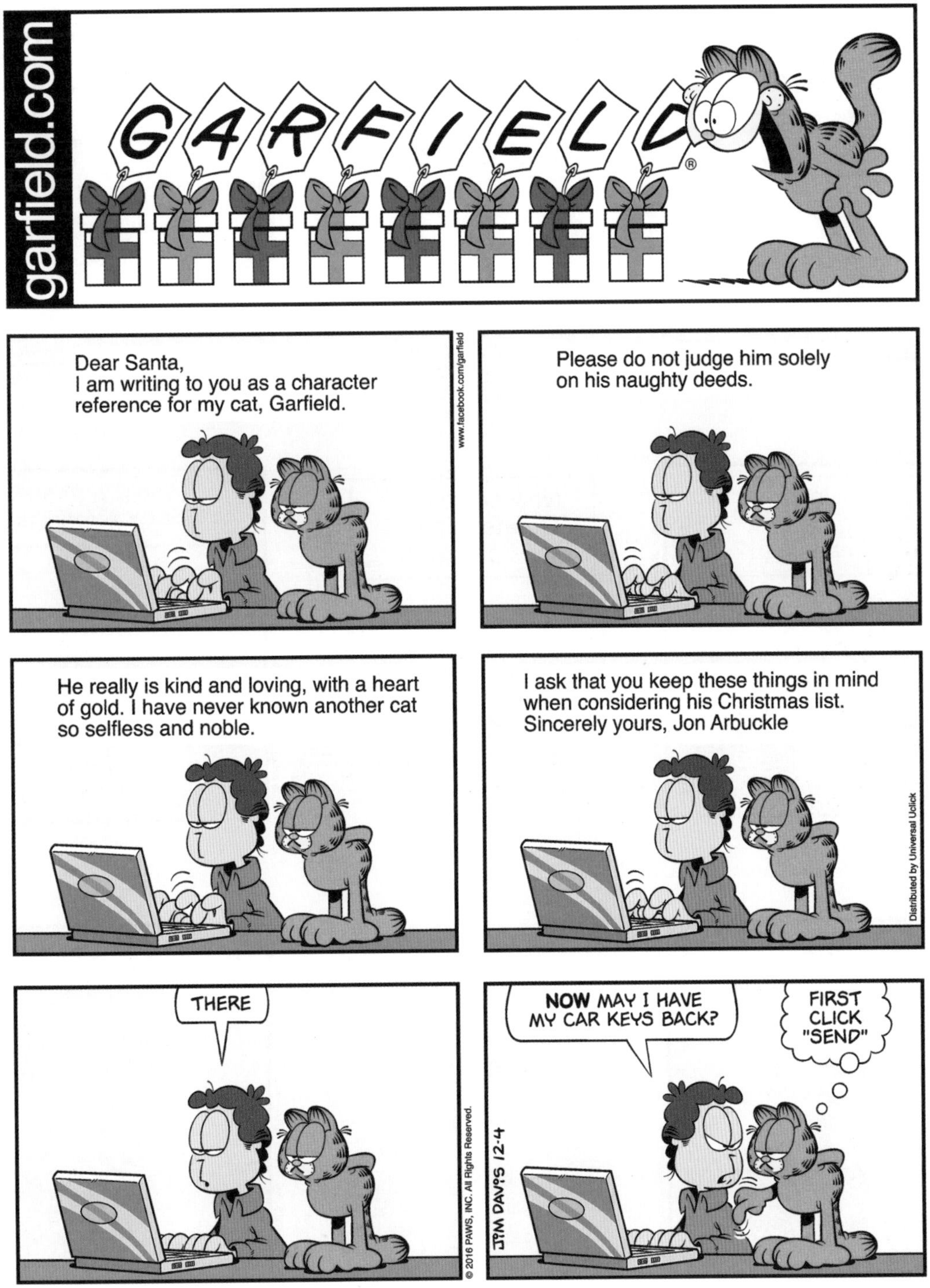
garfield.com
GARFIELD
Dear Santa,
I am writing to you as a character reference for my cat, Garfield.
www.facebook.com/garfield
Please do not judge him solely on his naughty deeds.
He really is kind and loving, with a heart of gold. I have never known another cat so selfless and noble.
I ask that you keep these things in mind when considering his Christmas list.
Sincerely yours, Jon Arbuckle
Distributed by Universal Uclick
THERE
© 2016 PAWS, INC. All Rights Reserved.
JIM DAVIS 12-4
NOW MAY I HAVE MY CAR KEYS BACK?
FIRST CLICK "SEND"

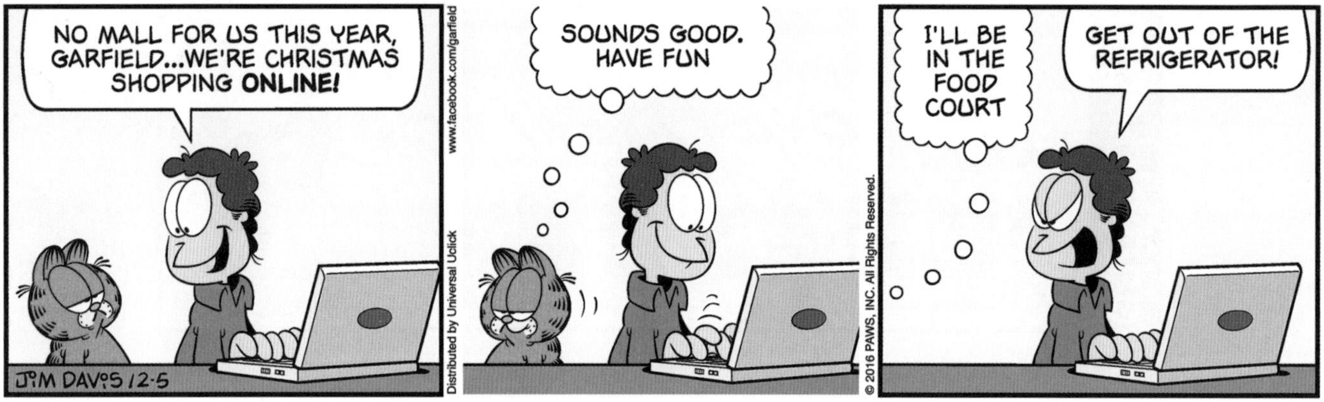
NO MALL FOR US THIS YEAR, GARFIELD...WE'RE CHRISTMAS SHOPPING **ONLINE!**
JIM DAVIS 12-5
www.facebook.com/garfield
Distributed by Universal Uclick
SOUNDS GOOD. HAVE FUN
© 2016 PAWS, INC. All Rights Reserved.
I'LL BE IN THE FOOD COURT
GET OUT OF THE REFRIGERATOR!

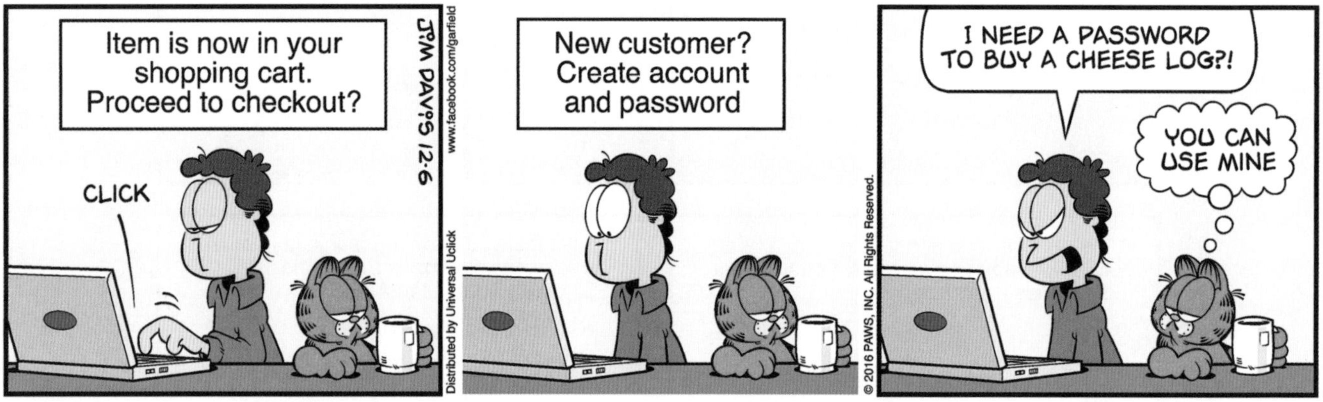
Item is now in your shopping cart. Proceed to checkout?
CLICK
JIM DAVIS 12-6
www.facebook.com/garfield
Distributed by Universal Uclick
New customer? Create account and password
© 2016 PAWS, INC. All Rights Reserved.
I NEED A PASSWORD TO BUY A CHEESE LOG?!
YOU CAN USE MINE

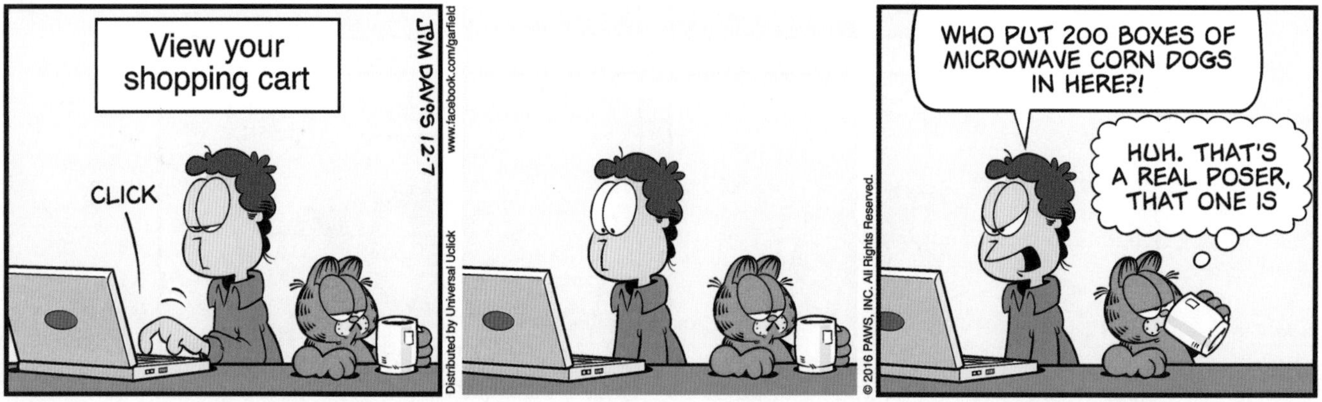
View your shopping cart
CLICK
JIM DAVIS 12-7
www.facebook.com/garfield
Distributed by Universal Uclick
© 2016 PAWS, INC. All Rights Reserved.
WHO PUT 200 BOXES OF MICROWAVE CORN DOGS IN HERE?!
HUH. THAT'S A REAL POSER, THAT ONE IS

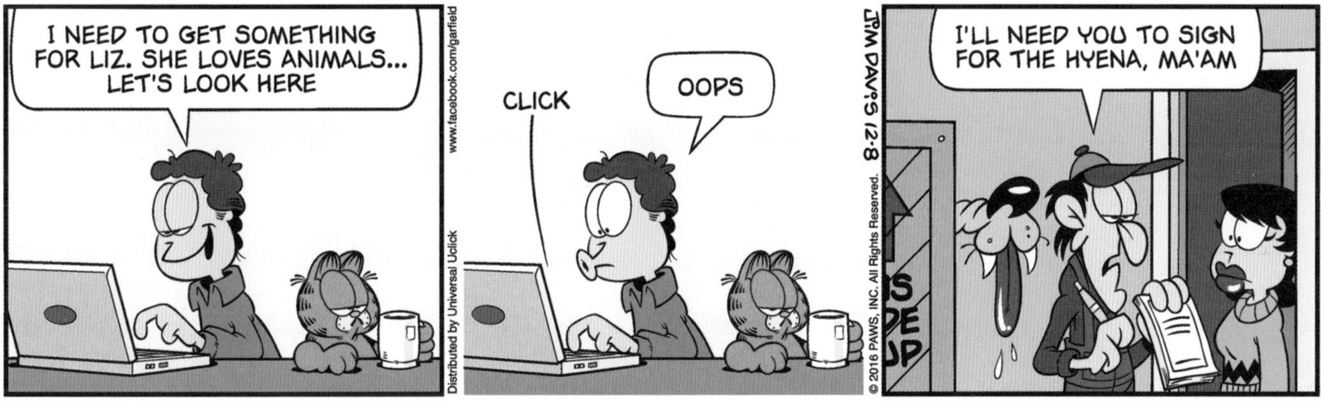

I NEED TO GET SOMETHING FOR LIZ. SHE LOVES ANIMALS... LET'S LOOK HERE
www.facebook.com/garfield
Distributed by Universal Uclick
CLICK
OOPS
JIM DAVIS 12·8
© 2016 PAWS, INC. All Rights Reserved.
I'LL NEED YOU TO SIGN FOR THE HYENA, MA'AM

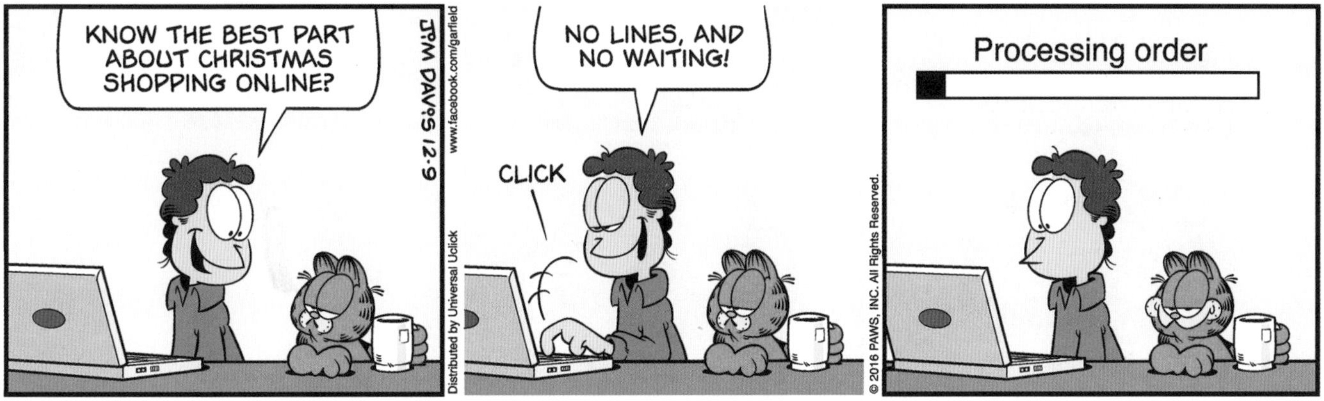

KNOW THE BEST PART ABOUT CHRISTMAS SHOPPING ONLINE?
JIM DAVIS 12·9
www.facebook.com/garfield
Distributed by Universal Uclick
NO LINES, AND NO WAITING!
CLICK
© 2016 PAWS, INC. All Rights Reserved.
Processing order

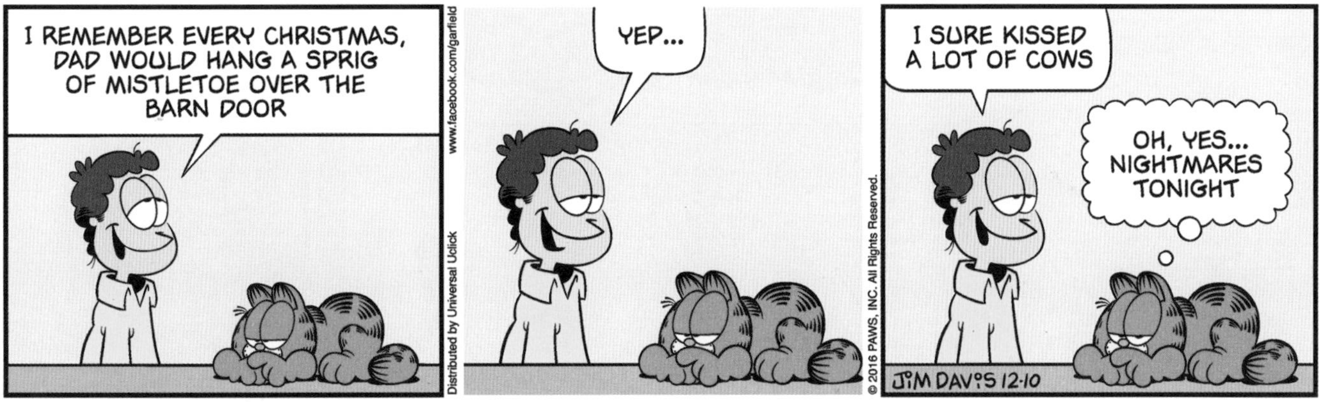

I REMEMBER EVERY CHRISTMAS, DAD WOULD HANG A SPRIG OF MISTLETOE OVER THE BARN DOOR
www.facebook.com/garfield
Distributed by Universal Uclick
YEP...
© 2016 PAWS, INC. All Rights Reserved.
I SURE KISSED A LOT OF COWS
OH, YES... NIGHTMARES TONIGHT
JIM DAVIS 12·10

Fat Cat Fan Art

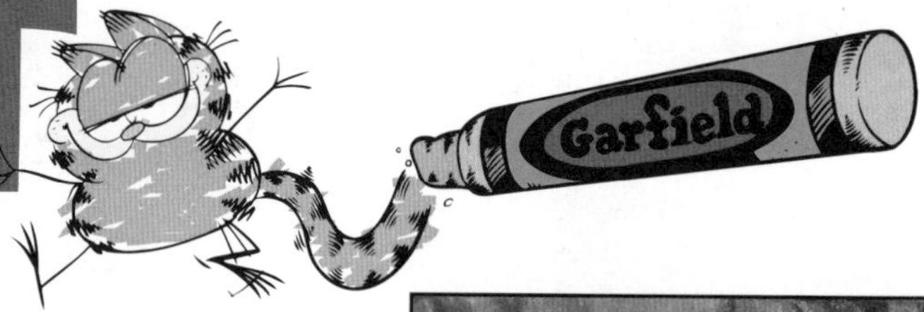
Garfield

Molly K.
Age 18
California

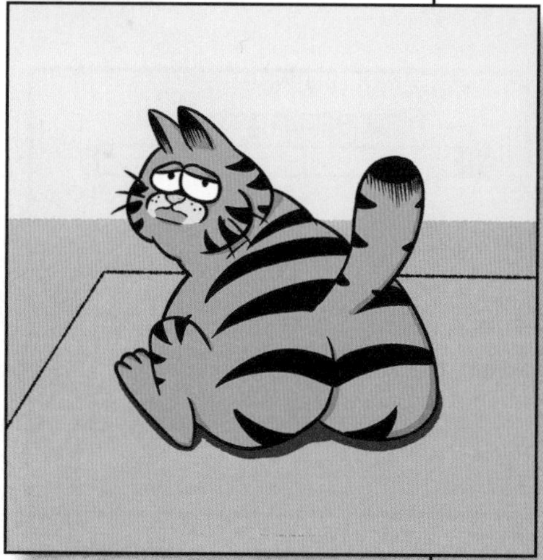

Cassy K.
Age 13
Canada

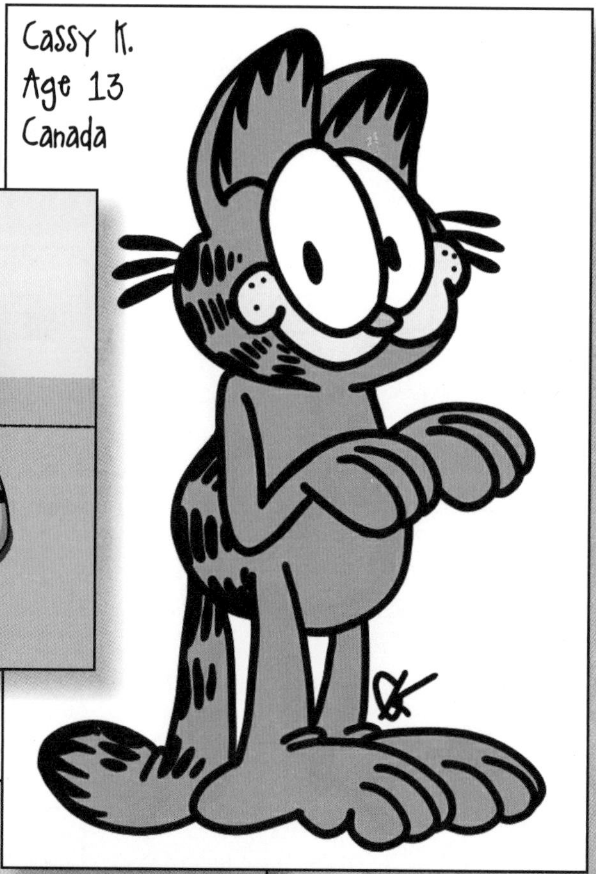

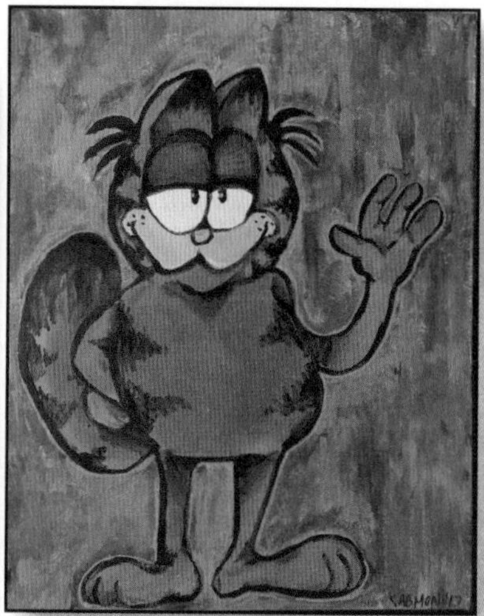

Sabrina M.
Age 16
California

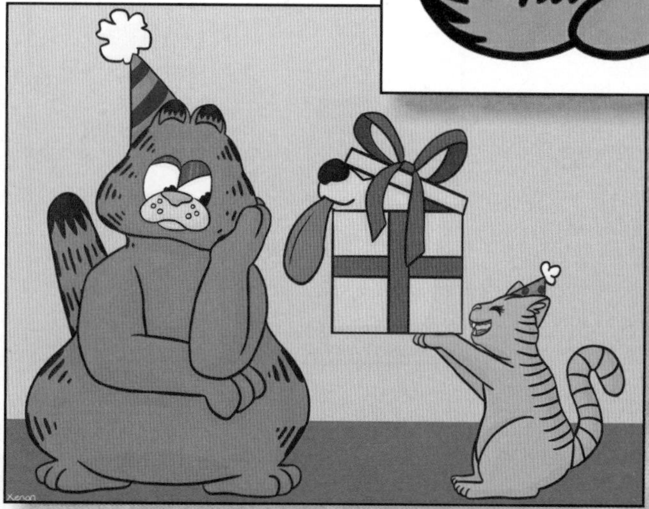

Xenon T.
Age 18
Canada

Julian H.
Age 23
Florida

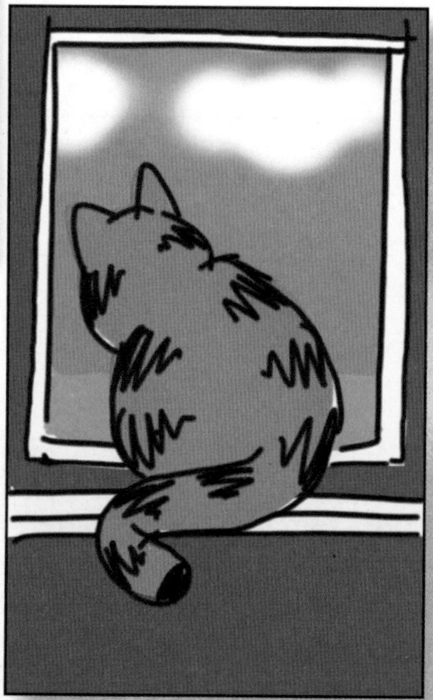

WATCH. READ. SHOP. PLAY.

DON'T FORGET THE SNACKS!

garfield.com

✳ *Garfield and Friends* and *The Garfield Show*

You can find your favorite episodes of *Garfield and Friends* and *The Garfield Show* on YouTube, Netflix, Cartoon Network, Boomerang, and on demand!

✳ The Comic Strip

Search & read thousands of GARFIELD® comic strips!

✳ Garfield on Social Media

Join millions of Garfield's friends on Facebook, Twitter, and Instagram. Get your daily dose of humor and connect with other fat cat fans!

✳ Shop all the Garfield stores!

Original art & comic strips, books, apparel, personalized products, & more!

✳ Play FREE online Garfield games!

Plus, check out all of the FREE Garfield apps available for your smartphone, tablet, and other mobile devices.

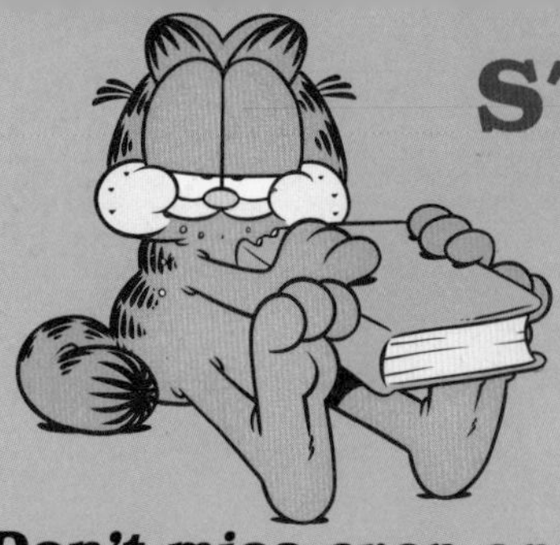

STRIPS, SPECIALS, OR BESTSELLING BOOKS . . . GARFIELD'S ON EVERYONE'S MENU.

Don't miss even one episode in the Tubby Tabby's hilarious series!

GARFIELD AT LARGE	(#1)	978-0-345-44382-3
GARFIELD GAINS WEIGHT	(#2)	978-0-345-44975-7
GARFIELD BIGGER THAN LIFE	(#3)	978-0-345-45027-2
GARFIELD WEIGHS IN	(#4)	978-0-345-45205-4
GARFIELD TAKES THE CAKE	(#5)	978-0-345-44978-8
GARFIELD EATS HIS HEART OUT	(#6)	978-0-345-46459-0
GARFIELD SITS AROUND THE HOUSE	(#7)	978-0-345-46463-7
GARFIELD TIPS THE SCALES	(#8)	978-0-345-46909-0
GARFIELD LOSES HIS FEET	(#9)	978-0-345-46467-5
GARFIELD MAKES IT BIG	(#10)	978-0-345-46468-2
GARFIELD ROLLS ON	(#11)	978-0-345-47561-9
GARFIELD OUT TO LUNCH	(#12)	978-0-345-47562-6
GARFIELD FOOD FOR THOUGHT	(#13)	978-0-345-47563-3
GARFIELD SWALLOWS HIS PRIDE	(#14)	978-0-345-91386-9
GARFIELD WORLDWIDE	(#15)	978-0-345-91754-6
GARFIELD ROUNDS OUT	(#16)	978-0-345-49169-5
GARFIELD CHEWS THE FAT	(#17)	978-0-345-49170-1
GARFIELD GOES TO WAIST	(#18)	978-0-345-49173-2
GARFIELD HANGS OUT	(#19)	978-0-345-49174-9
GARFIELD TAKES UP SPACE	(#20)	978-0-345-49178-7
GARFIELD SAYS A MOUTHFUL	(#21)	978-0-345-49179-4
GARFIELD BY THE POUND	(#22)	978-0-345-52558-1
GARFIELD KEEPS HIS CHINS UP	(#23)	978-0-345-52559-8
GARFIELD TAKES HIS LICKS	(#24)	978-0-345-52587-1
GARFIELD HITS THE BIG TIME	(#25)	978-0-345-52589-5
GARFIELD PULLS HIS WEIGHT	(#26)	978-0-345-52594-9
GARFIELD DISHES IT OUT	(#27)	978-0-345-52595-6
GARFIELD LIFE IN THE FAT LANE	(#28)	978-0-345-52600-7
GARFIELD TONS OF FUN	(#29)	978-0-345-52601-4
GARFIELD BIGGER AND BETTER	(#30)	978-0-345-52605-2
GARFIELD HAMS IT UP	(#31)	978-0-345-52606-9
GARFIELD THINKS BIG	(#32)	978-0-425-28516-9
GARFIELD THROWS HIS WEIGHT AROUND	(#33)	978-0-425-28559-6
GARFIELD LIFE TO THE FULLEST	(#34)	978-0-425-28564-0
GARFIELD FEEDS THE KITTY	(#35)	978-0-425-28569-5
GARFIELD HOGS THE SPOTLIGHT	(#36)	978-0-425-28574-9
GARFIELD BEEFS UP	(#37)	978-0-345-44109-6
GARFIELD GETS COOKIN'	(#38)	978-0-345-44582-7
GARFIELD EATS CROW	(#39)	978-0-345-45201-6
GARFIELD SURVIVAL OF THE FATTEST	(#40)	978-0-345-46458-3
GARFIELD OLDER AND WIDER	(#41)	978-0-345-46462-0
GARFIELD PIGS OUT	(#42)	978-0-345-46466-8
GARFIELD BLOTS OUT THE SUN	(#43)	978-0-345-46615-0
GARFIELD GOES BANANAS	(#44)	978-0-345-91346-3
GARFIELD LARGE & IN CHARGE	(#45)	978-0-345-49172-5
GARFIELD SPILLS THE BEANS	(#46)	978-0-345-49177-0
GARFIELD GETS HIS JUST DESSERTS	(#47)	978-0-345-91387-6
GARFIELD WILL EAT FOR FOOD	(#48)	978-0-345-49176-3
GARFIELD WEIGHS HIS OPTIONS	(#49)	978-0-345-49181-7
GARFIELD POTBELLY OF GOLD	(#50)	978-0-345-52244-3
GARFIELD SHOVELS IT IN	(#51)	978-0-345-52419-5
GARFIELD LARD OF THE JUNGLE	(#52)	978-0-345-52584-0
GARFIELD BRINGS HOME THE BACON	(#53)	978-0-345-52586-4
GARFIELD GETS IN A PICKLE	(#54)	978-0-345-52590-1
GARFIELD SINGS FOR HIS SUPPER	(#55)	978-0-345-52593-2
GARFIELD CAUTION: WIDE LOAD	(#56)	978-0-345-52596-3
GARFIELD SOUPED UP	(#57)	978-0-345-52598-7
GARFIELD GOES TO HIS HAPPY PLACE	(#58)	978-0-345-52602-1
GARFIELD THE BIG CHEESE	(#59)	978-0-345-52604-5
GARFIELD CLEANS HIS PLATE	(#60)	978-0-345-52608-3
GARFIELD CHICKENS OUT	(#61)	978-0-425-28515-2
GARFIELD LISTENS TO HIS GUT	(#62)	978-0-425-28557-2
GARFIELD COOKS UP TROUBLE	(#63)	978-0-425-28562-6
GARFIELD FEEDS HIS FACE	(#64)	978-0-425-28567-1
GARFIELD EATS AND RUNS	(#65)	978-0-425-28572-5

DVD TIE-INS

GARFIELD AS HIMSELF	978-0-345-47805-4
GARFIELD HOLIDAY CELEBRATIONS	978-0-345-47930-3
GARFIELD TRAVEL ADVENTURES	978-0-345-48087-3

AND DON'T MISS . . .

GARFIELD AT 25: IN DOG YEARS I'D BE DEAD	978-0-345-45204-7
GARFIELD'S JOKE ZONE/INSULTS	978-0-345-46263-3
GARFIELD FAT CAT 3-PACK/ VOL. 1	978-0-345-46455-2
GARFIELD FAT CAT 3-PACK/ VOL. 2	978-0-345-46465-1
GARFIELD FAT CAT 3-PACK/ VOL. 3	978-0-345-48088-0
GARFIELD FAT CAT 3-PACK/ VOL. 4	978-0-345-49171-8
GARFIELD FAT CAT 3-PACK/ VOL. 5	978-0-345-49180-8
GARFIELD FAT CAT 3-PACK/ VOL. 6	978-0-345-52420-1
GARFIELD FAT CAT 3-PACK/ VOL. 7	978-0-345-52588-8
GARFIELD FAT CAT 3-PACK/ VOL. 8	978-0-345-52599-4
GARFIELD FAT CAT 3-PACK/ VOL. 9	978-0-345-52607-6
GARFIELD FAT CAT 3-PACK/ VOL. 10	978-0-425-28558-9
GARFIELD FAT CAT 3-PACK/ VOL. 11	978-0-425-28566-4
GARFIELD FAT CAT 3-PACK/ VOL. 13	978-0-345-46460-6
GARFIELD FAT CAT 3-PACK/ VOL. 14	978-0-345-49175-6
GARFIELD FAT CAT 3-PACK/ VOL. 15	978-0-345-52585-7
GARFIELD FAT CAT 3-PACK/ VOL. 16	978-0-345-52592-5
GARFIELD FAT CAT 3-PACK/ VOL. 17	978-0-345-52603-8
GARFIELD FAT CAT 3-PACK/ VOL. 18	978-0-399-59440-3
GARFIELD FAT CAT 3-PACK/ VOL. 19	978-0-425-28561-9
GARFIELD FAT CAT 3-PACK/ VOL. 20	978-0-425-28571-8
SEASON'S EATINGS: A VERY MERRY GARFIELD CHRISTMAS	978-0-345-47560-2
GARFIELD'S GUIDE TO EVERYTHING	978-0-345-46461-3
ODIE UNLEASHED!	978-0-345-46464-4
GARFIELD'S BOOK OF CAT NAMES	978-0-345-48516-8
THE GARFIELD JOURNAL	978-0-345-46469-9
LIGHTS, CAMERA, HAIRBALLS!: GARFIELD AT THE MOVIES	978-0-345-49134-3
30 YEARS OF LAUGHS AND LASAGNA	978-0-345-50379-4
GARFIELD MINUS GARFIELD	978-0-345-51387-8
GARFIELD FROM THE TRASH BIN	978-0-345-51881-1
GARFIELD LEFT SPEECHLESS	978-0-345-53058-5
MY LAUGHABLE LIFE WITH GARFIELD	978-0-345-52591-8
GARFIELD'S SUNDAY FINEST	978-0-345-52597-0
AGE HAPPENS: GARFIELD HITS THE BIG 4-0	978-0-345-52609-0
GARFIELD COMPLETE WORKS: VOLUME ONE: 1978 & 1979	978-0-425-28712-5

New larger, full-color format!